Live Creatively
Fulfill Your Designed Destiny

Betsy Fritcha

Live Creatively - Fulfill Your Designed Destiny
Copyright © 2025 by Betsy Fritcha

ISBN: 979-8895311820 (sc)
ISBN: 979-8895311837 (e)

Writers' Branding
(877) 608-6550
www.writersbranding.com
media@writersbranding.com

Table of Contents

The cover design for this book is the creative design that my granddaughter, Ellesyn Fritcha designed when she was in high school. Look closely at this cover design that at first glance appears to be only a lion's head. However, through close examination Elle has creatively hidden depictions that emerge when you pay attention and look for what she creatively designed within the lion's head. Elle's creative design was inspired by The Creative God who lives in Elle.

Elle was asked by her high school administrators to paint a whole wall mural depicting the ideas people wrote down and gave her that they recalled when they were part of this school at some time in their lives. She creatively painted their ideas by inspiration. Elle's numerous creative art awards are displayed in various places in and around her home city. She as well has been publicly acknowledged for her artwork, athletic, and academic accomplishments through her local newspapers and TV Sport Reporters.

Elle recently graduated from college and is employed by a business who as well is aiding people in using their God-Designed creative skills to enhance people's lives in their personal environments so they can fulfill their God-Designed destinies which Holy God has innately put in each person ever born on earth.

Living and Creative God wants each person to discover and fulfill their Creatively Designed Destiny so that He can reveal Himself as The One True God Whose Creative Ability is seen through their accomplishments that overcome evil with GOOD and accomplishes His Good and Holy Intentions for all His Creations to eternally exist together in harmony and peace.

Introduction

What is written in this book is raw Truth for anyone who cares to rightly analyze Wisdom in order to creatively achieve their Designed Destiny.

So here goes!

Have you ever desired to live in an environment that was as perfect as you imagined it to be? A reality place where you could just be you? A place where you were free to create anything you could think of, and for it to remain and even creatively expand just the way you desire and envision? Have you ever tried to create an environment for yourself and your loved ones as you wanted it to be only to have others self-imposed ways forced upon you obligating you to conform to their way of thinking?

Do you truly have a strong desire to build and create something that is innately in you that you cannot seem to dismiss or erase?

Have you ever considered what it would be like to live in an environment free from opposition? What if this were possible? Would you seek to know how this could actually be accomplished?

Well, I have good news for you. This is possible. Creator God Planned for you to live in Perfect Harmony and Creativity for Infinity.

Every human being is Created in the Image and Likeness of a Creatively Unique GOD who formed within each person a definite designed pattern of creativity so that each person can form inventive ways to expand their lives that only they can complete for their personal enjoyment.

Creative God's *Will* for Creating humankind in His exact Image and Likeness is for His personal enjoyment of watching His Created people creatively create their own environment for Good purposes. He wants His Created human beings to mirror His Creative Ability He innately placed in them that is good and benefits them and others as well. He is not a selfish God. He shares His Creative Ability with people He Designed to be like Himself. Therefore, He wants to come long side you and be part of your life. He deeply desires that you create the environment you envision from the original design He innately placed within you before you ever born.

I write this book using my God-given and unique creative abilities to write what He designed in me. My desire is to enhance your creativity ability so you can learn how to creatively design and accomplish your Infinite destiny He Planned for you.

Creative God's Original Plan included creating humankind in His very own Image and after His Likeness for His Infinite Purpose to have someone like Himself who can create the environment they want to inhabit in the same way He does. God enjoys sharing His Creative Ability with you.

Watching you creatively accomplish your personal desires and intents for good that He placed in you brings Him everlasting Enjoyment.

You must know and understand, however, that there are sinister operations irrationally endeavoring to remove human beings from fulfilling their innately designed destiny. Consider rationally that one of these sinister operations is to remove human beings gender identity.

Is anyone asking why there is rampant perversion of sexual identity on earth today? Why are people cynically being pushed into deciding what gender they want to be?

Perverted culture is telling people that they can choose their gender electing to transgender from their born gender, and even declare they are nongender. Hogwash! Creative God created you to be the gender He wanted you to be. There is beauty and creativity in being male or female. Each gender needs the other and cannot be complete without the other's involvement. Just logically think this through! If there were neither male or female genders, you wouldn't be here.

If evil intent can remove humankind's gender uniqueness as either male or a female, they can no longer reproduce and have dominion of the earth to create their environment for good. Therefore, manipulative operations are being used through cultural savvy to convince humankind to become non-gender, which is totally ludicrous.

This sinister ploy of removing gender identity is to prevent humankind from achieving their innate creative ability to procreate their environment as they so choose. This threatening operation if allowed to be accomplished by human neglect, has the ability to stop humankind from creating a personally designed environment that suits their God-designed destiny. If humankind accepts this perverted plan, Creative God's intended destiny for them to create their environment for good purposes is thwarted and eventually shut down.

Along with this heinous maneuver, those who cannot be convinced to become non-gender or transgender are being duped into aborting their creatively conceived babies in the womb of their mothers. Each person's creative identity was planned by an Infinite Creator before they were ever born into this world and each has an innate destiny to fulfill.

Therefore, no matter how it seems or appears to be, nothing can stop these Created babies from fulfilling their predetermined Infinite destinies planned for them by Creative God. Sinister operations can never stop the created destinies of these aborted babies from being fulfilled. They immediately go into the Presence of their Heavenly Father and continue their created destinies. The Holy Bible states truth:

Jesus called a little one (child) to his side and said to his disciples, "Learn this well: Unless you dramatically change your way of thinking and become teachable, and learn about heaven's kingdom realm with the wide-eyed wonder of a child, you will never be able to enter in. Whoever continually humbles himself to become like this gentle child is the greatest on in heaven's kingdom realm. And if you tenderly care for this little one on my behalf, you are tenderly caring for me. But if anyone abuses one of these little ones who believe in me, it would be better for him to have a heavy boulder tied around his neck and be hurled in the deepest sea than to face the punishment he deserves."

Be careful that you not corrupt one of these little ones. For I can assure you that in heaven each of their angelic guardians have instant access to my heavenly Father. Matthew 18:1-6, 10

Jesus said to his disciples who were indignant that little children were being brought to him; and he said to them, "I want little children to come to me, so never interfere with them when they want to come, for heaven's kingdom realm is composed of beloved ones like these! Listen to the truth: No one will enter the kingdom realm of heaven unless he becomes like one of these." Matthew 19:13-15

Illogical and sinister operations deriving from a perverted being, namely the devil or Satan, presumes that if humankind accepts perverted and evil logic, they can no longer multiply and creatively create their infinite destines as Creative God mandated them to do. Read in The Holy Bible: Genesis 1:26-28, Psalms 8, Isaiah 65:17-25, Hebrews 1-2.

Blatant evil plots are being overtly spread with the intent of shutting down human beings from creatively creating their own environment as God Designed them to do. These evil plots also interrupt people from joining with other people's creativity for their shared enjoyment.

The devil cannot reproduce after his kind. He has to transform himself into a human being and present himself as a viable partner to cohabit with sexually. Any willing human woman who allows herself to illegally cohabit with him reproduces corrupted freaks who disrupts society. His perverted plan is to illegally fabricate a people and kingdom he can rule over.

This sinister and evil intent of removing gender identity is pretty stupid if you think about it with intelligence. If there are no longer human beings procreating to govern the earth as Creative God skillfully Designed them to do, eventually there will be no one left for him to cohabit with in making freaks; so, therefore, he will have no one left to rule an illicit and perverted kingdom of his irrationally imagined intent. Why would you want to conform to being a freak when you can creatively create and design your own environment for good as Creative God designed for you to accomplish for your personal enjoyment?

Yes, there is an evil devil whose intended purpose is totally wicked. He never relents in attempting to take creatively designed human beings away from their Creator's Good Plan for them. Each person needs to consider that when humankind creatively designs and creates their environment for good to enjoy both now and for Infinity, evil and sinister operations are closed down permanently.

The devil, never relents in attempting to corrupt human beings by lies and deception to gain power control over them so he can rule them by intimidation and fear. Will you allow yourself to be illicitly used for the devil's illegal plans, which eventually destroys you forever and ever stopping the creative ability you have been given by Creative God? Each person has to personally answer this question; and as well, give an account to their Creator as to why they chose evil over Good.

God of Heaven and earth Creatively Designed each human being with unique abilities to creatively design and create the environment in which they wish to live and enjoy for Infinity. He wants each person to know from His Heart of Love and Truth that you were Created by Him to live in Joy and Peace and Creativity in perfect harmony with Him and other people for ever and ever with no end.

God's Holy *Will* was established before He Created anything and before the world began. His Holy Plan can never be changed or permanently thwarted. He has sworn by Himself that His *Will* is True and established forever. He upholds His Name and His Word Eternally over all Creation: *The promises of Your Word are backed up by the honor or Your Name* - Psalms 138:2.

Therefore, God of Love, Truth, and Wisdom asked me to publish His Creatively Designed Intent, which is for humankind to know how to uniquely create and design their Eternal Destiny He intends for them to realize and accomplish. He is willingly and visibly revealing His Holy Plan for all who truthfully want to learn how to implement His Original Holy Intent for each person He Created in His Image and Likeness.

These are Holy ways of living that perpetuate and expand throughout Eternity.

Live Creatively – Fulfill Your Designed Destiny, entails Holy encounters producing divine revelations. Holy God is Sovereignly revealing how you can factually train yourself to Creatively live from Original Design both now and for Infinity. Creative God wrote down His instructions for Eternal Living from His Original Designed Intent in The Holy Bible. From Genesis to Revelation God lays out His Plan for Eternal Living.

He as well has innately designed into each person their Eternal destiny.

For You formed my inward parts. You covered me in my mother's womb. I will praise You, for I am fearfully and wonderfully made. Marvelous are Your works, and that my soul knows very well. My frame was not hidden from You. When I was made in secret, and skillfully wrought in the lowest parts of the earth Your eyes saw my substance yet unformed, and in Your book they all were written. The days fashioned for me, when as yet there were none of them - Psalms 139:13-16.

Therefore, what is spoken into existence is according to what redeemed humankind frames by The Father's Words they form and speak forth from their Holy desire intricately Designed innately within them.

Holy God's time has come to openly reveal, to those who obey His directions, how they are to fulfill His Creative Design for them as documented in The Holy Bible.

Says The Lord, "So shall My Word be that goes forth from My mouth. It shall not return to Me void or empty of fulfillment.

But it shall accomplish what I please, and it shall prosper in the thing for which I sent it. Isaiah 55:11

In the beginning was the Word, and the Word was with God and the Word was God. He was in the beginning with God. All things were made through Him, and without Him nothing was made that was made. In Him was (and is) *Life, and the Life was* (and is) *the Light of men. And the Light shines in the darkness, and the darkness did not comprehend it.* John 1:1-5

...the Word became flesh and dwelt among us, and we beheld His Glory, the Glory as of the only begotten of the Father, full of Grace and Truth. John 1:14

If you abide in Me [Jesus Christ, The Word of God made flesh, sent to earth by His Father to speak only those things the Father gave Him to speak – John 8:28-29] *and My words abide in you, you will ask what you desire, and it shall be done for you.* John 15:7

The Spirit of Truth has come, He will guide you into all Truth; for He will not speak on His own Authority, but whatever He hears He will speak; and He will tell you things to come. He will Glorify Me, for He will take of what is Mine and declare it to you. All things that the Father has are Mine; therefore, I said that He will take of Mine and declare it to you. John 16:13-15

Jesus Christ, the same yesterday, today, and forever. Hebrews 13:5

Your Father in Heaven is speaking Truth to those who choose to believe and seek Truth from the Words He continuously speaks to them:

But God speaks again and again, though people do not recognize it. He speaks in dreams, in visions of the night when deep sleep falls on people as they lie in bed. He whispers in their ear and terrifies them with His warning. He causes them to change their minds; He keeps them from pride. He keeps them from the grave, from crossing over the river of death. Or God disciplines people with sickness and pain, with ceaseless aching in their bones. They lose their appetite and do not care for even the most delicious food. They waste away to skin and bones. They are at death's door; the angels of death wait for them.

But if a special messenger from Heaven is there to intercede for a person, to declare that He is upright, God will be gracious and say, 'Set him free. Do not make him die for I have found a ransom for his life.' Then his body will become as healthy as a child's, firm and youthful again. When he prays to God, he will be accepted. And God will receive him with joy and restore him to good standing. He will declare to his friends, 'I sinned, but it was not worth it. God rescued me from the grave, and now my life is filled with light.'

Yes, God often does these things for people He rescues them from the grave so they may live in the Light of the living." Job 33:14-29.

For those who freely choose to truly believe, trust, and obey The Word of God who is *Jesus the Son of God who came in human flesh to do His Father's Will* the recorded Word of God is still being written because Holy Spirit is continuously speaking The Father and Jesus' Word of Truth into the earth through those who believe the Word of The Father and His Son, Jesus, and so speak their Words of Truth into existence.

And there are also many other things that Jesus did, which if they were written one by one, I suppose that even the world itself could not contain the books that would be written. Amen. John 21:25

These things that Jesus came on earth in human flesh to show us how to do are still being performed and recorded in the Books in Heaven. These things continue for Infinity through us who ask The Father in Jesus' Name.

Jesus says:

You did not choose Me, but I chose you and appointed you that you should go and bear fruit, and that your fruit should remain, and whatever you ask the Father in My Name He may give you. John 15:16

If you abide in Me, and My Words abide in you, ask whatever you will, and it shall be done for you. John 15:7

Ask and it will be given you; seek, and you will find; knock, and it will be opened to you. For everyone who asks receives, and he who seeks finds, and to him who knocks it will be opened. Matthew 7:7-8

Have faith in God. Truly, I say to you, whoever says to this mountain, 'Be taken up and cast into the sea,' and does not doubt in his heart, but believes that what he says will come to pass, it will be done for him. Therefore, I tell you, whatever you ask in prayer, believe that you receive it, and you will. And whenever you stand praying, believe that you have received it, and you will. And whenever you stand praying, forgive, if you have anything against anyone; so that your Father who is in Heaven may also forgive your trespasses. Mark 11:22-26

For if you forgive men their trespasses, your heavenly Father will also forgive you; but if you do not forgive men their trespasses from your heart, neither will your Father forgive you. Matthew 6:14-15

Truly, truly, I say to you, he who believes in Me will also do the works that I do; and greater works than these will he do, because I go to the Father. Whatever you ask in My Name, I will do it, that the Father may be glorified in the Son; if you ask anything in My Name, I will do it. John 14:12-14

I (Jesus) have spoken these things to you while I was with you. The Counselor, Holy Spirit, whom the Father will send in My Name, He will teach you all things, and bring to your remembrance all that I have said to you. John 14:25-26

I, Paul (and all of us who are in Christ Jesus) *who am a fellow elder and a witness of the sufferings of Christ, and also **a partaker of the glory that will be revealed*** 1 Peter 5:1

What is written in this book, *Live Creatively – Fulfill Your Designed Destiny,* connects humanity with Infinity to accomplish what Holy God has always intended, which is to encompass and unite Heaven and earth as one complete Circle of Life. These supernatural encounters I transcribe is by inspiration of Holy Spirit – 2 Peter 1:20-21 2 Timothy 3:16-17. Therefore, in my wholehearted obedience to my Lord and my God to write this book, I am *a **partaker of the Glory now being revealed***.

Through these God-selected Holy encounters God Almighty took me into, He is manifesting what already exists in the invisible realm into the visible realm of earth through the obedient actions of His Righteous ones to whom The Lord is openly revealing what to do and speak for Him. Therefore, what already exists as invisible in the Spirit realm is now operating in Holy ways and is becoming visibly operational on earth. In this, God Almighty is bringing into visibility and tangible form the fullness of His Manifest Creative Glory to make Himself known in wholeness and usefulness which fulfills His Originally Designed Intent to fill the whole earth with His Glory. When this occurs, evil is eliminated thus fulfilling God's Holy Intent.

It is not the purpose of this book to humanly explain the Divine encounters I experienced by the *Will* of Holy God. The purpose of this book is to show a Holy Creator Who intends for those He Created in His Image and Likeness to Creatively fulfill their Originally Designed Eternal Destiny. By humankind's obedience to use their innately designed creative abilities, the heavens and the earth can be restored to Supreme God's Original Intent.

Because Holy God's Original Design and Plan for earth and the heavens has been perverted through evil intentions, Holy God is now in the process of restoring His Original Design for Heaven and earth to operate together in perfect harmony.

Creative God truly wants humankind, whom He Created in His Image and Likeness, to know how to permanently eliminate evil that stole their rulership of the heavens and earth which shut them down from creatively designing their environment for Good. Therefore, in accordance to His Perfectly preordained *Will*, Creative God of Heaven and earth is presently showing how He is displaying His Power that is eliminating evil in all its forms. Creative God is doing this by replacing evil ways through the creative ability He innately Designed in each human being.

Holy Divine occurrences are displayed throughout the entire Holy Bible and are recorded for our learning. God's Son, Jesus Christ, came from Infinity and became a human being by being born from the womb of a woman in order to display Holy Divine occurrences that are attainable for human beings.

Jesus Christ the Only Son of God, willingly said *YES* to His Father's request to become human flesh by the incarnation of a miraculous birth that causes Him to be both human being and Holy God all at the same time. **DO NOT** attempt to understand this with your mind. You can't.

Holy Divine encounters recorded in The Holy Bible were written especially for those who would be living at the time when evil was expressing its best shots. Creative God's specific time has arrived to fully reinstate and accomplish one Righteous Kingdom Rule between Heaven and earth. The evolution of evil has diminished Holy Knowledge almost to the point of annihilation.

Even so, in the midst of evil being permanently eliminated, Creative God is intervening and making Himself known in the fullness of Wisdom and Knowledge. Holy God's ordained time has arrived for Him to openly and visibly reveal how it is possible to Creatively exist both now and beyond the ages of time.

As you choose to train yourself in Godliness, the Holy accounts as documented in The Holy Bible along with what is written in this book, *Live Creatively - Fulfill Your Designed Destiny,* come alive. There are, as well, other Holy books presently being written and published that The Lord is raising up to reveal Himself in the fullness of Revelation Knowledge and Wisdom.

I humbly, yet with Supreme God's Authoritative permission, record in this book, *Live Creatively - Fulfill Your Designed Destiny,* some of the Holy encounters I personally experienced which reveal God's Holy Purpose of making Himself known in the Glory He has in Heaven and is presently transmitting onto earth at this time in history. These holy encounters align with Biblical Truth and Wisdom.

Supreme God's Holy Intent is for you to know with understanding that you were Originally Created with an innately designed creativity that He fully intends for you to achieve so that you bring into existence what you create in the same way He does.

Supreme God envisioned the earth and the heavens and then spoke them into existence. All through The Holy Bible Supreme God is inviting human beings Created like Himself to imitate Him in using their innately Designed Creative ability in the same way He does, which is to creatively create their desired intent by speaking what they envision into existence by the words they speak. His Righteous Purpose is for humankind to occupy Infinity free from sin and evil so Heaven and earth operate in one complete Circle of Life that brings Him Glory and humankind enjoyment.

Ponder these words in The Holy Bible taken from The Passion Translation:

Lord, you know everything there is to know about me. You perceive every movement of my heart and soul, and you understand my every thought before it even enters my mind. You are so intimately aware of me, Lord.

You read my heart like an open book and you know all the words I'm about to speak before I even start a sentence!

You know every step I will take before my journey even begins. You've gone into my future to prepare the way, and in kindness you follow behind me to spare me from the harm of my past.

With your hand of love upon my life, you impart a blessing to me. Wherever I go, your hand will guide me, your strength will empower me. It's impossible to disappear from you or to ask the darkness to hide me.

You formed my innermost being, shaping my delicate inside and my intricate outside, and wove them all together in my mother's womb.

I thank you, God, for making me so mysteriously complex! How thoroughly you know me, Lord! You even formed every bone in my body when you created me in the secrete place, carefully, skillfully shaping me.

You saw who you created me to before I became me! Before I'd ever seen the light of day, the number of days you planned for me were already recorded in your book.

Every single moment you are thinking of me! How precious and wonderful to consider that you cherish me constantly in your every thought!

When I awake each morning, you're still with me. Psalm 139

May each person reading this book be personally stimulated and invigorated to pursue Holy and Creative God to learn how they can creatively create their own unique personal environment, and then join their personal creativity with the Holy creative ability of others and in agreed conjunction enjoy an enlightened Infinity.

The Lord God of Creation has openly revealed Himself to me since early childhood. I simply accepted Him each time He presented Himself to me. I openly and honestly convey Him in my writings as the only way I to know to identify Him: Love and Truth.

The Lord Sovereignly trained me to know His Voice and His Holy Ways through His unchangeable Word by means of the Inspirational Power and Wisdom of Holy Spirit. Read 2 Timothy 3:16-17; 2 Peter 1:16-21; and Romans 15:4 in The Holy Bible. My personal Holy creative encounters align with

His Holy Word of Truth as found in The Holy Bible. Holy God desires for each person to know Him in intimacy so they too can have their own personal celestial encounters with Him.

In all these Holy encounters, I personally interact with my Sovereign God whom I have known on intimate terms since early childhood when He came to me in an orphanage. In obedience to Him, I accurately record in this book some of my most recent Holy interactions with Him.

Holy God is revealing Himself to me according to His innately Designed destiny for my life both now and for Infinity. What I write in this book are transcendent Holy celestial encounters He has allowed me to have part in for His Purpose of revealing how Heaven and earth are to be reconciled so they operate as one complete Circle of Life throughout Infinity. I continuously agree to allow Him to Live and Move and have His Being in me and through me however He desires. I pray you, the reader, also allow The God of Infinity to work in you those things that are pleasing in His Sight so you can fulfill your intended and designed destiny.

My desire in all my writings is to accurately relate Holy God Who is Love and Truth as He has Sovereignly chosen to show Himself to me. He deeply desires to personally make Himself known to each and every person so that each of you fulfills your Creatively Designed Destiny. I trust God of Love and Truth to reveal Himself to you in these writings in a way that is meaningful to you so that you Eternally fulfill the Holy destiny for which He Created you. May Creative God be truly Glorified as each one of us attains our Eternal Creative Destiny.

The Lord made it clear to me that what I am writing in this book is to be accomplished in cooperation together with those living in Highest Heaven with Him and those who live upon the earth. Keep in mind that to God there is no separation (disconnection, detachment, severance, dissociation) between Heaven (Spiritual) and earth (natural).

What is vividly being made known in this book is to be distributed so that others know that Creative God is fulfilling the Truth He has spoken and revealed throughout all the ages of time. He is tangibly making Himself known on earth and in the heavens in powerful and noticeable ways. All that He has spoken and revealed through all the ages of time is being fulfilled because His Truth is founded on Wisdom and Revelation Knowledge based on His personhood.

Because evil intent has upset Creative God's Original Plan for Heaven and earth to cooperatively function together for Good, The Lord is Creatively revealing how He intends to restore and reconcile Heaven and earth back to His Original Intent so, together in harmony, Heaven and earth operate as one Holy Creation for Eternity.

For He has made known to us, in all wisdom and insight the mystery of His Will, according to His purpose which He set forth in Christ as a plan for the fullness of time, to unite all things in Him, things in Heaven and things on earth. Ephesians 1:9-10 The Passion Translation

For in Him (Christ Jesus) *all the fullness of God was pleased to dwell, and through Him to reconcile to Himself all things, whether on earth, or in Heaven, making peace by the Blood of His cross.* Colossians 1:19-20

Creative God's Holy Purpose for using Words and displaying tangible Actions, is to cause redeemed people to learn how to regulate and maintain His Creatively Designed Creation with Love, Authority, Justice, and Harmony that makes for an enjoyable Infinity.

I was pondering within myself how what I was writing of my celestial Holy encounters which involve harmonious operations between Heaven and earth would be understood and known as The Lord intends.

Eternal and Living God let me know that is not up to me whether or not His Creative Ways are understood. It's up to me to obey Him to publish these experiences so that His Creative Ways are known as to how Heaven and earth are to Creatively function for Infinity. He further made me to know that these supernatural or beyond natural activities He took me into are cooperative maneuvers that are to operate between Heaven and earth as one Holy and complete operation for Infinity. I willingly and continually submit to Him. I allow Him to continually reveal to me what I do not know that I need to know in order to bring Heaven and earth back into complete harmony to function as one complete Circle of Life for Eternity.

What I am writing in this book by the inspiration and direction of Holy God is to favorably and distinctly build an indisputable Foundation of Truth for others to build on who come after me.

Creative God is making Himself known through what I am writing in ways that He wants to be known. He is displaying His sure Foundation of Truth and Justice that opens Eternal Ways for Creative Living for those who fully desire to know Truth so they can creatively design and maintain their innately desired intent that continues for Infinity. Faithful obedience reaps rewards for those who obey what Creative God is revealing through these writings that honestly reveal His Holy way to achieve true and joyful living that lasts forever.

For these Truths to operate in one's life, it is imperative that each person makes a heart decision to receive Salvation from sin and evil that the Father offers through Jesus' Blood Sacrifice and as well wholeheartedly forgive all who have trespassed against you as Your Father in Heaven has totally forgiven you so you can receive from Him all you ask and desire. When this heartfelt and decisive choice is honestly made before Almighty God and publicly confessed before another person, then you have the ability to mature in Eternal Ways that can never be erased.

When you truly and honestly make this Eternal decision, and so desire above all else that you want Holy God to be the Source of your Life, then His DNA - **divine nature assimilated** lives in you and imparts His Wisdom Truth into you that continually empowers your RNA – **revealed nature achieved** to creatively design and bring into existence your intended and good desires that fulfills your designed destiny.

Wisdom Truth is imprinted into your DNA - **divine nature assimilated**. Your **revealed nature achieved**, is Holy God's innate DNA causing you to accomplish your designed destiny for the GOOD of His Creation and all humankind, who He Created to be like Him in nature and ability.

This is an ongoing operation from intimate relationship with Him so you learn for yourself what your own personal design entails. The Father's DNA abiding in you causes you to be like Him in nature and ability which ignites your RNA to create from the original design He innately placed in you before you were ever born. What you design and create blesses your Father in Heaven and helps humankind.*

Holy God is a Father who delights in listening to His children He Created to be like Himself. He is a Good and Favorable Holy Being properly caring for His children He made to be like Himself. He endows them with Holy rule, dominion and stewardship over whatever they creatively create to inhabit for Infinity.

Supreme and Living God knows you in the way He Created you to exist for Infinity, so He graciously and intimately interacts with you in your own personal way of communicating with Him. You just have to choose to do so. Don't allow yourself to be swayed from reaching out to Him no matter how weak your first attempts may be to know Him in ways you have not known Him. Ask Him honestly and openly to reveal Himself to you in Creative Ways. Keep on asking Him no matter how much you may *think* you know Him and His Ways. Asking Him for more Knowledge and Wisdom to use in Creative Ways is an ongoing Way of Life for Infinity. Start practicing!

Read on to find out how The Lord God of Creation wants to be known to those who choose to listen to Him with the purpose of obeying His Word of Truth and Wisdom.

Hear Him!
See Him!
Choose to obey Him!

I highly recommend Lance Wallnau's teachings that train you how to connect the natural and supernatural realms into everyday existence to achieve what God has innately designed in you to accomplish both now and for Infinity in cooperation with Heaven and earth. www.lancewallnau.com

The Immeasurable Holy
Operations of Supreme God

Disruption of the Earth

Have you've noticed! The world has gone crazy and is totally out of the control of any sort of significant law and order. Everyone living by the world's standards is doing whatever they think is right for them with no consideration of how others choose to live. Anarchy and chaos are overtaking and consuming any kind of decency and peaceful living that has been the norm for centuries. There is a heinous disregard toward any kind of legal authority and rule of order.

Is anyone asking, "Why is there all this disruption on earth? Is there any answer to counteract all this disruption?"

I want to offer the only meaningful and concrete answer that there is. In the beginning of what is commonly known as the world, a Supreme Creator defined immutable laws that were to be adhered to so that there would be no chaos and disorder on the earth and in the heavens He created to be lived in and to be ruled by Peace and Harmony. These immutable laws included set boundaries that formed a solid sense of rule and order.

I was asking The Lord why I was seeing storms, fires and winds, volcanoes, earthquakes, and rocks on and within the earth, as one violent operation, all seeming to erupt in violent upheaval all at the same time.

As I quietly waited in His Presence, I knew innately and emphatically that the earth is thrashing and convulsing as in the pains of birth. Through all this upheaval Holy God is birthing His Kingdom Rule of Righteousness in the heavens and on the earth. He is causing all forms of evil entities to be vomited out of their secret hiding places where they think they cannot be seen and so cannot be detected.

The Lord flooded me with His Love assuring me that I do not need to fear all this disruption because these things have to happen so that Righteousness can reign on earth to displace all evil ways that keep people from fulfilling their designed destines He placed in them for the good of His Creations.

I began to praise Him for His Great Strength and Power. He made me to know deep within me that when Holy praises are given to Him, He is empowered even more to display His Authority in the face of His enemies and *all* their clandestine evil. I had an enlightened understanding that Holy Praise empowers Creative God to Act Judiciously. Holy Praise propels Him into Action. His Mighty Power Acts that are presently being seen on the earth flow out of the increased Holy praise being voiced on earth through the people who know Him on intimate terms. Along with Holy increased praise through His Holy people, Creation is crying out to their Creator. The maneuvers and operations of the winds and waves, thunder and lightning, and fire are giving Him praise. This is why the rocks are crying out and joining the praises of God's Holy people. God's Holy people's praises are combining with the praises and cries of His Holy Creation which empowers Him into full forward motion to rout out all evil entities from their hiding places.

I recognized The Lord was placing Truth inside me. He revealed to me that the earth is convulsing to rid itself of evil. Blood is crying out from the earth for vengeance. Lifeblood is a form of praise God hears that forces Him to Act in Holy Vengeance and Wrath against those who cause Lifeblood to be spilled.

Holy God, The Father, asked His only begotten Son to come on earth in human flesh and allow His Holy Life-Blood to be poured on the earth to pay the penalty for the sin of iniquity that invaded His creatively Designed Creations. Yeshua or Jesus Christ, God's only Son, said a heart YES and agreed with His Father to become the Holy Blood Sacrifice that would pay the penalty for the sin of iniquity that invaded His Creation. Because Jesus willingly agreed, The Father told His Son, *"Vengeance is Mine. I will repay, says The Lord."* The Father's time has come to express His Holy Vengeance against all wickedness and evil that caused His Holy Son's Precious Life-Blood to be spilt. Holy Justice demands retribution. The Father's Authorized Holy Vengeance is against all evil entities who caused His Son, whom He loves, to spill His Blood to redeem His Creation.

My Lord and my God, how excellent is Your Name and Your Word! We rejoice with You and exalt You before all the heavens and the earth. You alone are worthy of ALL Praise, Honor, and Glory. Be magnified in our praise and worship to You alone! Your Love to us empowers us to praise You even more. We join with Jesus' in praising and thanking You for avenging His Holy Blood and for delivering us from all evil, and for seating us with you in heavenly places to Rule and Reign with You in all Righteousness, Peace, and Joy. This is The Kingdom of God!

God Is Working in Unseen Ways

Holy God is working in Ways that cannot be seen by those who choose not to submit to His Way of doing things.

When you ask God to show you what He is doing on earth at this time, He will show you in unexpected ways. It won't necessarily be through pleasant ways. You must know that when your circumstances become unpleasant, God is carrying you and is with you to deliver you from what is coming against you. This is the time to intimately know God of Love and Truth so you can trust Him unreservedly. God is presently disrupting things the way we know them to be so He can get us to recognize the way we have been doing things is not working.

We must know that Holy angels are on assignment because people are crying out to God in their pain asking Him to help them. God is answering these prayers and bringing to us what is needed to accomplish His Creatively Designed *Will*.

In the midst of unpleasant situations, learn to look for God's abundant Blessings He is pouring out on you to be far more than you expect or can contain. God intends for you to share these Blessings with others. However, you must keep your focus on God, not on the Blessing of provision just for the sake of having the Blessing. When you do this, the abundance of His Blessing of provision continue flowing and coming to you for His Purposes. You must know this and trust God. You should count on this as you trust God in what He is saying to do so that His *Will* is accomplished by what you say and do in obedience to His Holy directives.

Partaking in God's Glory Being Revealed

God Almighty is manifesting what already exists in the invisible realm into the visible realm of earth through the obedient actions of His Righteous ones to whom The Lord is openly revealing what to do and speak for Him. Therefore, what already exists as invisible in the Spirit realm is now operating in Holy ways and is becoming visibly operational on earth. In this, God Almighty is bringing into visibility and tangible form the fullness of His Manifest *Creative Glory* to make Himself known in wholeness and usefulness so the whole earth is filled with His Originally Designed Intent which shuts down all evil. Those who wholeheartedly obey The Lord are partaking in His Glory that is being revealed.

Halting Old Methods

The Lord opened up my understanding to know that upcoming generations are to be trained in His Creative Ways so that they follow their creative bent that He innately designed within them. He related to me that those who choose to operate in Creative Ways are stopping OLD methods and bringing in the NEW ways that are presently being released on earth. OLD ways and methods no longer work. NEW methods and ways must come forth to replace what people presumed would work but now recognize does not produce good and lasting results.

For NEW ways to be established it is imperative not to look back or return to past ways. We must learn God's NEW ways and act in NEW ways that produce Good and lasting results.

What was done in the past is gone and so can never be repeated. When the NEW is being done congruently, it is being accomplished and lasts for Infinity. Creative God lives in Infinity where there is no past, present, or future.

Jesus said in The Holy Bible:
Why do you keep looking backward to your past and have second thoughts about following me?

When you turn back you are useless to God's kingdom realm. Luke 9:62

Lord, I choose to walk in Your Creative Glory expansion believing You to work in me and through me what I cannot accomplish without Your intervention. I rely on Your Glory Fire Presence working within me to flow out through me. I choose not to look at my circumstances on earth, but to expect Your Holy Provision from Heaven to operate through me.

Bringing in New Ways

In order to walk into the NEW, our lives must be simplified. We must let go of OLD habits and ways of doing things. We cannot stay in OLD ways or the ways we are used to doing things, which includes daily chores. We must make a concrete effort to put into practice doing things that will bring His NEW ways into tangible manifestation.

Here are some practical checkpoints:

Pray daily and often! Praise God continuously! Trust God in all your ways! Envision God's Divine Orders to you which determines your daily activities! Cease from daily labors beyond what is necessary – let things go!

Do not allow yourself to deter from these practical checkpoints! Do not speak unnecessary or idle words!

Speak Words of Authority that cause people and angels to help you! Act in Love toward all people!

Daily refurbish these directives by integrating these practical ways into your everyday life so in the midst of your unsettling circumstances you align your life with God's Ways to truthfully live. Making a concerted effort to diligently practice these activities in your life causes you to go forward on a level path in accomplishing your divine destiny that is innately within you.

It is imperative that you allow God's thoughts and plans to be integrated into your life so you can fulfill your creatively Designed Destiny that continues for Infinity. Make a quality decision within yourself to keep expanding yourself in God's Creative Design that is implanted in you by His doing.

Keep silent of all unnecessary or idle words so that when you do speak, the desires you want to occur flow and manifest into tangible form from your Holy intent. Keeping silent and not speaking unnecessary words continually increases Holy God's Creative Energy and Power so that when you do choose to speak into your circumstances, Holy Fire Power emanates from the sound waves in your voice that designs your Holy intent for the present and for Infinity.

These Holy operations cause you to recognize in fullness of understanding that when you speak and talk by God's Creative Glory residing in you, what you speak causes God's perpetual Creative Energy and Power to activate, which brings His Righteous Kingdom on earth. Then His Intended and Designed *Will* for redeemed humankind to rule the heavens and the earth in Holy Dominion both now and for Eternity can be accomplished.

God's time of acceleration for the expansion of His Creative Glory to operate on earth is here. Therefore, what has been known dimly can now be known in fullness so His Kingdom is established on earth to function as it functions in Highest Heaven. This expansion of God's Creative Glory fills the whole earth with His Knowledge and Glory and fills the whole earth with people who know Him.

Written in God's Books

God has Books in Heaven that contain the record of His Originally Designed Ways He intends to be fulfilled. What is recorded in these Books in Heaven does not change. Therefore, God is seeing to it that all His Original Plans recorded in these Books is being made known at this time on earth so that what is written in the Books is accomplished, and completed Forever.

What is written in some of these Books reveals your ordained destiny that Holy angels can go to and see what is written about you so they can then arrange your circumstances for these to be fulfilled. You may ask God to send His Holy angels assigned to you to go and open your Book to see what is written about you that needs to be done so you can fulfill your Creatively Designed Destiny.

Each person's destiny is written in the books, and there is more than one book written about each person. You have a book with your name on it that contains and reveals your ordained destiny that Holy angels can go to and see what God has written in your book for you to accomplish. Your circumstances are arranged by God and His Holy angels to assist you in fulfilling your ordained destiny.

However, there are other books written pertaining to your responses to God's directions to you. These other books record your obedient actions and your rewards for faithfulness and obedience to Holy God.

There are also other books carrying God's Designed *Will* that reveals your assignments He has ordained for you to do in accomplishing His Designed *Will*. There are created beings Designed by Supreme God who carry Wisdom and Prudence. You can call on Wisdom and Prudence to enlighten what you don't know that you need to know. Then, these books can be opened to reveal what is written in them for you to do. This is to be done when activities on earth dictate that it is time to fulfill what God has written in His Designed *Will* Book that you need to carry out for His Glory to be known and seen on earth that dispels evil.

Lord, I ask You to put in my heart the desire to ask You what is written in the Books for me to accomplish for Your Glory and Honor. You are surely worthy of Praise. How Awesome and Magnificent You are Lord! There is none like You. Show me what is written in the Books, Lord. Thank you.

Manifest Glory Operations

Holy God is no longer acting in former ways. OLD ways have ceased through God's divinely appointed interference. God is once again unleashing on earth His Creative and Original Ways. He is presently bringing His Original Ways of operating on earth back into public view. There are those who recognize that their way of thinking and doing no longer works. Therefore, they are ready to change their former habits and thinking to align with God's Original Way for them to creatively function on earth and in Heaven.

Holy God's Original and Creative Ways can operate through each person who allows themselves to trust Him and also trust themselves in working out how to incorporate and release their Creatively Designed Holy destiny. Through each redeemed person using their innate God-given creative ability, the earth and the heavens are being restored, renewed, and replenished to function as Supreme God Originally Designed.

O, Lord my God, I trust You and I choose to trust myself as I pursue using the Creative Design you placed in me before I was born. Keep me from all forms of pride and deception so I can serve You in uprightness and prosperity all my days to make You known in all Your Glory and Power. Thank You.

Molecular Restructure

Beginning in January 2018, God's Holy Presence came into my home and remained for three months. His Presence was so heavy and powerfully within in me, upon me, and around me in my home that I could barely function in the natural.

During this three-month timeframe in 2018, God's Holy Presence was tangibly and powerfully evident in my home. One morning I awoke overpowered by God's tangible Presence. I was stunned to the point of numbness and inability to do daily tasks of getting ready for a new day. I pushed on through to do the things that had to be done and then went to my Prayer Room. I said, "Why is this happening to my body? Why am I so physically stunned like this, Lord?"

The Lord caused me to know that He was restructuring the molecular structure system of my body so He could take me where He wants me to go to accomplish a higher purpose He has for taking me into places. I asked Him why He was doing this to me.

He let me know that He was doing this so my body can transport back and forth from earth to Heaven in a transformed molecular structure to accomplish a purpose He had for me to do what I could not otherwise do without a molecular structure in my body. I asked if this meant I was going to die. He assured me that I would not die the way I was thinking. I knew by Holy Spirit that my body, soul, and spirit would still be intact so I could properly function both in Heaven and on earth.

Therefore, I submitted to Holy God. I knew Him so well in full trust and assurance that I knew this was from Him for me to do. Therefore, I gave God permission to work in me whatever pleases Him in using me as He *Wills*. I chose not to stop this flow of Power and Authority that was transforming the molecular structure of my body. I expressed to The Lord that I would receive all He was doing in me, around me, and through me for His Holy Purposes.

I fully trusted Holy God in releasing myself to Him and in allowing Him to transform my molecular structure to operate in higher degrees of Creative Glory. I cannot explain this nor do I totally understand this. I just yielded in worship to my God who I fully trusted. I was immensely enjoying His Holy Glory Fire Presence that was in me and all around me. He supplied the Strength I needed to do ordinary tasks when I needed to. To Supreme God alone be all the Honor and Glory forever and ever! This encounter and others of like nature that The Lord has taken me into since childhood, are detailed in this author's book, *Infinite Destiny Truth and Wisdom*.

I know in Truth and with understanding that The Lord restructured my physical body in a higher molecular form to carry in fullness the Power and Authority of Heaven so that when He transports me by Holy Spirit encounters to be on the scene in the Spiritual realm or in natural situations where He wants to bring change for Good that what I obey Him to do in cooperation with Him is accomplished. The Holy Bible gives accounts of this happening with Elijah and Philip, Jesus, and Paul for whatever Good purpose our Father in Heaven had for their encounters.

Greater Works

I asked The Lord how I was to do the works that Jesus did: disappear into the clouds and vanish, walk out of the midst of a crowd when people were trying to kill him, come back and forth from Heaven to earth as He has openly revealed to me are the ...*greater works*... Jesus said we would be doing to bring Supernatural Acts on earth to make Almighty God known in all His Glory and Power to shut down Satan's evil.

I have read about Kathryn Kuhlman's life that when she walked into a place, people would be powerfully influenced and touched by Holy Spirit sometimes without her saying a word. I have never understood how this could happen. I always pondered how this happens and to some degree asked for this to occur for me even though I had no understanding how this could happen. I recognize now that The Lord was revealing a foretaste that this is indeed possible. The circumstances on earth are such that He is manifesting the fullness of supernatural happenings through obedient people so wickedness and evil is kept from being dominant and His Glory is manifested in Influential Power.

There are Holy Bible accounts of Jesus, when He lived on earth, at times vanishing out of the midst of a crowd of people who were trying to kill him; and after He was resurrected from death, disappearing into the clouds ascending back into Heaven. Paul, the apostle, had an encounter in the third heaven and came back to earth and gave an account of what happened to him in the best way he could explain. He just honestly told what he knew happened to him even though he did not fully understand.

Jesus spoke that we who would come after Him, would do … *greater works…* than He did because He was going back to His Father in Heaven and would send Holy Spirit who would live in us permanently; and therefore, we would do even greater works than He did. Jesus knew His Father's *Will* and knew the time would come when these supernatural occurrences would need to be done to save many people's lives during the time Satan was attempting to annihilate and destroy people and everything on earth so he could rule a kingdom of his own making.

When evil operations are taking place on earth, trusting God to work through miraculous ways is a must so that He can be seen and known in Power manifestations that outdo Satan. Even though Satan is permitted to do supernatural things, God Almighty is greater than anything Satan could ever do.

The times we are currently living through dictate that Holy God is doing supernatural occurrences that are greater than Satan's evil to show Himself as Supreme God over all forms of wickedness and evil.

How marvelous are Your Ways in our eyes, O Lord.

Gabriel Brings Visionary Glory Box

During this time of intense Holy Presence in my home in 2018, I awoke at 2:15 a.m. worshipping The Lord expressing my love to Him. As I lay in bed, I saw a Pure White substance. I could not distinguish exactly what it was.

I became aware of an angel I saw way up high in the heavens. He was Pure White and had wings. He was wearing a Pure White robe with his knees bent like he was carrying something. He emerged out of a Pure White Substance that appeared to me to be a Glory Cloud. Then I saw another Pure White object shaped in rectangle form also emerging out of this Pure White Substance pointing downward as if coming down toward earth from Heaven. I knew this angel was coming to me and bringing me this rectangle Box. I was puzzled by what I saw.

I asked The Lord to reveal to me what I was seeing. He related to me that this was an angel coming to me emerging from Pure White Substance and bringing me a Box containing Visionary Glory. The Lord said I could open this Box anytime I wanted.

I asked, "What is Visionary Glory?"

The Lord openly revealed to me that Visionary Glory is Living Substance. Visionary Glory exists in the Spirit realm and is actual Living Substance. The Substance of Life exists in reality form in the invisible Spirit realm and can be brought into tangible manifestation by calling into being with words what is seen from Visionary Glory so that what could not be seen before can now be seen and known. Visionary Glory is actual Living Substance that can be displayed into material manifestation by spoken words. I suddenly understood that the words I regularly declare *I release the Glory Influence to displace the powers of darkness and replace them with the Ruling Presence of Almighty and Living God* are actually manifesting Living Visionary Glory Substance on earth to displace evil operations.

Visionary Glory is Living Substance that can be seen and acted upon. It is real, not imagined. When the Box containing Visionary Glory is opened, what is seen from Visionary Glory can be brought into our circumstances and as well over situations we hear about in the natural. We are to do or act on what is seen from Visionary Glory which is Living Substance.

By acting on what is seen from Visionary Glory, Living Substance is brought on earth from Heaven that displays God's Justice on earth. We are to call those things that are not seen in the natural as though they are because these things that are invisible to us on earth exist as Living Substance. These invisible things exist as Living Substance and can come into visible form to be used on earth for Good purposes. This is accomplished by words that are spoken from what is seen from Visionary Glory. It is God's Holy *Will* that this be done in order to displace the powers of darkness. It must be made known that what is seen from Visionary Glory is actual Living Substance that is to be spoken into existence on earth to exalt Holy God and eradicate Satan's evil.

Visionary Glory is increased as we obey and go and do what Holy God is revealing must be done in our circumstances. Visionary Glory guides us in seeing what to do or say in every situation or circumstance we are in or up against. We are to count on this and act like Visionary Glory is there because it is. If we don't act like Visionary Glory is there, it remains invisible and unusable and therefore cannot be used as God intends for it to be used for His Holy Purpose of eradicating evil in all its forms.

Visionary Glory is invisible Living Substance that is alive and active and can materialize into tangible matter to be used on earth in our circumstances when what is seen from Visionary Glory is spoken into actual existence. What is seen from invisible Visionary Glory can be spoken into visible matter or form that is fully operational on earth.

Elijah, Elisha, and Jesus operated from Visionary Glory to do what seemed to be miracles to people on earth but is who God is the Great I AM to whom nothing is impossible. Visible and invisible are both alike to Him.

Holy God is in the process of merging both visible and invisible realms back to the Original State of Glory before Satan disrupted His Designed Plan for earth. There was no visible and invisible in Creation until Satan flaunted his rebellion before humankind and they accepted this rebellion as reality. Rebellion forced Holy God to conceal invisible Glory Substance from visible form so that what intrinsically resides in Glory Substance could not be used for evil purposes. Humankind became content to accept only operating in visible form when there is so much more available to them to be used for good purposes and holy reasons that enables visible and invisible realms to manifest as one complete and holy operation. Nevertheless, Supreme God already had a set Plan in motion to reconcile and re-establish visible and invisible realms as one complete operation so that evil would not remain forever and so stop God's Holy Creative Designed Plan for people's lives that goes on for Infinity.

Holy God's predetermined time has come to reconcile and restore the visible and invisible realms to function from Original Design in operating as one solitary complete operation. God's Holy Purpose for Heaven and earth to function together as one fluid operation Originated from His Uniquely Designed Purpose He formed before the foundation of the world. Jesus' Holy Blood Sacrifice redeemed humankind to live in Visionary Glory. Those who accept God's Holy Redemption from evil and walk with Him in Blood Covenant relationship have the ability to operate from Visionary Glory *if* they so choose. In order for Visionary Glory to operate in the Way God Purposed from the beginning of time, redeemed people must choose to operate in Visionary Glory. At this time on earth, Visionary Glory operations must be activated so that every form of dark and perverse evil is permanently eradicated.

Ask Holy God to grant you fullness of understanding from Revelation Knowledge and Wisdom to know how to creatively operate in Visionary Glory. When you act in accordance to what He reveals to you, you receive what you ask of Him.

As I was compiling and recording all The Lord is speaking to me, *suddenly*, understanding opened to me. Instantly, I knew that the angel descending to me with a Pure White Box containing Visionary Glory Substance was Gabriel. In this Visionary Glory Box Gabriel brought to me are the Good things or works that God Planned before the foundation of the world that are to be accomplished at this time on earth when God's Word of Authority is being fulfilled by His doing.

Visionary Glory is Living Substance which can be Creative words or acts in the form of words, pictures, prayer to verbalize, specific healing pronouncements, a Blessing, a Righteous Judgement announcement. When the Glory Box containing Visionary Glory Substance is opened, what is seen from Visionary Glory can be released into your immediate circumstances, or over situations you hear about, or in which you are personally involved by God's doing. By speaking or acting on what you see in the Visionary Glory Box, Holy Creative acts are being performed by the words you speak and the actions you perform.

Remember when you were a child and imagined all kinds of things that your teddy bear or superman doll could hear you and knew what you were saying or that you could fly or jump off a tall building and land on your feet in one piece without any kind of harm or walk on or lay down on white clouds in the sky. When I fly in airplanes, I still imagine myself playing on the white puffy clouds. Well, transfer this into using your imagination to design, frame, and speak into reality existence what you imagine. God Created this innate ability in us to imagine and create into existence what we envision. This is why young children are so tuned into their imagination. They so want what they imagine to be real just as you did when you were a child. If you have young children, encourage them to develop their imagination to dream and to integrally form into actual manifestation what they see inside them that to them is real because it is real. Visionary Glory that Holy God innately Created within each human being is to be used for good purposes, and not for evil purposes.

God, The Great I AM, has no limits as to how to release and transport Visionary Glory, which is Living Substance. As you ask Him to know, when you are in a situation you need to know, you will know what word or act needs to operate in the situation you find yourself. Then you step out and do what you know to do trusting Visionary Glory to operate and meet the need at hand.

God's Visionary Glory Substance is amazing and overwhelms our finite minds. We must trust and rely on God's Holy Wisdom to empower us to obey what we see and know to do from Visionary Glory, which is Living Substance that sustains Life.

O, Lord, comprehension of Your Visionary Glory Substance is amazing and is overwhelming to our finite minds. We trust and rely on Your Holy Wisdom to empower us to obey You. Thank You for revealing Yourself to us in Visionary Glory, which is Living Substance that sustains Life. I thank and praise You God of my life.

Life is Invisible Substance

Substance of Life resides in Holy Spirit who essentially exists in The Father and in Jesus, His Only Son. If we love God and keep His commandments, Father, Son, and Holy Spirit abides is us and we abide in Him – Galatians 2:20. Jesus said to His disciples, *"Loving Me empowers you to obey My word. And My Father will love you so deeply that we will come to you and make you our dwelling place. When the Father sends the Spirit of Holiness, the one like Me who sets you free, He will teach you all things in My name."* John 14:23-26; 17:20-23.

Therefore, we who are created in Holy God's Image and Likeness can create material matter from the Substance of Life that exists in the invisible realm by Jesus' *Faith* abiding in us. Jesus' Faith abiding in us enables us to believe in Holy Spirit's Creative Ability to operate The Father's *Willed* Design through us.

Jesus manifested The Father's Substance of Life innately residing in Him when He spoke into visible form what appeared to be invisible: water into wine, expansion of food. Jesus spoken words caused the water to become wine and food to multiply so that the Substance of Life would manifest into useable material form on earth. Jesus' spoken words caused water to become solid matter for Him to walk on, bread and fish to multiply, and people to come back to Life from the dead. Jesus did many other things that are not recorded in the Bible according to John 21:25.

Jesus Created what was needed in a situation by *Faith* in His Father's and Holy Spirit's Ability to manifest tangible matter from The Substance of Life residing in them. Jesus knew His Father and Holy Spirit dwelled in Him also. Jesus knew that when He spoke from the Substance of Life residing in His Father and Holy Spirit and in Him as well the very thing He spoke that was tangibly alive in Heaven but was invisible on earth would manifest into tangible matter that would sustain Life on earth. Faith manifests invisible substance into visible matter. Faith acts upon what is genuinely believed.

From this Truth, those redeemed by Jesus' Blood Sacrifice who freely choose to speak and act by Jesus' Faith abiding in them can create material matter from the invisible Substance of Life. When we truly believe Jesus' Faith abides in us, then we can step out in Jesus' Faith and creatively speak into material existence the tangible objects we desire to exist in our environment that brings us enjoyment.

I know by Holy revelation knowledge that we who are Created in True God's Likeness and Image can create things from Visionary Glory which intrinsically is Substance of Life Who resides in The Father as Holy Spirit and Jesus and flows out from them into those who are redeemed by Jesus' Precious Blood so together as one Holy operation Creative manifestations come into existence to be joyfully used for God's Glory and Pleasure as well as for our benefit and enjoyment.

The Substance of Life is invisible until we speak into tangible existence whatever words or material objects we see from Visionary Glory and then speak into material existence. What exists in the invisible realm and we see by Visionary Glory comes into existence on earth by our Holy creative desires and spoken words. We must truly believe that we can create what we desire by Jesus' Faith permanently residing in us who are redeemed by Jesus' precious Blood sacrifice. Therefore, we can accept with no doubting that it is Jesus' Faith in us doing the creative work through us (Galatians 2:20). When we truly believe and act from this premise, Supreme God's inherent creativity indwelling us cannot be affected by Satan's evil influence.

We *must* truly believe that we can create what we desire by Jesus' Faith permanently indwelling us that does the creative work through us – Galatians 2:20. Then, because we truly believe this, Supreme God's inherent creativity that He placed in us cannot be affected by Satan's evil influence. We are Holy as He is Holy with the ability to Create our environment as we desire. Supreme God Created the heavens and the earth for humankind to rule and have dominion over by the words He spoke. Consider what is written in The Holy Bible in Isaiah 65:17-25, Psalms 8, Hebrews 2:1-9, 1 Peter 1:13-21.

Faith is The Substance of Life causing or producing material things we desire, that are yet in invisible form, to manifest into visible manifestation that can be used on earth. The ability to bring invisible objects into visible form flows from the innate Holy passionate desire that issues from GOD'S Faith abiding in you, which is actual Living Substance.

When you are *born again* into New Life in Christ Jesus (John 3:3-8), the law of the Spirit of the Life of Christ Jesus lives in you enabling you to creatively create what you envision that is innately within you to draw from (Psalm 139). Ruminate and digest Romans 4-8.

Your passionate desire is outlined in vision form from your innate creativity or imagination that Holy God Creatively Designed in you before you were born. Your creative vision emanates into material manifestation from the Holy words you speak and actions you perform by Jesus' faith residing which is Living Substance. Your Holy innate desire sees what you want from your creative imagination and so forms into material manifestation by the words you speak. To be specific, Your Holy words emanate and materialize or manifest into visible form from the innate desire that is in your heart. This innate desire is formed by your creative imagination residing in the Substance of Life known as faith. What you form and create from Living Faith is to be used for Good.

Our innate desire to generate what we creatively envision by Holy Spirit's Substance of Life transports the invisible structure of what we envision into visible manifestation and testifies to the innate creativity Supreme God Designed in us before we were born (Psalm 139). What we speak from the Living Substance of Life from the faith of Father, Holy Spirit, and Jesus indwelling us is what opens up to us the realm of Visionary Glory Influence that brings into material existence on earth what we create with our words from the Substance of Life Who is the very Source of Originality.

Holy God's Creative Glory Influence is Favor. Favor is an actual Living Substance that truly exists in the invisible realm in visible form and must be called into manifestation from our desired intent and spoken words. God's Creative Glory Influence transposes the Substance of Life into material manifestation on earth by our desired intent and our spoken words. Favor is a Living Substance that causes the atoms that make up the physical world to respond to our spoken words.

Whatever we construct from our Holy creative imagination and then speak into existence from Visionary Glory issues from the Substance of Life and so structures or forms into visible manifestation the Holy creative words we speak that can be used on earth for good.

Our innate Holy desire to create what we envision creatively frames what is invisible to us but has not yet been Created into material matter. Creating into material manifestation what we creatively envision is possible through our confident expectation or hope that this is possible through the *Faith* of Jesus and His Father, and Holy Spirit indwelling us. *Faith* is a Living Substance that permanently resides in The Father, Holy Spirit, and in His Son Who indwell us. Therefore, our *hope* or confident expectation is anchored on their *Faith* indwelling us. Thereby, we positively know our desired intent is certainly being fulfilled. We frame our Holy desired intent from what we see from Visionary Glory. Then we bring into material manifestation our desired intent from the Substance of Life residing in Father, Son, and Holy Spirit by the words we speak through the Faith of The Father, Jesus, and Holy Spirit indwelling us.

Living Substance in invisible form is still tangible matter that can be spoken into material manifestation into the earth through the emanating Substance of Life abiding in Father, Holy Spirit, and Jesus Who indwells each true believer who trusts and relies on Holy God and His Holy Word.

Engage yourself to come into The Father's Presence and profess that Jesus' Blood Sacrifice stands for you on the Mercy Seat allowing you direct access to your Heavenly Father. From intimate relationship by being in The Father's Very Presence, you participate with Him in creating into tangible manifestation what you see by Visionary Glory that exists in invisible form within The Substance of Life. This is what is better understood as procreating with The Father to generate Holy Life or Fruit into the earth and the heavens that remains Eternally.

What you see from Visionary Glory is the Substance of Life that essentially exists in The Father who dwells within you. From Visionary Glory emanating from the Substance of Life, you speak with words your intended desire you want to bring into material manifestation. What you frame from Visionary Glory actualizes into visible matter that can be used on earth by what you see in invisible form from being in The Presence of The Father's Voice. This is to be an ongoing operation causing material things to happen around your life for Eternity. This is how you procreate with Holy God throughout Infinity.

The Father's Voice has a unique pattern which is the Source of Creative Origin. Sound is the Pattern of The Father's Voice which forms a frequency that attracts to Original Design. Matter can only be created from The Substance of Life residing in The Father (Genesis 1). When you are in the Presence of The Father, you learn to know His Voice and so can creatively speak from within His Voice speaking to you. From the words that you hear or see from within His Voice, you speak. What you speak has the ability to creatively form tangible matter that emanates from The Substance of Life residing in Father, Holy Spirit, and Jesus. Your voice emanating or coming from within His Voice is what brings into material existence on earth what you frame by your Holy words because Father, Jesus, and Holy Spirit's residing Presence indwells you, and so you are in Him, and He is in you (John 17:21-23).

Because Jesus' *Faith* resides in us along with the indwelling Life of Father and Holy Spirit, we have the intrinsic and essential belonging ability from our Holy position in Jesus to be able to procreate with our Father in creating our Holy desired intent that formulates into visible manifestation by the Holy Words we speak.

Thank You, Lord, for showing me Truth about Visionary Glory. Now that I understand how Visionary Glory operates, I ask You for an increase of Visionary Glory to use on earth to displace the powers of darkness in every situation I find myself or I observe or You send me or take me.

Invisible Atoms, DNA, and Transmuted RNA

In the invisible Spirit realm, tangible atoms formulate from Living Substance and produce Life in invisible form that are undetected to us who live in the physical realm on earth, but nevertheless, tangibly exist in the invisible realm. Invisible atoms are actual Living Substance that truly exist. From this undeniable Truth, invisible atoms are to be observed by the Faith of Father, Holy Spirit, and Jesus permanently residing in redeemed humankind. When these invisible atoms are observed, the actual Living Substance that is invisible to us on earth is to be brought into material manifestation by pure and holy words of decree and creatively designed actions so that the innately Creative destinies God innately designed in humankind can be performed on earth and for Infinity.

The Creative ability for humankind to Create as Supreme God Creates comes from DNA (*divine nature assimilated*) transmuted into RNA (*revealed nature achieved*). Therefore, because humankind is Created in Holy God's Image and after His Likeness, they too can create in the same Way He Creates. Supreme God Creates from what He speaks from The Substance of Life that essentially resides within Himself, and also resides in Holy Spirit and in Jesus, His Only Son who altogether abides in us.

Therefore, the innate DNA (*divine nature assimilated*) and RNA (*revealed nature achieved*) abiding in redeemed humankind must flow together in harmony to be able to bring invisible substance into tangible matter and form to be used on earth. This harmonious action engages Spirit world with physical world to bring the Kingdom of God that exists in invisible form in Heaven into the material realm on earth to become the visible Kingdom of God on earth.

Faith and *hope* are RNA (*revealed nature achieved*) and is the building block that sets every material thing in place and holds together the structure of our spoken Holy words. From RNA the creatively created object can be visibly manifested on earth by the Holy words we speak from The Father, Holy Spirit, and Jesus' *faith* abiding in us Who has the essential ability to manifest into visible manifestation our heart's intent and desire. DNA (*divine nature assimilated*) in us manifests what we frame by our Holy words from RNA (*revealed nature achieved*) in us.

From this reality, you can have confidence that Supreme God's DNA (*divine nature assimilated*) lives in you by Jesus' *Faith* indwelling you that reveals to you that He and The Father and Holy Spirit reside within you, and so you are one with Him. Therefore, you can truly believe Jesus' Faith abiding in you is DNA (divine nature assimilated) transforming within you as RNA (revealed nature achieved).

Consequently, from this Holy position of relationship Jesus' Living Faith abides in you, and His DNA (divine nature assimilated) becomes RNA (revealed nature achieved) that is exhibited through you. Therefore, you have the essential ability through Jesus' Faith Living in you to creatively design whatever you imagine and structure by His Visionary Glory that lives in you, which are the Holy words of decree you speak and the inventive actions you perform from what you see through Jesus' Visionary Glory abiding in you.

At Moses' request, *"Show me Your Glory"* Holy God revealed His Glory to Moses. Supreme God responded to Moses request by saying, *I will make my Goodness go before You...* (Exodus 33:18- 19). God's Glory is His Goodness. God of Glory wants to be known as I AM WHO I AM, Who is Goodness Personified. Therefore, everything Holy God does and speaks lines up with His Goodness. Therefore, Holy God abiding in you and you abiding in Him manifests His Goodness residing in you that becomes affirmative action by the holy words of decree you speak and the creative actions you take.

Drawing on God's Glory Substance

In a dream, I saw a tube shaped in bent form with each end open. I saw a creamy white substance in the tube. I saw people activity but cannot remember the details.

I asked The Lord, why the tube was shaped like this? Why was it not straight?

Holy God revealed in my heart that He does not pour Glory Substance into people until they seek Him. Each person redeemed by Jesus' Holy Blood Sacrifice who personally seeks to know Living God by choosing to live in His Presence, can draw on His Glory Substance as one would draw substance from a drinking straw. Those who choose to live in His Presence can draw on His Glory Substance that empowers them to speak holy words of decree and to perform creative actions by Glory Fire Power that dispels darkness and compels Light to perform everlasting Life in them.

Gabriel Brings Glory Fire Messages

I awoke feeling myself smiling widely. Then, I saw a head and face pop and vanish before my visionary eye space. This head had dark brown curly hair and face was translucent white. I thought, *"It's Gabriel! The angel of God's Presence."*

Because of previous Holy encounters with the angel of God's Presence, Gabriel, I knew this was Gabriel bringing Glory Fire Messages to me. Gabriel carries God's Holy Fire Presence and expounds His Messages of Authority that Holy God wants disseminated. These Messages of Authority ignite and release Glory Fire Power, causing people living in sin to hear and recognize Holy God's Message to them. If they choose to respond to God's Authority Message to them, they receive Holy Power that changes their circumstances by empowering them to walk out of darkness and come into His Marvelous Light of Truth and Love that has everlasting benefit. The free-will choices each person makes whether good or evil establishes their temporary and Eternal destiny.

Glory Fire operations are God's intentional doing, not any persons. As people truly desire and then allow God's Holy Fire to demolish all that has consumed their thoughts and emotions based on lies causing deep-seated pain, they are set free. These ingrained deceptive thoughts and false beliefs have set up an idol in their heart that has replaced True God in their lives. God's Holy Glory Fire consumes all the dross within people's lives when they truly want these things removed from their lives and so prove this by turning to Him asking for His help.

When God's Word is spoken, Glory Fire is triggered causing sparks to fly that ignites stony hearts triggering slumbering people to seek God above all else. When those hearing the words of Truth, Light, and Life you speak and then seek

True God with all their heart, they will find Him. Holy words of Life spoken by decree and performed by creative action exposes the devil's darkness in people and encases these lies with Holy Glory Fire Power that consumes deceptive lusts embedded within them, stemming from deeply rooted wrong beliefs and unholy desires. When people who have been held captive by unholy desires and wrong beliefs are set free because of seeking Holy God with all their heart, Glory Fire Power continuously operates around them so former ways of darkness can never return to harass them if they continue to live in holiness and Truth.

God's Voice carries Holy Fire. Holy Glory Fire ignites and consumes all that is not of God. God's Love is a burning Fire that cannot be quenched. His Holy Fire consumes all it touches with either all-consuming passionate Love for Him or death, which is Eternal separation from Him. Gods' Glory Fire causes people to make a free-will choice to either choose Eternal Life or Eternal death. Each person freely chooses how they respond to God.

Holy Glory Fire is Passionate Love personified igniting people to choose to walk in God's Ways of Holy Living *if* they will. That is why God is seen as a Pillar of Fire and people feel as if Fire is burning within them. This Glory Fire is a Holy Fire of consuming Passion that is Pure and all- consuming, burning up all that is not of God.

God's Holy Glory Fire replaces the passionate fire of lust and self-gratification that holds people captive to deception and lies. God's Holy Glory Fire burns out this dross and replaces it with His Passionate Love that remains within them. Holy Fire is Love that produces tangible manifestations of Life and Truth.

Each person who is cleansed by God's Holy Fire is now free to offer God unending praise, worship, and thanksgiving for eternally delivering them from false beliefs and the idols embedded in their hearts that were taking them away from Living God, Who Loves them with passionate and Everlasting Love.

Pure and Holy worship expressed to God allows Him to act in agreement with your personal praise worship to Him, and this is what restores Heaven and earth as one complete circle of Life as He Originally Designed.

True unadulterated worship that focuses on True God allows you to eat from the ...*Tree of Life*... from which all Created Substance flows. Eating from the ...*Tree of Life*... truly Creates unending Life and productivity.

Eating from the ...*Tree of Life*... enables you to create what you desire. Eat and create! Eat and create is the way of Life throughout Eternity. Worship sustains Life forever. The fig tree refused to worship God and it withered and died permanently for not bearing fruit that remains. This fig tree failed to transmit a message God Commanded it to give.

Consider this, your Pure unadulterated worship to Holy God exposes evil entities who defy Supreme God that causes them excruciating and unending torture because they wrongly desire to be worshipped. Continual pure Praise and Worship to The Lord God of Heaven and earth tortures them even more. So bring even more pure praise and worship to Holy God. This pleases Him and blesses you.

The Council of the Godly

There are those in Heaven who are seated in the Council of the Godly in the Court of Heaven at the request of Holy Spirit. Those from earth who are brought into this Council at the request of Holy Spirit join the Council of the Godly in

Heaven. This is a joint operation between Heaven and earth. This Council cooperates together to fulfill God's Purpose of Ruling His Righteous Kingdom as one complete Circle of Life.

Those living on earth who are being led by The Spirit of Holy God hear His summons to join Heaven's Council of the Godly. From this Holy encounter, they make a free-will decision to come into this Council and join with Heaven's Council of the Godly. All those attending this Council are held accountable by Almighty God.

God says in His Holy Word, *Bring all who claim Me as their God, for I have made them for My Glory. It was I who Created them. Bring out the people who have eyes but are blind, who have ears but are deaf. Gather the nations together! Assemble the peoples of the world! Understand that I alone am God. There is no other God. There never has been, and there never will be. I, yes, I am The Lord, and there is no other Savior. From eternity to eternity I am God. No one can undo what I have done.* (Isaiah 43:8-9a, 10-11, 13 NLT).

As it is in Heaven so it is on earth. The Court of Heaven has Judged Satan forgotten forever. Therefore, Satan can never again attack or accuse anyone on earth or in Heaven who legally stands in Jesus' Judicial Blood Sacrifice that covers their sins in the Court of Heaven forever.

It has been decided in the Court of Heaven that the devil and all his evil is to be abolished in the ...*lake of fire*.... Therefore, no longer do people have to continually deal with evil. They can permanently live in Peace, Joy, Love, Harmony and Rest with Holy God and others of like mind and heart in conjunction with all God's Creations of Beauty. Those who belong to God and so have cast away their self-desires and unholy ways, have willingly chosen to forsake self-promotion and unholy ways. Therefore, they are no longer subject to Satan's attacks and unwarranted accusations before Heaven's Judicial Court. Through the judicial acts of redeemed people in cooperation with the Court of Heaven, Satan is permanently banned from the Court of Heaven. These combined Holy Judicial acts ensure Satan's Eternal annihilation.

Holy God is divulging secret things at this time of events on earth so people know that Life is never-ending, and that their lives have a purpose whether they are living on earth or in Heaven. Redeemed people made in God's Image and after His Likeness rule from Heaven's Courts whether they are abiding on earth or in Heaven. Heaven's Court operates eternally.

Revelation knowledge originates from the Substance of Life that is now being unveiled and revealed for end-time operations between Heaven and earth. Therefore, Revelation knowledge originating from the Substance of Life operates through those who have ears to hear and eyes to see what Holy Spirit is doing through them and this is what transmits a tangible witness of observable holy operations between Heaven and earth. Heaven and earth work in cooperation to establish God's Righteous Kingdom on earth and in the heavens.

What Holy God is presently revealing is true and stands in His Council of Justice and can never be changed. People on earth need to truly recognize this. When they do, Heaven and earth can operate as one complete operation with no apparent separation. When the devil and all his evil activity is shut down, Holy God is Glorified forever and ever! Praise and thank Him for this!

Your Ways are unsearchable, O God of Heaven and earth. I give all praise and thanksgiving, honor, and Glory to You alone, O Lord of Might and Power.

What Do Angels Know

The Lord caused me to know that people and angels learn and grow together to enhance each other. People and angels working in cooperation exchange with each other to gain fuller knowledge and understanding as to how to collaborate in performing His *Will* on earth and in the heavens. These operations between people and God's Holy angels in Heaven are increasing in greater dimensions and are releasing unveiled Truth from Heaven.

These joint Heaven and earth operations are bringing back into alignment God's Circle of Life to complete His Original Intention for Heaven and earth to exist as one Holy and comprehensive operation. The combined obedience between Heaven's angels and redeemed people on earth immensely blesses God.

Lord, I willingly join and cooperate with Your Holy Created angels and beings in performing Your Holy *Will* on earth and in the heavens. Be Blessed, our Lord and our God in our combined obedience to You.

Procreating by Perverted Angels

While in my kitchen preparing my breakfast, I was worshipping The Lord with songs on a music album. I was not consciously aware of anything in the Spirit realm. I was just normally going to eat my breakfast. As I was eating my prepared meal, Divine revelation *unexpectedly* erupted up in me.

Suddenly, I knew that Satan and the angels who followed him in rebellion against Living God have knowledge of how to procreate. I knew in certainty, had they stayed in their Supreme God- ordained position and place for them, they could have used Holy knowledge for Good.

I knew with opened understanding that Holy God is unmistakably and astoundingly notifying all evil angels to their faces that they used His Holy Knowledge of procreating for their own selfish desires, and now He is stopping them. Supreme God is fully releasing Holy Knowledge to redeemed humankind on earth by informing them that He Created them with innate Creative ability to procreate with Him. He is divinely revealing to redeemed people that what they desire from the Holy intent in their hearts and so speak what they see from Visionary Glory, is what procreates with Him in restoring the earth and the heavens back into Original Design. Procreation with Holy God comes through an established and ongoing relationship with Him.

Legitimate Holy Procreating

In the very beginning of Creation and time God Supreme Sovereignly Created Adam in His very own Image and Likeness and endowed him with innate creative ability to procreate Good in the same way He does. Then, He brought every living creature He Created to Adam to see what Adam would name them (Genesis 2:19-20a).

God of all Creation Created Lucifer as a Holy angel of Light, Knowledge, and Wisdom and also placed within him creative ability. But Lucifer betrayed His Creator and obstinately used his endowed free-will to dishonor and pervert God's Holy Knowledge of Creativity. He misused this Holy Knowledge for his own selfish desires and as well persuaded other angels to join his coup against God's Kingdom of Righteousness.

By Lucifer's blatant self-centered rebellion, evil intent was illegally formulated. Lucifer chose to covet Creative Knowledge to use for his own selfish desire to promiscuously procreate to fulfill his evil lusts. He falsely and illegally set up an illegitimate kingdom of his own device. This was the origin of evil intent.

Then he slyly came into the Garden of Eden and duped humankind by saying, ...*has God said!*... By these words, Lucifer was saying to Adam, I also have knowledge of how to procreate from personal desires. If you listen to me and do as I say, you will be like God as I am. Lucifer's perverse image of self-importance was already in his heart. He formulated unholy personal desires by perverting Holy knowledge God revealed to him in order to fit his own evil desires.

When you, who are Created and Designed in God's in Image and after His Likeness, receive God's redemption from evil by accepting His Son's innocent Blood Sacrifice that forgives all your sins and iniquities, you now live in Blood Covenant with Him. Therefore, you now have personal relationship with Creative God and can creatively formulate, frame, express, verbalize, voice, communicate, convey, devise, and invent, your personal Holy plan that is good for you and for others. You together with others who have been redeemed by Jesus' Precious Blood Sacrifice, can now creatively and visibly bring into existence the good you desire. Acting from your innate creativity completes God's Holy Plan for earth to exist in wholeness and productivity.

Indelibly implanted within each person is the creative ability to procreate with God. As each person communes with God in intimacy, He imparts within them His Holy Seed of creativity in freshness and newness. This is Holy and genuine procreation. From mutual intimate interaction with God, a Holy seed of innate creativity is deeply imparted within each person. This Holy seed of innate creativity is implanted within each person through their intimate communion with Holy God. Then what is implanted within them from procreating with

Holy God is to be combined with the Holy Seed of creativity implanted within others who have procreated with Holy God.

The combining of people's creativity from procreating with Holy God works together for good to accomplish God's Perfect *Will* for earth and Heaven to flow in one complete Circle of Life. In Truth, Holy people procreating with Creative God and then joining together to manifest what they creatively procreate eliminates evil falseness by routing out all evil entities still vying to stay in charge as they see it. This process creates new heavens and new earth. Holy procreating replenishes the earth and restores what has been devastated by evil thus making a new earth where Righteousness dwells Eternally. This is how God's Righteous Kingdom is established on earth as it is in Heaven, and how His *Will* is done on earth as it is in Highest Heaven so that one complete Circle of Life can flow unceasingly. This is the Way of Life for Eternity. When Heaven and earth are reconciled and restored as one complete operation as Holy God Originally Planned and Designed before the beginning of time, harmony reigns Eternally.

Thoughts Are Doings

The Lord put on my heart to ask Him this question: "Do thoughts have sound waves?"

So, I asked Him. *Suddenly*, understanding opened to me. I knew in the very essence of My being that existence is energy that emits sound waves, and these sound waves create whatever I think. Thoughts and sound waves are one and the same. Thoughts are sound waves that emanate Creative Energy, which is the very Essence of Holy God whose Name is I AM WHO I AM. Creative Energy exists according to God's predetermined law or established principle of thermodynamics: the changing of a Living Substance from one form to another.

Humankind is Created in God's Holy Image and Likeness. Therefore, they have the same ability as He has to emit sound waves from thought intentions within the heart where decisions are formulated. I knew in unchangeable Truth what a human being thinks in their heart emits sound waves that creates good or evil.

You must know that creative ways of thinking are ingrained into the human psyche by a God who Created humankind in His Image and Likeness to be creative. Therefore, people emit sound waves that create whatever they are thinking in their heart good or evil. God's laws of thermodynamics cannot be changed. Proactive God has given human beings a free-will to decide to selfishly create what benefits their egotistical agenda over the Good He wants for them. However, there are also people who choose to creatively create for good purposes for themselves and others.

When people declare aloud what they want to have happen in their environment, whether for good or for evil, what they speak is transmitted into the atmosphere around them as a decree. This decree of intention takes on an existence from what they speak from the thoughts in their heart.

The Holy Blood Jesus shed on The Cross redeems sinful mankind from perverted thinking. This is the only remedy that cleanses them from *all* unrighteousness. Supreme God created mankind to *think* good in their hearts and to creatively design good things for their enjoyment and God's Pleasure. As redeemed people rightfully think, they transmit sound waves that create good. God's Righteous thoughts are Holy doings that always create Good, not evil.

It must be recognized that both righteous thoughts and unrighteous thoughts that are transmitted into the atmosphere of the first and second heavens and into the earth are picked up and acted on either by those who have Holy Spirit living in them or by those who adhere to evil agendas.

Supreme God is presently disrupting evil in all its forms causing evil to bow to His Kingdom of Righteousness so that that evil cannot persist or continue. When those redeemed by Jesus' Blood Sacrifice declare aloud what they want to have happen in their environment that is for good, what they speak is transmitted into the atmosphere around them. Their righteous thoughts and spoken words against evil and for good notifies Satan and his hordes that they are being permanently judged.

The Lord reminded me of a recent instance in Walmart when I spoke healing to a young man being pushed in a wheel chair by his mother. Holy compassion rose up in me causing me to ask God to make him whole. However, there was no indication that He was made whole at that moment. As I pondered this encounter before The Lord, He instilled in me that to Him it is always *now*, the present. God Eternal is not limited by time. What rises up in me to do from what He reveals to me in any situation I am in is accomplished in His Sight even though I may not see the things I pray, think, and speak being done in my time as I think they should be done. It is always *now* or in the present to Him even though to me on earth, it is yet future.

The Lord especially made me know that because the things I want to do are in my heart, I am doing them. This is how He sees it. Therefore, I emphatically knew that what I spoke from the righteous intentions in my heart healed this young man and made him whole. God marked him healed and made whole by the inaudible words I spoke that were in my heart. My Holy thoughts are sound waves that create what I think in my heart even though they are not spoken aloud. God hears these thoughts that are Living words to Him and He Acts on these Holy inaudible words. This is Eternal Life in action.

I know the thoughts in my heart are doings and emanate from an upright heart that has been cleansed through Jesus' Blood Sacrifice; therefore, I have the assurance that the good things I think are performed. My Holy thoughts emit sound waves and bring into being the good desire that is my heart through the words I speak and the actions I take. This is operating in Eternal Ways. Only the Pure in heart see God in Eternal Ways. When our hearts are Pure, we do Eternal things that are good and transmit sound waves that formulate the good intention in our heart.

God's Mesh of Communication Wires

God has communication wires that glow as Pure white Glory Light. These Glory Light communication wires cannot be separated. They are intertwined and work together into one complete message no matter when they are spoken times past, times present, or times yet to come.

At this time of polluted thinking and words, there is a mesh of unholy communication wires that are hindering God's mesh of Glory Light communication wires from fully operating as He Originally Designed.

God's Glory Light mesh of communication wires are being confiscated by complacency and acceptance of polluted communication wires that operate through compromise. When emphatic action is taken against this polluted mesh of wires, God's flow of Power and Energy causes Creative Action that annihilates the polluted mesh of wires.

Continuously plugging into God's communication wires of Glory Light through praise and worship to Him ignites His

Energy and Power to flow causing action to occur. What you think and speak creates your desired intent. Thoughts are doings, and so are words of action. Holy God is I AM WHO I AM. He is always present and continuously in motion or action. I AM is perpetual Power and Energy that flows and never ceases and so causes Action whether or not this Power and Energy is acknowledged or accepted by His Creations. This is why there is no cessation of existence. Perpetual Energy continuously Creates whatever is thought or spoken.

Thank You, Lord. I choose to continuously plug myself into Your communication wires of Glory Light Energy and Power. Therefore, I am Blessed indeed to walk in the Holy capacity of Your communication wires that creates action that gives You all the Glory. I trust you to keep me in Your Higher Way of living on earth that establishes Your Righteous Kingdom in the heavens and on the earth. May my thoughts and words, always Create action. So be it, Lord!

Creative Glory Acts

Through Holy Divine encounters, Holy Spirit is teaching me how to supernaturally transport from the material realm into the invisible realm to accomplish The Lord's Holy Purposes. Being supernaturally transported means to vanish in the natural flow on earth to flow with Holy Spirit by being supernaturally transferred from one place to another in order to minister Holy God's Purpose into the situation for which He wants to manifest Himself to bring His Light of Life and Love.

These Holy encounters do not derive from New Age philosophy of astral transport. New Age teachers have tapped into this truth of Holy Spirit transportation, and so are using legitimate Holy Spirit Ways for illegitimate and unholy purposes. God's infallible Laws He instituted to maintain His Creation cannot be changed. However, God's Laws that He indelibly established to govern His Creation can be thwarted and used for evil purposes.

There are those who have tapped into God's indelible Laws to selfishly promote themselves for monetary gain, fame, and power. New Age philosophy that is being publicly disseminated and transmitted is another form of deception. Deception is twisted truth portrayed as legitimate. Deception is truth intertwined and wrapped in lies. Satan is a master of deception. He is a liar and a deceiver. The Lord wants those who may be deceitfully using illegitimate power to turn to Him so they come out of darkness into His Marvelous Light and use His legitimate Laws of Power for good rather than for selfish purposes. Satan is a deceiver and a liar who makes himself appear as Light and Power attracting those who do not know Truth to fall prey to his wiles. Jesus Christ is the only Way, Truth, and Life that human beings should live by (2 Corinthians 11:13−14).

In John's Gospel chapter 8:44-45 in the Holy Bible, Jesus emphatically exposes Satan as a deceiver and a liar:

For you are the children of your father the devil, and you love to do the evil things he does. He was a murderer from the beginning. He has always hated the truth, because there is no truth in him. When he lies, it is consistent with his character; for he is a liar and the father of lies. So when I (Jesus) *tell the truth, you just naturally don't believe Me!*

Supernatural transportation is being legitimately transferred by Holy Spirit to a specific location to minister for The Lord in helping someone in distress they cannot get free from, or to answer the questions in their hearts that they are asking. There are documented accounts in The Holy Bible of God answering the cry of someone's heart by supernaturally sending His servants to them. Read some recorded accounts in 1 Kings 18:10-12, 2 Kings 4:1-7, John 2:1-11, and in Acts 8:26- 40; 16:6-10. There are as well other recorded accounts in The Holy Bible of supernatural operations to meet people's desperate needs that override the human spirit and demonic influence to accomplish Holy God's *Will.*

I said, "Lord, I am traveling on a road less traveled. I know factually that I am walking properly in Holy relationship with You. Therefore, I want to know Truth concerning how to be supernaturally transported to carry out Your *Will* on earth and in the heavens. How do I discern where to walk into this supernatural transportation point and so be taken where You want me to be to minister Your Word of Truth? Where is this supernatural transportation point for me? Do You want me to come into a higher level of this? If so, I want to be used by You to meet people's profound and deepest needs. How am I to do this? I ask You, Lord, to bring me into a higher level of discernment to learn how to mystically transport into situations to accomplish a Holy Purpose You have for taking me into situations to meet the need in a circumstance to accomplish Your *Will*. Reveal more to me that I do not yet understand so I can move to a higher level of discernment in being supernaturally transported to cooperate with You in accomplishing Your *Will* and Holy Purposes for what is needed in a situation. Thank You."

As I surrendered my will to The Lord, He opened understanding to me and answered me. He opened comprehension to discern Truth in knowing that I am to submit to His *Will* in each encounter He takes me into. He revealed to me that there are different levels of being supernaturally transported just as there are differing levels of maturity.

The Lord made me to know that I am supernaturally transported into situations within the dreams and visions that occur in the Spirit realm. He also revealed to me that supernatural occurrences happen in my circumstances in the natural realm of this world. Nevertheless, these are both supernatural encounters bringing God's Life of Truth into the situation where I find myself either in my dreams and visions in the Spirit realm or in my natural circumstances.

He let me know that when I am taken into situations by Holy Spirit in dreams or visions or in the natural, these encounters are actually occurring for the purpose of bringing His Truth into a situation. When He transports me into a circumstance in dreams or visions, it is for the purpose of carrying out His *Will* in a circumstance so His Purpose is accomplished without interference from the demonic realm or human souls thinking their own thoughts.

I know emphatically by Holy Spirit that these Holy encounters will continue and that I am to allow Him to use me in this way so His Holy *Will* is accomplished in the situations He transports me into for His Holy Purposes to be accomplished in each situation He takes me into.

I responded, "Yes, Lord! As You have spoken to me, let it be done for me. I am willing to be transported in whatever way You choose to send me to accomplish a good work in the place you take me. I don't hesitate to tell You I do not understand in fullness all You have spoken to Me concerning Spiritual journeying for Your Purposes. Keep me from supposing I know when I really don't know how to obey You to carry out what You are revealing to me. Impress in me to ask You what I need to know. Thank You!"

Personal Holy Supernatural Encounters

As directed by The Lord, I have been concentrating on being transported by Holy Spirit to accomplish God's *Will* in bringing Heaven to earth. I know that these Holy encounters from The Lord have happened to me, on occasion, over the years. Yet, I am sensing there is more The Lord wants for me to accomplish in this area because The Lord spoke to me that there are different levels of being transported into situations that I need to know and experience to accomplish His *Will*.

The Lord instilled deep with me that every time I pray, I am being transported and taken on the scene to transform the situation from darkness to Light. I understand that when I come on the scene through my prayers, I see by Holy Spirit what to ask and then declare. Thus, I know how to pray in every situation that arises. When I open my mouth and speak, Holy Spirit instantly transports me into the situation as if I was presently in the situation. I know that the more I pray, the more my words are being transferred into the place God is taking them to change the circumstances for good.

By Holy Spirit Operations, Heaven and earth are linked in cooperation to fulfill all Righteousness in accomplishing One Eternal Circle of Life as Supreme God Originally Designed. Therefore, Satan cannot interrupt this Flow or these Holy maneuvers (planned and controlled movement, skillful strategy, or scheme – secret plan, an orderly combination of things on a definite plan).

Speaking words, which is praying, transfers you into the situations of your choosing. You can freely pick and choose the scenarios you want to become a part of in prayer declarations. Other times, Holy God chooses where He wants to take you to accomplish a Unique Purpose He has in a particular situation. Holy angels transport your words into the situation to bring Light that dispels darkness.

Holy angel messengers take the words you speak or declare in prayer and imprint these words on the hearts of humankind who are refusing Holy God in these very last days of time on earth. This is happening so people know the Truth of God's Word and so are without excuse. God's Words you declare in prayer, are forcing people to accept or reject the Holy words you speak. God's Holy angels are taking these words and imprinting them in their hearts. No person will speak to them, but the Holy words spoken are taken by God's Holy angels and imprinted on rebellious hearts, and these words alone will speak to people so they have no excuse before God. Every person will have heard of Supreme God, and they will know it. No one can excuse themselves before Holy God at the time He calls every person to give an account of their lives to Him (Romans 1:18-32 Jeremiah 17:10 Revelation 2:23).

Holy God's spoken Word is alive and active and working, and always Lives before Him in the atmosphere. Thoughts are spoken words. So words either thought or spoken, do not desist or return void or empty of fulfillment (Isaiah 55:11). God's Word does a work of dividing and separating the thoughts and the intents within the hearts of people (Hebrews 4:12-13). If people say they have never heard God's Word, it is because they refuse to hear and give heed to His Word spoken to them or imprinted on their hearts Romans 1:18-32.

As I continuously yield to The Lord, I increase in learning how to supernaturally transport into a higher level to accomplish God's Holy purposes. The Lord is making known to me that there is so much more He wants to do in the realm of the supernatural with my cooperation, which seems to me to be supernatural, but to God is the only Way He interchanges.

I follow Righteous Protocol in going back and forth from the natural realm to the supernatural realm by saying, "Through the Blood of Jesus on the Mercy Seat, I have Legal Authority to go into the spiritual realm and then come back into the natural realm. I stand in My Righteous Authority through The Blood of Jesus interceding on the Mercy Seat, I step forward into the spiritual realm as an act of my will. Through Jesus' Faith that dwells in me, I give The Lord permission to take me where He wants to use me for His Glory and someone else's good. I, as well, give myself permission to supernaturally transport through time and space to accomplish The Lord's Holy *Will* in the circumstance for which He is transporting me.

God chooses when and how to supernaturally transport us where He wants to use us to release His Word and Love and Power into situations. When we step into the spirit realm through the Blood of Jesus, we wait on The Lord to see where He wants to take us to accomplish His *Will* in the situation. Supernatural encounters may or may not be immediate. They may occur in dreams and visions during the night or during the daytime. Supernatural encounters can happen in earth's natural circumstances that we are naturally part of or He sends us into. When we obey Holy Spirit's directions in the situations, the supernatural encounter is completed. Then we step back into the natural realm knowing that God's *Will* was accomplished by our obedience in allowing Him to supernaturally transport us into situations as He so chooses.

Holy Spirit Adventures

I was obeying Holy Spirit operations by command of The Lord to not fear to do what He is asking me to do because it won't look like what I have been doing. He let me know that I am to trust Him in taking me to places through Spiritual journeying for His Purposes of halting evil entities in their tracks who are defying Him and attempting to steal His Creation for their own pleasure. He revealed to me that He is God of Might and Power and that He is no longer allowing evil entities to defy Him. As I submit my will to obey Him in doing His *Will His Way*, He is operating Glory Fire Power through me to annihilate all evil entities who are vying for illegitimate Power control over His creations.

The Lord is now using people fully committed to doing His *Will* His Way to bring an end to all those who are vying for illicit power control. He let me know that by my trust in Him, He is taking me places by transporting me into a situation to speak for Him. This is a Spiritual journey, not a natural physical journey on earth.

I knew emphatically that I was to let go of myself and hold on to The Lord as a matter of total surrender. This was not a matter of my doing anything, but a willing surrender of myself to The Lord by sanctified trust. Then I felt a heaviness and sleepiness while attempting to do housework. I could not shake this or go on doing what I was doing.

I knew I was to stop what I was doing and just sit down and take a nap. The Lord let me know that this sleepiness was from Him. I obeyed what I was feeling and sat down and took a nap. Later, The Lord revealed to me that because I obeyed Him in taking a nap, He saw my obedience as preparation to be taken into Holy Spirit encounters for His Purposes, and He would be expanding me and taking me places in the Spirit realm to do a Holy work needed in the situation.

Personal Supernatural Encounter

I awoke this morning from a reality encounter in the Spirit realm that was still vividly alive in me. As I was waking up, these words reverberated all through me, *I see this man and I am pleased with him.* I saw myself walking down the corridor of a hospital and walking into someone's hospital room. I saw this person's family was there, and they were weeping because of this person's sickness that seemed to be unto death. It became crystal clear to me that I was to speak these words over this person, and I did: *This sickness is not unto death. It is for the Glory of God to be seen. This is another opportunity for your family and other people to believe in Jesus' as Savior and Lord.*

When I was fully awake, I got up and went to my Prayer Room for the purpose of coming into the Council of the Godly as He has mandated I do often. I drew near to Almighty God approaching Him through The Holy Blood of Jesus which is the appropriate and proper protocol to come into His Presence and into the Council of the Godly. I worshipped The Lord by giving Him Praise and Thanksgiving to honor Him. Then I picked up my Bible and began my daily Bible reading in the Gospel of John. I began reading in John chapter 9 and read through chapter 11. *Suddenly*, the words Jesus spoke in John 11:4 and then verse 15 rose up in me and became so alive in me:

Lazarus' sickness will not end in death. No, it is for the glory of God. I, the Son of God, will receive glory from this. Lazarus is dead. And for your sake, I am glad I wasn't there, because this will give you another opportunity to believe in Me. Come, let's go see him.

I then put these words together with the account I read in John 9 of the man who was born blind being healed by Jesus and Jesus saying that this man being born blind was for the Glory of God to be seen.

While still pondering Jesus' words in John's Gospel, The Lord led me to 1 Kings 17 to the story of Elijah raising the widow's son from death; and, the woman saying to Elijah, *Now I know for sure that you are a man of God, and that the Lord truly speaks through you.*

Instantly, I knew that these words I spoke to this man and his family was for The Lord's Glory to be seen so this man, his family, and other people would be given another opportunity to believe in Jesus as Savior and Lord.

Suddenly, I recognized this supernatural encounter concerned an actual personal situation happening in a family, one of whom, I was ministering God's Love and Truth. Their loved one was suffering from post-traumatic syndrome from being in war zones. I shared this with the one person in this family to whom I have been ministering God's Love for this entire family. I shared with this person that the suffering man's immediate family was to speak these words over their loved one. She said she would relay this to them. I knew in actuality from our conversations that I would not be accepted by this entire family if I were physically on the scene with them. Therefore, I literally saw and knew in reality that God was working in this family's circumstances to fulfill His Word to them because of our agreed prayers for this situation.

I realized the Scriptures I read in John 9 and 11 along with 1 Kings 17 focused on God's Glory. I saw in truth The Lord was answering what I asked Him recently from the Words that so powerfully rose up in me to ask Him, "Transpose me, Lord, into a higher realm of Glory Influence in both supernatural and natural Holy encounters to accomplish Your Purposes. Thank You."

The Lord let me know I created an atmosphere of Glory Influence when I obeyed speaking His Words He gave me to speak in this supernatural encounter where He placed me. My obedience allowed Holy Spirit operations to manifest to help these people in their dire situation. To God alone be all the Glory and thanksgiving.

Steering Wheels - Magnetic Force

During the night, I found myself in another reality encounter I did not fully understand. I was holding on to a large steering wheel and flying through the air being taken to places. I could feel the sensation of a very strong magnetic force in my body pulling me through the air causing me to fly around and go to places as I held tightly to the steering wheel. I could not pull away from this strong magnetic force nor could I let go of the large wheel or stop myself from flying. I was laughing with glee and thoroughly enjoying this very strong magnetic force that was pulling me around and taking me places as I held tightly to the steering wheel. I wanted to keep doing this and didn't want it to stop.

While I was flying at whirlwind speed, I looked to my right to see where I was going and what was around me. I saw what seemed to me to be an angel with long flowing hair streaked with subdued colors of emerald green, silvery blue-gray, and brilliant white. Yet I saw me holding onto this steering wheel and flying through space at a whirlwind pace being taken to places by this strong magnetic force. I couldn't determine if the angel was the magnetic force or if the angel was carrying me even though I was holding the steering wheel. This angel was laughing with glee and enjoying this flight. As I was flying through the air, I kept seeing that the steering wheel had a straight cross bar in the middle at a right angle. I didn't understand this.

Eventually I came back down to earth and as I stood there, I saw standing side by side a small sized steering wheel and a large sized steering wheel. The small sized wheel looked exactly like the large wheel. Both were perfectly round circles that had soft comfortable suede-like padding with tiny holes in the suede material, but the large steering wheel had a bar in the middle that was at a right angle going from southwest to northeast. The small steering wheel was a clear circle with no bar in the middle. I looked at this wondering what it meant. I didn't know why I was seeing side by side a small steering wheel and a large steering wheel that had a right angle cross bar that was not in the small steering wheel.

I knew I could take hold of the small sized steering wheel that looked just like the large steering wheel minus the right-angle cross bar. I did take hold of the small wheel, but nothing happened. I just stood there holding the small steering wheel. There was no force or power. So I let go of the small wheel and took hold of the large wheel. As soon as I took hold of the large wheel, I was instantly pulled by a great magnetic force and was again flying through the air going places.

Later, as I was pondering this, I instinctively knew that I could take whichever steering wheel I wanted – the small or the large. I knew the small wheel was the way I wanted to go. I knew that large steering wheel was greater than the small-sized steering wheel and would take me where I could not go myself. I knew as well that I could not go the way I wanted to go if I took hold of the large wheel.

I deeply pondered what the bar at a right angle inside the large steering wheel going from southwest to northeast meant. The Spirit of God rose up in me. Instantly, I knew that the bar in the middle of the large wheel gives strength to the circle or steering wheel. I knew that the bar going from southwest to northeast represents that I am looking from the earth up to God in Heaven, and this is what causes a magnetic force that works in cooperation with God and gives me strength in taking me where I cannot go myself. Because it is at a right angle means that I am doing things the *right way*, which is God's Way. This is what causes the magnetic force to take me to the places where God can work His Purposes in the situation.

God is making known that He wants to burst through and break off the bondages in people's lives. People are drawn as a magnet to those who are totally free from the effect of evil all around them. Those who carry Glory Fire Presence speak Holy words that draw people to hear what they speak. Therefore, they are not to withdraw or pull back from speaking God's Holy Word. Holy Glory Fire Presence emanates through holy words of decree spoken and creative actions performed. This is what burns constraints so bridges can be built between God and people. Speaking from Glory Fire Presence allows a River of Life to flow through those who allow God to flow through them as He *Wills*. As God flows through those who allow Him to, God's Holy angels show up and listen, and go to perform the words spoken by their mouths.

These words rose up in my spirit: **Don't consider and Go! Just Go and Flow! In the Flow is the Know!**

The Lord is revealing that people are not to consider how to go, or go doing what they consider to do or do what has always been done. Each one is to go flowing with God in The River of Life and Truth so intuitively they know *when* to go, *where* to go, and *what to do and say* in every situation they find themselves.

Declare over yourself continuously, **I will always be in the right place, at the right time, with the right word, among the right people!**

WOW! Lord! What secret things you reveal to me. I love You.

Pure Worship Creates Glory Substance

In a reality dream, I was in a place among people observing them. I was mulling over what I observed happening among these people. A misty substance or cloud emerged and floated by me flowing or floating around in this place among the people. I watched people being healed, delivered, and set free. They were instantly transformed and brought out of darkness that enabled them to see Light.

Then, I saw the same rectangle Box I previously saw at a distance coming down from Heaven. However, now it was close at hand in the place where I was. Instantly, I recognized the Visionary Glory Box was carrying Visionary Glory, which are words to say and, actions to do for the need at hand. I knew that I was to open this Visionary Glory Box to see how to operate Glory Influence.

At this point, the dream ended and I was awake. I emphatically knew that from now on I am to open this Visionary Glory Box containing Visionary Glory in every situation or circumstance The Lord places me or takes me, whether in the invisible realm or in the visible realm.

I intuitively knew that worshipping and praising God creates Glory Substance. Pure and Holy vessels offering Pure worship to God brings His Glory Fire Influence on the scene bringing Light that eliminates every form of darkness. Darkness is evil that has a form that causes sickness and death. Glory Fire Influence brings God's Substance of Life in the form of Light that eradicates darkness.

At the moment people see Light, they truly understand Truth and they choose God, The Light of Life. When they choose Holy God, the darkness in them is immediately transformed into Light; and they are changed from darkness to Light causing them to be free and come out of darkness into His Holy Light. This is why there is always Holy mist surrounding God. Only Purity and Holiness Creates Glory Substance. When Holy Mist, which is Glory Substance, comes into a situation darkness flees and people are healed, delivered, and set free.

Redeemed people, who live Holy lives and who are obedient to God, have the innate ability to cause Glory Mist to manifest around them. This Glory mist may or may not be visible, but rest assured it is present. Glory mist flows into situations when redeemed people give Holy God, their Creator, Pure and Holy worship. God gladly receives this Pure worship to Him. Pure worship expressed in praise creates a Holy Mist, which is the Substance of Life. The Substance of Life brings Glory Fire Influence that manifests a molecular change in the atmosphere and so restructures darkness to become Light. From God's Light or Holy Mist, emanates the Substance of Life causing creative happenings. From the invisible Visionary Glory Substance of Life, actual material objects can be creatively formed and brought into visible and tangible substance on earth by specific words of decree spoken and creative acts performed that bring into visible and tangible substance on earth by specific spoken words that bring into material existence human body parts, water, food, gold, spheres of dominion, and creative miracles of all kinds in many forms.

Spoken words cause quantum physics to activate transforming the invisible Substance of Life back into its Original form of Light bringing molecular change into visible matter that can be used on earth as Originally Designed and Created by Holy God.

Pure and Holy worship to Holy God creates quantum mechanics that causes living frequencies to vibrate with Life-giving Energy. Only Holy and Pure worship to Creative God creates Light that transforms the invisible Substance of Life into tangible matter that turns the darkness of evil back into Light in original form.

This occurs when God's Created Holy angels and Blood-redeemed people Created in God's Image and Likeness offer Him Pure and Holy worship. This combined Pure worship to Him causes the Creative Substance of Life to manifest into material matter which appears - to human beings living in the material realm as Creative Miracles but is Almighty God's only Way of Life. When mist or clouds of Light known as Shekinah Glory Influence comes into a situation God's Holiness manifests and eradicates the darkness of evil in all its forms and brings Light that Creates.

Thank You, Holy God for Holy Revelation Truth. Increase our ability to offer You Pure and Holy worship so that, through our obedience to flow in Glory Fire Influence operations as led by

Holy Spirit, evil is eradicated and the earth and the heavens are transformed back into Original forms of Light which establishes Your Holy Kingdom of Righteousness that Reigns for Eternity.

Transporting Visionary Glory

In another reality dream, I saw myself pushing a grocery cart. I saw this over and over. I also saw others around me pushing grocery carts.

The Lord instructed me to know that His redeemed people are transporting Visionary Glory Influence everywhere they go. Visionary Glory operates when you are around people in the circumstances where God places you, or where you go by choice, or are invited. Visionary Glory does not operate in isolation. You carry God's Presence into your personal situation. Redeemed people carry Holy God's Presence that creates an atmosphere of Glory Fire Influence all around them in their circumstance that tangibly removes all that is not of Him. Each redeemed person bringing God's Holy Presence into a situation must remember to open the Visionary Glory Box carrying Visionary Glory Influence and then speak or act from what you see or hear from Visionary Glory Influence. When this is done, Glory Fire Influence carries your spoken words of decree and creatively designed actions into your current situation or circumstance and brings lasting change for Good.

Visionary Glory is transported into your present circumstance by the Holy Creative words you speak, the visions or pictures you see that show you prayer to verbalize, specific healing pronouncements, a Blessing or a Righteous judgement to decree. Know that Glory Influence Flows out of your body, shines on your face, and transports through your smile, and manifests through your words. I cried out to The Lord, "Lord, why are there times when I don't see immediate visible manifestations when I speak? I know and truly believe that the Substance of Life exists in the invisible realm in a form that manifests into visible matter by the words I speak?"

Visionary Glory is transported into your present circumstance by the Holy Creative words you speak, the visions or pictures you see that show you what to do: prayer to verbalize, specific healing pronouncements, decree a Blessing or a Righteous judgement. Know that **Glory Influence Flows out of your body, shines on your face, and transports through your smile, and manifests through your words**.

I cried out to The Lord, "Lord, why are there times when I don't see immediate visible manifestations when I speak? I know and truly believe that the Substance of Life exists in the invisible realm in a form that manifests into visible matter by the words I speak?"

The Lord let me know that when I speak, my Holy and Anointed words cause manifestations that I may or may not see. No matter what is happening around me, I am to keep my focus on Him, not on whether or not I see immediate manifestations. The Lord is revealing that Visionary Glory operations are launching the new heavens and new earth to replace the devastation from evil. Visionary Glory is bringing into manifestation Eternal Living.

Unused Words in Visionary Glory Box

The Lord openly revealed to me that there are still unused words in this Visionary Glory Box that are to be spoken to create what is needed on earth during the time Satan is attempting to shut down Holy God's Creative Ways of Living for Good.

My spirit was greatly stirred to know more about these unused words. So in all boldness I asked The Lord to reveal more to me concerning the unused words in this Visionary Glory Box that I instinctively recognize need to be spoken so they create and bring into manifestation what is needed on earth when Satan is attempting to shut down what God Created for Good and evil is blatantly being flaunted.

These words rose up in me to declare: "In Jesus' Name and by the Power of Holy Spirit, I release the Glory Influence to displace and stop the powers of darkness that would halt any request I decree. Amen! Glory be to You O Lord God Most High!"

Intuitively, I knew that the unspoken and inaudible Holy Words contained in the Visionary Glory Box are being spoken by Supreme God. I strongly sense in my spirit that Almighty God is releasing these unused words contained in the Visionary Glory Box. I knew by revelation knowledge rising in me that these unused Words, are not being heard by human or demonic hearing. Nevertheless, these unused words are underway and are actually happening without the devil's or people's knowledge so that Holy God's Will for heaven and earth to be reconciled together as one operation is not thwarted.

Supreme God is soundlessly speaking these unspoken Holy Words contained in the Visionary Glory Box. These unused words being spoken by Holy God releases Shekinah Glory Power that is causing *sudden* destruction bringing to an end all things as they are now so that the new heavens and the new earth can be established by the Visionary Glory operations being spoken into material existence by God's redeemed people.

Religious Spirit and Human Will Join

The Lord is issuing a warning to all those who are diligently pursuing Him in relationship, to learn how to walk in Eternal

Ways of existence, that they are to be fully aware that the unsanctified human will and the religious spirit are uniting and working together. These unholy spirits are presently increasing their combined operations to work in unison to shut down Holy Glory Fire operations flowing through all of those carrying Glory Fire Influence by the Power and Life of Holy Spirit.

The Lord is warning that this will happen through people we presently trust or have formerly trusted by association who, for whatever reason, allow unholy spirits to influence them. Subtle deception is at work in a greater degree and manner trying to get those carrying Holy Glory Fire Influence off target. Casual trust can no longer be accepted by immaturity and blind acceptance.

The human will can be transformed by the religious spirit operating under the radar undetected. Its deceitful maneuvers ensnare unsuspecting people who just go to church to look acceptable to others and, yet, truly believe they are acceptable to God. The unholy operations of the religious spirit are altering the rational thinking of many people and so are holding them captive to a form of religion without Holy Power manifestations because they do not know The Lord on Holy intimate terms.

To those who do not detect this joint operation between the unsanctified human will and the religious spirit, the power of this unholy alliance is increasingly deceiving those *playing church* which keeps them entwined in half-truth and half lies.

Alert discernment wrapped in Holy Love must operate in those carrying Glory Fire Presence enabling them to detect unholy operations deceitfully working in people who are not awake and watching. Those carrying Glory Fire Influence are to adhere to God's Holy Word when they are around suspicious people so as not to fall prey to deceiving ways that pulls unsuspecting into its web. Absorb and heed God's Word in Romans 16:17-20 Hebrews 13:9a Ephesians 5:6-11 Colossians 2:8 2 Timothy 3:1-9 Luke 21:8 Matthew 24:4-12.

An increased number of people walking in Glory Fire Influence are being sent by The Lord to come on the scene in Power demonstrations. This causes the religious spirit and the human will to become stirred and unsettled causing them to increase their joint effort to stay in charge of church operations as they see it.

At this point of delusion, deceived people who are so ingrained in deception openly accept the half-truth and half-lies from this unholy alliance as Truth. So they see no need to repent because they sincerely, although wrongly, believe they are fine. They mistakenly and confidently believe that those walking in Glory Fire Influence are in deception; therefore, they have the unmitigated right to turn and attack those walking in Glory Fire Influence. Those who allow themselves to be held captive to deception will betray those who are powerfully carrying Glory Fire influence.

Jesus warned that those doing this will think they are doing God a favor:

I have said all this to you, to keep you from falling away. They will put you out of the synagogues; indeed, the hour is coming when whoever kills you will think he is offering service to God. (John 16:1-2).

They went out from us, but they were not of us; for if they had been of us, they would have continued with us; but they went out, that it might be plain that they all are not of us. (1 John 2:19).

This is why those who are walking in Glory Fire Power must remain alert in every area of their lives. Deception is no respecter of persons. Its ploy is for all people. It is imperative to stay alert by walking in Truth as recorded in The Holy Bible. Pure worship to Holy God from an undefiled heart washed clean by The Blood of Jesus keeps you alert to all forms of pride and deception.

In a dream, I was with another Holy woman of God who ministers The Lord's Life and Truth wherever she goes alone or we go together as He leads us. In this dream, we were together watching an old lady sitting on a low stool fixing a bicycle rim or tire. I saw us saying to her, "We will pay you." She said, "I don't want you to pay me." We said, "We want to pay you. You deserve to be paid." She kept saying, "I don't want to get paid." We kept on talking with her. She adamantly said, "I don't want to hear what you are saying."

Suddenly, I saw in such vivid vibrant colors, teams of horses go by me. There were six horses to a team. They were in full speed ahead, seemingly flying past me. They caught my attention. I felt like I wanted to go after them. They appeared to be pulling stagecoaches full of people one after another. I saw many, many activities like you would see at a Country Fair all going on at the same time, and this scene was so vibrantly alive and in full vibrant colors. I so wanted to be part of this. I felt so very, very happy. I didn't want what I was seeing to ever end.

I said, "I am going after the horses. I love horses, and I am going after them." So I got in my car and headed after the horses which I could see in the far distance. They went so fast I couldn't catch them. So, I stopped going after them and turned around in a driveway to return to where I was. I recall the driveway was not a straight driveway but completely rounding in front of a beautiful architecturally-designed house. The rounding patio looking driveway was made of pretty pinkish textured of bricks of smooth yet imprinted design. As I turned around to leave the textured driveway, I saw the yard had lush green grass and was well-manicured. Vibrantly beautiful flowers lined the driveway and were closely aligned along the driveway where I was turning around to head back to where I was. I was looking out my window watching the driveway trying to stay on the driveway so as not to smash the vibrant flowers or get in the beautifully-manicured yard. I was captured by the beauty of this driveway and how closely it was aligned with the vibrantly-alive grass and flowers. I didn't know why I was so particularly drawn to these. I just was. So much so that I was looking down at them from my driver's window to make sure I did not drive over them as I was turning around to leave the driveway.

Next, I was back again with my ministry friend. We were again in the presence of the old lady fixing the bicycle. We said to her, "We know! You don't want to be paid." She said, "Now I do. I want to hear what you are saying." We said, "We don't have anything to tell you." I was puzzled by the old lady formerly not wanting to hear, and now wanting to hear what we had to say; and our saying we don't have anything to tell you. I pondered this dream for days. I almost dismissed it because I did not understand it.

Then The Lord opened my understanding. I perceived in my spirit that this old lady's reaction was the typical reply that the unsanctified human will that is aligned with the religious spirit speaks. They want to hear on their own terms when they want to hear. Then when they decide they want to hear, The Lord doesn't have anything to say to them. They missed His timing in what He wanted to say to them. The happy times are going on without them. They can't join in the happy times that are happening at a fast pace because they didn't want to hear what The Lord wanted to personally speak to them when He came to them individually or through others He sent to them with His Glory Fire Influence to make Himself known to them with His Glory Fire Influence to make Himself known to them as He wants to be known. His Holy Desire is for them to turn to Him with all their hearts (Mark 12:30-31).

I also see that if we who are speaking to others what The Lord is saying also do not get on board with the fast-paced activities The Lord is doing at this time, we too will get left behind to do our own thing.

Religious Spirit Rendered Powerless

The religious spirit aligned with the unsanctified human will attacks Glory Fire Operations. Jesus was publicly shut down so many times by the religious spirit operating through unsanctified human wills. At this time on earth, the Authority of Jesus is being released and carried out through His redeemed people who carry His Glory Fire Influence by being obedient to do ...*the greater works*... of Power and Glory that Jesus said we would do after He ascended back to His Father (John 14:12). Those who are obedient to do ...*the greater works*... are causing the religious spirit to be shut down in all its forms through their Holy Glory Fire operations being carried out under the guidance of Holy Spirit.

Through a Holy and uniquely orchestrated assignment, The Lord came upon me mightily. Spirit tongues flowed through me all day long. This was an unusual day. I knew Glory Fire operations were being performed in cooperation with Holy God. I let these Holy Spirit operations flow into me and out through me. The Power and Presence of The Lord Almighty was evidently on me the entire day. I just flowed with His directions. Travailing, groaning prayer fell on me as Fire. I could not stop this nor did I want to. The Lord revealed to me that this was His Glory Fire operating through me to render the religious spirit inoperative and unable to keep God's fully committed people captive and in bondage to its illicit tactics.

Holy Glory Fire operations continued through me and intensified in cooperation with my friend The Lord brought into my life to walk alongside me in ministry. Even though we were not physically together at this time, we kept in contact by texts to each other. I was keeping her updated on what The Lord was doing through me that was bringing the religious spirit's stronghold of illegal influence into subjection to God's Holy Authority so God's redeemed people are released from lies and deception. The Lord arranged our circumstances so we would come into Holy agreement with each other and with Him in rendering the religious spirit permanently powerless to operate in any form. We joined our hearts and words together in Holy agreement. In the mouth of two or three witnesses shall every word be established (Deuteronomy 19:15, 2 Corinthians 13:1).

These Spirit-led actions are part of ...*the greater works*... Jesus said we would be doing when He returned to sit at His Father's Right Hand and sent us Holy Spirit (John 14:12-14).

During the night as I lay in my bed, I was rehearsing the Glory Fire operations against the religious spirit that The Lord did through me today in agreement with my Holy friend. I heard myself asking The Lord, "Is the religious spirit now rendered powerless by the Mighty Acts You did through me against this ugly spirit and in agreement with You and my Holy friend, or are we to continue bombarding the religious spirit to stop it from operating?"

A clean and Pure fragrance permeated my room as I lay on my bed. I knew it was the sweet fragrance of Heaven being released. I deeply breathed in this sweet and Pure fragrance. I kept doing this. I could not get enough of this smell.

I indelibly knew that the fragrance of Heaven is now released to encompass God's redeemed people. Therefore, they are now free to follow Him *if* they so choose. People can no longer be held captive by religious spirit ways unless they choose to stay complacent to its wiles. God's Holy operations have set people free to see and hear Holy God's Voice above the clamor of the religious spirit. Therefore, even more of ...*the greater works*... Jesus declared His disciples would do can come forth through them.

Through the obedient actions of my friend working in cooperation with me in obedience to The Lord's directions, God's Holy anger was unleashed and His Holy Wrath spent on this religious spirit who has held His people captive by strangulation so they could not see or hear Him. Now those who choose to comply with Holy Spirit's direction are free from the entanglement of the religious spirit. They can accurately know The Lord in Truth and openly experience His Love for them in going forth doing ...*the greater works*... they now have the uninterrupted ability to carry out.

If people receive what The Lord is openly revealing concerning the religious spirit being permanently rendered powerless, they are fully released to follow Him and as well to operate ...*the greater works*... as Jesus said we would. Count on this: no more unsanctified human will and religious spirit operating together to keep God's people captive to lies and deception.

The religious spirit has been dealt a powerful blow that restrains its unholy actions against God's Holy people causing all the redeemed in Heaven and on earth to rejoice together. No longer can people excuse themselves; nor can they blame God for their selfish decisions. Only those filled with Holy Spirit who receive what has been accomplished against the religious spirit will agree with God and so flow in this Holy knowledge.

The Lord made it evidently clear to me that everywhere God's redeemed people go, we are to declare the religious spirit powerless to operate. We are to forbid this religious spirit to lie and deceive us. Each redeemed person is to emphatically state to this religious spirit that it no longer has any power to operate its lies and deception to keep God's Holy people captive to its evil lies. We are to continually remind this religious spirit that it has been permanently dismantled by declaring loudly and openly with bold Authority:

Supreme God and I have come into agreement against you religious spirit. I legally demand you by the Authority of Almighty God to let God's people GO! You no longer have any power to lie and deceive, or strangle God's people! Says The Lord, "Let My people go!"

The religious spirit has been dealt a powerful blow and has been rendered permanently powerless by the obedience to Holy Spirit led operations.

All Glory, Power, and Dominion is Yours, Supreme God of Creation. I know in Truth that agreeing with You in unified agreement renders the religious spirit powerless in all its forms and so seals on earth and in the heavens Your Kingdom of Righteousness and Justice. Praise be to Almighty God forever and ever! AMEN!

Hallelujah!!! Amen and Amen multiplied many times over!

Church Leaders and Religious Spirit

However, the religious spirit is still active in organized churches because there are those who worship God with their lips while their hearts are far from Him. In doing this, they hold the form of religion, but they deny God's Power to work Truth in them because they allow their human will to override God's Word. When the religious spirit aligns with a strong human will, a powerful alliance is formed causing deception to operate unleashed. People who are in captivity to the spirit of deception willingly surrender their minds and their wills to believe lies. This leads them deeper and deeper into a place where they are unmercifully held captive to deception. They become completely satisfied with the way things are done and have always been done. The human spirit who is held captive to the influence of the religious spirit just keeps on thinking all is well when it is not. Therefore, The Lord is strongly warning people to be alert and to not relinquish their God- ordained authority against this all-consuming religious spirit. Its wiles are insatiably after people who truly belong to Holy God, attempting to get them to give in to its wiles so they don't take a stand against its unauthorized stranglehold and as well, do not operate the *...the greater works...* Jesus said they are to do.

However, The Lord is openly disclosing that there are church leaders who recognize the rampant deception of the religious spirit that is operating in the organized church. Therefore, they are not satisfied with the way things are being done that is against Bible Truth, and so they are choosing to come out of the organized church. It is hard for them to do this in front of their children who have been brought up in the church scenario. However, these leaders are following Holy Spirit leadings trusting their children to The Lord believing He will cause them to eventually understand the decisive stand their parents are taking against the actions of the human will aligning with the religious spirit who control the operations of their church.

Parents must honestly and openly tell their children why they freely chose to leave the church they have perhaps attended for years and years. The Lord wants parents to tell their children why they are leaving the organized church and that it is also to OKAY for the children to leave as well. The Lord wants the youth, children and young adults to know why their parents are leaving the established organized church's traditions, many of which are based on deception and all-out lies perpetuated by the religious spirit who harassed and basically deterred Jesus when He lived on earth.

The Lord is at work in all of those obeying His directions. Therefore, those who wholeheartedly follow the direction of Holy Spirit are being linked together in ways that have never before been considered. Even though these Spirit-led individuals may not be in tangible proximity with one another, God sees them as true believers in Yeshua Ha'Mashiach who are united as one united entity who are working together with Him in accomplishing His Will His Way. Therefore, they are not forsaking the assembling of themselves together during these horrendous times of upheaval to eradicate evil. Closely observe in your own circumstances how God is doing this. Then praise and thank Him for working in and through each one of us separately yet altogether as one when we obey His directions to us individually.

Thank You, Lord Supreme of Heaven and earth for openly revealing Yourself in Majestic Glory Operations. To You alone be all the Glory and Honor throughout Eternity.

Satan Rendered Powerless

I recalled two reality encounters The Lord openly allowed me to observe. The first encounter was on January 19, 1992. The most recent dream was on November 3, 2019. I will begin with the most recent reality encounter that confirms and fulfills the January 19, 1992 reality encounter.

November 3, 2019

DREAM: Satan Stands Impotent Before You

In a dream, I was alone at home working at my kitchen sink. I was deeply engrossed in what I was doing and was not fully cognizant of the knocking I heard on my pantry door between the kitchen and utility room. I automatically said, "Who is it?" I mechanically went over and opened the door not looking because I was engrossed in what I was doing and so automatically went back to what I was doing at the sink. When I finally did look over at the open pantry door, I explicitly saw a man standing in my pantry. He had not yet walked through the door. He was just standing there. He was totally naked, and had no hair on him or his head. He was on crutches, and his right foot was in a blue walking cast. He had no sex organs whatsoever. There was only what looked like skin covering the part of his body where sex organs would be normally. But he looked like a man in appearance. He had a man's haircut and look. He began walking through the door and walking toward me. As I got behind my kitchen island and began heading toward my back door, I cried out, "Get away from me! Stay away from me! Don't you touch me!" With this, I awoke from this dream.

This scenario lingered and remained before me for days. I kept seeing this naked man standing before me over and over. I could not dismiss it. Therefore, I knew it had to have significance and that The Lord wanted me to know something that I did not know. I have been so occupied caring for my husband who had total shoulder replacement, I have not had time to pursue The Lord on the meaning of this dream. This morning, I had time to go up to my Prayer Room. I brought this dream before The Lord asking Him to show me what this means.

As I rested in the Presence of The Lord, I knew that what God is giving me to speak and do for Him is causing Satan to stand naked, exposed, crippled, and impotent before me. I knew explicitly that all forms of his evil are being rendered powerless.

Immediately, I recalled the horrible dream I had on **January 19, 1992** when The Lord began openly speaking to me and giving me revelation.

On this date, I was waking up from an appalling dream I was having that was in such explicit detail that I could not bring myself to even think about it. It was so vivid that I could not shake it from my memory or forget it. I was crying out to God to erase it from my mind. It was so vividly awful that I didn't want to see it or remember it. But it wouldn't go away.

I was crying so hard I scarcely heard the words The Lord was speaking to my heart. I just wanted to forget it, but I couldn't. It kept playing over and over in my mind's eye. As I awoke and got up, I could not get away from this horrible dream. I was greatly disturbed by it. Then I finally realized that God was trying to tell me something. I cried out, "My God and my Lord, what are You telling me?"

The Lord explicitly, plainly, and clearly spoke to me. He said that His Body was allowing themselves to be raped right at the point of fruitfulness and giving birth to what He planted within them. He further revealed that His Body was being raped by their engaging with the lust of the world right at the point of bearing fruit and this is what was causing them to allow themselves to be raped so they can't bring forth what He implanted within them that is right at the point of fruitfulness.

I cried out asking, "O, Father, what do You want me to do about this?"

I knew intuitively that God, our Father, was going to expose the cause of the rape and show openly that the one who is raping His people is Satan but that he is impotent and powerless and cannot complete or perform the act of raping His people to the point of losing their fruitfulness.

I asked, "How are You going to do this?"

He let me know that this will only be accomplished through affliction that will cause pain and suffering to His people.

I asked, "How does this involve me?"

Instantly, I recalled a previous dream I had had on March 14-15, 1991, where things were at the point of devastation, yet God was using me to *build and plant*. I also recalled His Word to me on October 13, 1983, from Isaiah 14:24-27, 32 about the affliction that He was going to use to drive His people to Himself because they would have no place to flee but to Him; and He would be waiting for them in Zion, a place of refuge where His Presence dwells. He related to me that this pain of affliction is GOOD as it will cause His people to run to Him when they have nowhere else to turn. He stated that after this short affliction comes birth that brings forth fruit from the seed He implanted in His redeemed people so He is seen as Potent and able to perform the ACT of planting seed in the womb of His people that bears fruit. He wants to be seen and known as All- Powerful and able to bring forth the fruit of the womb He implanted within His people that brings forth good fruit that remains.

O, Lord my God, I see this recent dream on November 3, 2019 is confirmation and the fulfillment to the 1992 dream. In truth, Satan is permanently defeated when redeemed people bear Holy fruit for God's Kingdom that remains.

Hallelujah! Your Word endures forever. AMEN

Time to Construct and Create

Before going to bed, and seemingly all night long, I was entwined or wrapped around a cylinder-shaped substance that appeared as blue vapor mist. I sensed strongly that The Lord God was wound around me and we were creating, producing, formulating, generating, constructing, and building. We spun and twirled and rolled flying through space. We were being transported through space. This was so exhilarating and satisfying. I didn't want this to end and it seemed as if this would never end.

This sensation of spinning and twirling and being transported through space lasted all night long. I wanted this to go on forever. The entire time I was spinning around and around wrapped around this cylinder and blue vapor mist being transported through space, intense Holy Spirit-tongue praying flowed out of me. These strong and forceful tongues never stopped. They just flowed and flowed as if they would never stop. I felt so wrapped in the intensity of His Love and was immensely enjoying this.

I could not shake this visionary yet tangible encounter all day long. Finally, I stopped and wrote this down. When I finished writing this encounter down, these words rose up in me: *construct and create.*

Then I had another dream. I saw a place where people were so joyous and were refurbishing their run-down dwelling places and their meeting places saying to each other with great joy and enthusiasm, "Now we can do this." They were referring to me and expressing how I gave them courage and comprehension to know how to creatively *construct and create* what has been devastated because of what I said to them.

In this dream, I was not there with them doing this restructuring. I wanted to be but was just observing them doing this. It appeared to me that I was excluded in the refurbishing, yet I was with them in all they were doing. I so wanted to be with them and join with them in what they were doing. But I saw all this at a distance.

The Lord revealed to me that He is encouraging me through this dream to know there are those whose lives are being empowered by Holy Spirit to believe the Holy knowledge He is revealing through me to give them so they can *construct and create* new ways to refurbish the old habitations in their lives that have been devastated by evil. *Suddenly*, it became clearly evident to me that this is where things are on earth right now.

The Lord has spoken to me many, many times in various ways over many years that the time would come when He would use me to *build and plant* to restore the devastation caused by evil. Because of all the recent revelation that He took me into, I now have more understanding of His meaning that the time would come for me to *build and plant*. I now have fullness of understanding to know that to *build and plant* means to *construct and create* new ways when everything has been devastated and appears as though it cannot be rebuilt because people are pretty much convinced that the devastation can never be reversed. He has spoken to me for years that He would use me to refurbish new ways in people's lives when it appeared that everything on earth was devastated and people were saying things on earth could never be restored.

The Lord Almighty is revealing that His Time on earth is here to *construct and create* new ways in people's lives in order to restore and rebuild the foundations that have been ruined and devastated by evil operations. This obvious devastation is causing people to turn to Him. Therefore, I know with certainty that His Time has come to *construct and create* new ways in people's lives in order to restore the foundations of Righteousness that have been destroyed by evil devastation.

Holy Wisdom and Knowledge is being opened by The Lord to His redeemed people so they know how to *construct and create* a fresh environment when everything as they know it to be is devastated. Holy Knowledge and Wisdom is being unleashed to know how to use Visionary Glory to creatively *construct and create* new heavens and new earth. Humankind is Created in God's Image and after His Likeness. Therefore, they innately have creative ability residing within them that gives them the capacity and the capability to *construct and create* what they envision by the Holy desire in their hearts that they release into visible manifestation by the words they speak and the actions they take. This is exactly the Way Supreme God Creatively Created the heavens and the earth.

Creative Glory manifests through people's innate creative ability enabling them to *construct and create* what is needed to rebuild and refurbish right in the midst of the seeming devastation all around them. It doesn't matter to creative people that there is devastation all around them. They are operating by Holy Knowledge and Wisdom by the Creative Glory that is innately Designed within them.

The time has come for people redeemed through Jesus' Blood to step out in Jesus' indwelling (permanently present) *Faith* residing in them to creatively *construct and create* the desire in their hearts that refurbishes their environment as they want it to be. Their *Faith* enterprises (creativity, innovation, originality) enable them to construct and create their environment in ways that please them which cause Supreme God's Creative Glory Power to be magnified and exalted so He is seen and known as a Righteous God who Loves His Created people enough to allow them the freedom to *construct and create* their environment in ways they enjoy.

Lord, I appeal to You. Reveal to me in Truth how this will begin. It is one thing to know this, but another thing to know how to do this. Are there people with the mindset that this is possible? Do they surmise this is underway? Is their unsettled discontent in the ways things on earth are at this time stirring them up to seek more Knowledge and Wisdom from You?

Show me tangibly how to know if this is already underway. I explicitly surrender and yield to You to know what is next in fulfilling Your Word to me that after devastation is the time to *construct and create* to restore what has been devastated by evil. Hasten my knowing, Lord. Help me to understand how this is to be done in fullness. Thank You.

Holy Spirit revelation knowledge opened to me and enlightened my understanding to know that during the unprecedented times on earth when everything on earth and in the heavens is being shaken to remove all forms of evil, God The Almighty Creator of Heaven and earth is exhibiting His unique, Great, and Awesome ...*signs, wonders, and miracles*... that outdo Satan's counterfeit signs and wonders. His Holy and Anointed ones ordained by Him are speaking His Word of Authority in Heaven and upon the earth. This Holy interchange between people living on earth, redeemed people in Heaven, and Holy angels in Heaven is releasing an abundant and tangible supply of untainted Power manifestations that provide and restore any needs people on earth have during the unparalleled times when God is pouring out His Holy and Just Wrath to eradicate all evil.

Seeing and experiencing the fulfillment of God's Word causes The Lord's Holy people and angels to cry out to Almighty God of Heaven and earth, "Holy, Holy, Holy, Lord God of Sabaoth,

Lord of hosts. You alone are Almighty God of Heaven and earth! Heaven and earth are full of the Glories of Your Majesty. Your Kingdom is an Everlasting Kingdom and Your dominion endures throughout all generations. You alone are The True and Living God who is worthy to receive All Glory, Honor, and Power and Dominion, for You alone Created All things and by Your Will, they exist and were Created. Amen and Amen!"

Almighty and benevolent God of all Creation, You are Glorious in all Your Ways. You alone are able to make all Grace, Knowledge, and Wisdom abound to us so that at all times in all ways, we have everything we need to abound in every good work for the Praise of Your Glory. Amen and Amen!

Unlocking Supernatural Provision

I was randomly reviewing what The Lord has spoken to me concerning His Righteous Kingdom on earth as it pertains to operating in supernatural provision. Luke 12:32, 42 immediately rose up in me:

Fear not, little flock, for it is your Father's good pleasure to give you the Kingdom.

Who then is the faithful and wise steward, whom his master will set over his household, to give them their portion of good at the proper time?

The Lord is letting it be known on earth and in the heavens that all those who heed His directions, are His faithful servants to whom it is His Good Pleasure to give them the Kingdom. Each faithful steward has ownership of all Holy God's possessions. His faithful and obedient servants have all they need at the proper time and so are able to dispense what is needed both physically and spiritually. God has commissioned Holy stewards to dispense food at the proper time to any who have a need. They are set in place over all God's possessions as Righteous stewards who have management and charge over food distribution.

Each one of these Holy stewards may do as they freely choose in meeting the needs of people. Natural circumstances are worsening. It will become evidently clear that supernatural provision needs to operate in full provision to provide people's pressing requirements. Old ways of providing people's needs have passed away. Now is the New Day of supernatural provision so God's Holy Ways are seen on earth. To most, this seems supernatural. To Supreme God it is His only Way to provide.

Supernatural provision occurs through those who are found faithful by Holy God. These faithful and obedient servants are set by God as His loyal stewards over all His possessions. Shekinah Glory is powerfully removing all forms of evil. Supernatural operations expedited from Visionary Glory release Creative Glory operations to activate and bring into tangible use all the necessities needed for those who belong to God during this time of horrendous and unprecedented upheaval to eradicate evil. It will be known who belongs to God when it is seen that all their necessary needs have been met by Creative Glory operations. God's abundant supernatural provision meets the required needs of His redeemed people living on earth during all the upheaval that is removing all evil. Supernatural provision flows from Visionary Glory.

God's Visionary Glory operates in fullness using these Eternal Rules:

FAITH: in God's Ability to supply
RESPONSE: to hear with focus what God is saying
ACTION: to do what Holy God says to do when He says to do it

Holy God is openly revealing working Knowledge and Wisdom to all who heed His Holy and Just revelation operations. Keep asking Him how and when to do what you innately have the Authority and Power to do through His Presence indwelling you.

Supernatural Acts Defy World's Logic

In the midst of openly praising and worshipping The Lord, I understood distinctively that all those operating in Visionary Glory are *a sign and a wonder* to show evil principalities, powers, rulers of darkness, and spiritual wickedness in high places that Holy God's Power is superlative and belongs to Him alone, and they cannot touch those who belong to Supreme God in what they are obeying Him to do. His Holy Authority working through His redeemed people is dispensing Justice that dispels darkness and evil and displays His superlative and indispensable Light.

Those who unflinchingly obey Almighty God's Holy directions override the natural system used on earth that these evil powers control by their unholy supernatural operations. Supreme God's Power manifestations defy the world's logic. No longer are things as usual: financial needs being met or supplied through natural means of the world banking system or by those working the religious system by receiving the tithe and offering from people through using God's Word to receive their financial ministry support and as they propose, give to the poor.

No matter how this has worked in the past, it is no longer a viable way to receive necessary provision. Almighty God is closing down the world's financial systems, governmental systems, medical systems, and religious systems who are propagating themselves for self-profit even though they do not believe they are doing this. Deception causes delusion that even takes Holy Scripture and twists it for selfish reasons. Glory operations are being carried out through those who belong to Holy God as they do Creative acts in obedience to His Holy directions. These Glory Fire operations override the world's system of operation. Those operating from Visionary Glory release God's Holy and essential provision to meet people's needs both now and for Infinity.

To God alone be All the Glory, Honor, Power, and Dominion Forever! Amen!

Kingdom Shift Back to Original Design

I am coming into increased understanding that all The Lord has openly revealed to me, and taught me, and sent me to do for Him through the years is currently being confirmed and validated as He promised me. He is clearly showing me how procreation is being done through redeemed people who operate Visionary Glory. In doing this, they are creatively creating the new heavens and new earth that restores and replaces the devastation caused by evil. This creative restoration brings God's Holy Kingdom back to Original Design that remains for Infinity.

The Lord is presently unveiling hidden revelation that He revealed and spoke to His Holy prophets and had them record at the time He spoke to them which is written in The Holy Bible as we know it today. He has purposely concealed recorded revelation knowledge in The Holy Bible until the time was ripe for this veiled information to be made known for the purpose of fulfilling His Word of Truth. Present world circumstances dictate that the proper time has arrived to uncover these concealed revelations so they are fulfilled as He previously voiced.

Therefore, The Lord is unveiling hidden revelation to those redeemed by Jesus' Holy Blood so they know how to operate Visionary Glory by their innate creative ability He endowed in them before they were born. When they use their innate creative ability by operating Visionary Glory, the new heavens and new earth are created from the desired Holy intent flowing out of their inborn creativity. By doing this, they are utilizing their God-given creativity and Holy Authority to remain in dominion over the part of earth where they choose to reside both now and for Eternity (Revelation 21-22).

God's Original Designed Intent for redeemed humankind to creatively create their own environment is in process of being completely fulfilled. When redeemed people frame the Holy desired intent in their heart by spoken words of decree and creatively designed actions they receive from Visionary Glory Influence, their holy intention manifests into material form and creates the environment they desire that brings themselves and Holy God pleasure and enjoyment resounding for His Glory throughout Infinity that has no end.

Contemplate Job 22:28 (TAB): *You shall also decide and decree a thing, and it shall be established for you and the light* [of Gods favor] *shall shine upon your ways.*

From their Holy Designed and Creative position in Christ Jesus, redeemed and renewed humankind can construct their desired intent and bring into material manifestation on earth what they frame from the Holy words they speak from Visionary Glory. This brings Supreme God Great Pleasure and Enjoyment to have someone like Himself to fellowship with who creatively creates in the same Way He does. This is His Purpose for Creating humankind in His Image and after His Likeness.

God is Uniquely Creative. He Sovereignly elected to Creatively Design humankind with a free-will to creatively create and manage the Garden, where He placed them, in any way they desired. But human beings used their free-will and listened to the devil's wiles thereby succumbing to his lies that they would be like God in knowing good and evil. God knew evil. However, He never intended for humankind to know evil. The devil betrayed humankind by causing them to believe they could be like God if they knew good and evil. This is true deception at work. The devil is always tricking people into agreeing with him, and this leads them into complying with his selfish will above God's Holy Will, making what he is doing through them by deception appear as their idea, and so he stupidly thinks this excuse him from being detected. The devil even lies to himself to comply with his selfish will above God's Holy *Will* so that it appears as if it was their idea. In this way, he stays under the radar undetected and lets them take the blame for his rebellious evil.

Deception is truth mixed with a lie. God Almighty did not want the people He Created in His Image and Likeness to know the maneuvers of evil so they would be free to use their creative abilities for Good purposes that could never be taken away from them. However, people's disobedience to His Perfect *Will* for them caused sin to enter earth. Their willful rebellion caused them to temporarily lose their ability to creatively create Good things that would remain forever.

Nevertheless, Holy and Living Love came to our rescue. He immediately revealed His Holy Plan to redeem us from Satan's evil (Genesis 2-3). God's Holy and Righteous Goodness drove humankind out of the Garden because if they remained in the Garden in their fallen state of existence, they would remain in this Eternal State that would allow them to Eternally create evil. Thanks be to God who delivers us from ourselves.

For humankind to fulfill God's Original Creative Design in creatively creating their environment as they so choose, a Holy transformation of thinking and speaking must take place in our finite minds so this can occur. We must choose to allow ourselves to transition into Creative Infinity by an act of our free-will. This can be done when Father, Son, and Holy Spirit's essential and actual abiding Presence resides in us. His abiding Presence dwelling in us transforms our thinking so we think and act as He does. As we submit to our Righteous God-head: Father, Son, and Holy Spirit, His Infinite Creative Ability Intent continuously operates in us for good.

Even before we were born, God had a plan for our lives. He intentionally Designed within us our creative ability to transform our environment into what we creatively construct from our Holy desire by the words we speak. As we continually allow the fullness of Supreme God's Presence indwelling us to transform our thinking, we are Creative Infinity activated and realized. This creative ability remains in redeemed people when they graduate to Heaven and continues to operate through them for Eternity. This creative ability also exists within all living beings Supreme God Created and endorsed with His Stamp of approval.

Creative God Originally Designed for the entire company or assembly of beings in Heaven along with humankind on earth to flow together with Him in creatively creating a beautifully and creatively designed environment for all of us to enjoy together for Infinity. Each God-Created Holy being is uniquely fashioned so that our creative abilities flow together to fulfill God's Predetermined Plan for His Creations to exist together in perfect harmony. Therefore, His intended purpose is for all His Created beings to work together as one united and Holy Plan according to their uniquely and Creatively Designed aptitude.

Prayer:

In Jesus' Name, I call forth a shift back to Original Kingdom Living. According to Hebrews 12:22- 24, I call out to heavenly Jerusalem, the city of God in Heaven, the cloud of witnesses in Heaven, innumerable company of angels, the general assembly and church of the firstborn, to God the Judge of all, to the spirits of just men made perfect, to Jesus the Mediator of the new covenant, and to the blood of sprinkling that speaks better things, to come and join in accomplishing together our Holy Assignments from Supreme God. I entreat you to come to us and exchange Holy facts with us to establish Kingdom Living back to its Original form so that Holy God's Planned Intention for the heavens and earth to cooperate together in one complete and Holy Circle of Life is completed for Infinity. Amen!

I truly, and deeply, and innately perceive and therefore wholeheartedly believe by Holy Spirit of Supreme God abiding in me, that there are those of you who have had or are having dream or vision encounters where you are creatively creating or designing something for good *that you know, that you know, that you know* is real. In fact, it is so real that to you, it is already a done deal. Yet you stay quiet about this hesitating to share this with anyone, but you feel you are about to burst if you don't release this creative intent so deeply ingrained with in you.

I lovingly implore you not to hide this any longer. Instead, go forward in some way no matter how small or insignificant these dreams and visions may seem to you. Move forward with what is burning in your heart to do or to share with others concerning your creative vision or dream. **Without a vision, the people perish**. You may have the very vision that will keep people from perishing and that will enhance them to come into the fullness of their God-given creativeness.

We all need each other to enhance our lives and fulfill the God-Created destiny He Creatively Created in us that is to be achieved for Infinity.

Imagination is The Key of Creativity.

What you creatively imagine grows and blossoms into fruit that brings fruitfulness to your God-given creative intent. You have the ability to bring this creative imagination into actual being by the words you speak and the actions you take. Keep reading and rereading this book to prepare yourself to fulfill your creative destiny.

When you step out and do what is in your heart to do and then meet head-on what you suppose is failure, just remember it is not failure. It just shows you that there is still more to be learned for your creative design to be achieved. Always learn from supposed mistakes. No mistake is a mistake. Mistakes are just training opportunities. Keep pursuing. Each step you take and each endeavor you explore is leading you to attain your innate creative design that you clearly know will help others. Keep on seeking and asking all kinds of questions to God and to people. No question is a dumb question. It proves that you are seeking Wisdom to know how to continue fulfilling your God-ordained Creative Destiny.

The Lord's Seven Spirits have eyes full of Wisdom and Knowledge. Wisdom is empowered by Prudence who imparts Knowledge into all the Seven Spirits who carry you into the situations on earth to accomplish Holy God's preordained Plan. God's time is here for those He Created in His Image and Likeness to operate in supernatural ways that are opposite of the world's ways. God's Holy Ways bring righteous gain for the Holy Purpose of reconciling Heaven and earth back into His Originally Designed Intent.

It must be made known explicitly that God's Creative Plan for Heaven and earth to flow as One Complete Circle of Life has been hijacked by Satan. He selfishly perverted his Creative ability endowed in him by His Creator. Satan used his God-Fashioned creative abilities for his own selfish gain. He wrongly set out to make a name for himself by persuading others to join in with his deplorable plans to build a false kingdom of his own making.

Satan's evil creativity destroys. Supreme God's Holy Creative Ability expands and establishes GOOD outcomes for His Creations.

Through redeemed humankind creatively designing and procreating their environment by Holy means, God Almighty is reversing the evil intent in the hearts and minds of mankind put there by Satan in his attempt to control them for his own selfish purposes of building his own evil empire.

Supreme God Originally Designed humankind to combine their creative efforts to create an environment they desired to inhabit for their social enjoyment. The following Biblical account reveals the creative capacity that innately resides within each human being.

*Now the whole earth had one language and one speech. And it came to pass, as they journeyed from the east, that they found a plain in the land of Shinar, and they dwelt there. Then they said to one another. "**Come, let us** make bricks and bake them thoroughly." They had brick for stone, and they had asphalt for mortar. And they said, "**Come, let us** build ourselves a city, and a tower whose top is in the heavens; let us **make a name for ourselves**, lest we be scattered abroad over the face of the whole earth."*

*But The Lord came down to see the city and the tower which the sons of men had built. And **The Lord said, "Indeed, the people are one and they all have one language, and this is only the beginning of what they will do; now nothing they have imagined will be impossible for them.** Come let Us go down there and confuse their language, that they may not understand one another's speech."*

So The Lord scattered them abroad from there over the face of all the earth, and they ceased building the city. Therefore, the name of it was called Babel because there The Lord confused the language of all the earth; and from there The Lord scattered them abroad over the face of all the earth. (Genesis 11:1-9).

People on earth at that time were attempting to use their innately God-created abilities to build and create a city for themselves to enjoy. However, Satan thwarted their good intentions of creatively creating a city for themselves through their innate creativity by duping them by evil deception and lies based on self-importance that caused them to selfishly want to stay in one place and not spread out into all the world. Holy God had bigger plans for the whole world, not just for one region on earth.

At this time on earth, Holy God is intervening within corrupted history and making Himself known as Supreme God. He is releasing Holy Revelation Knowledge and Wisdom as to how He intends to restore back to Original Design what He Creatively Created for humankind to achieve.

Through what is written in this book and through what others as well are writing from what The Lord is revealing to them, The Lord is openly revealing how He is fulfilling His Holy Originally Designed Plan for humankind and Heavenly beings to unitedly work together in complete harmony, peace, and creativity in order to creatively create the environment they desire to inhabit for Infinity.

Overseers in Charge of Cities

The Lord poured out to me knowledge that was unknown to me which opened my understanding of things I do not know that I need to know as I asked Him to do. He poured into me a download of Truth from His Holy Word, The Bible, as recorded in Matthew 8:5-11, Luke 7:1-9, and Luke 19:11-27, Jeremiah 3:17, Revelation 21:2-7; 22:1-6. Then He went beyond human understanding by mystically revealing Himself in the way He and His Righteous Kingdom truly exists.

Jesus' parable in Matthew 8:5-11 reveals a centurion who understood authority and how to wisely use his authority for the good of his servants. Jesus was astounded that this centurion so rightly understood Kingdom Authority. Seeing the faith and action of this centurion so blessed Jesus because most in Israel, to whom He was sent, did not understand Kingdom Authority because they were so full of themselves.

In Luke 19:11-27, Jesus told this parable to His disciples because they supposed that the Kingdom of God was to appear immediately. Therefore, Jesus related to His disciples that there was a nobleman who went into a distant country to obtain for himself a kingdom, but before he left, he called ten of his servants and gave them money and told them to go and trade and bring him an increase on his investment by investing what he gave them until he returned. The nobleman was expecting a return on his investment. There were those who decided that they didn't want this nobleman to reign over them when he became king. So they sent a delegation after him telling him they did not want him to rule over them when he received his kingdom. When the nobleman did return having received the kingdom, he commanded these servants to give him an account of what they gained in trading with the monetary investment he entrusted to them. Some were good stewards of what was entrusted to them because they multiplied what they were given and received a return on his investment to give him. The nobleman rewarded them according to the return on their investment. Then, he gave them authority to rule over cities in his kingdom. Some would rule over ten cities, some over five cities. Those who did not want the nobleman, to rule over them were brought before him to give an account of what he monetarily entrusted to them, and those who had nothing to give him in return were slain before him for not giving him a return on his investment he entrusted to them.

This story or parable Jesus told has Eternal impact and significance. Jesus is talking about the Kingdom of Righteousness that His Father gave Him to Rule. He is Truthfully stating that those presently living on earth who invest in His Holy Kingdom are setting themselves up to receive Eternal rewards that include ruling over cities for Infinity.

In Jeremiah 3:17, The Lord gave Jeremiah a message of hope to give to His people:

Jerusalem shall be called The Throne of The Lord, and all the nations shall be gathered to it, to the name and presence of the Lord in Jerusalem and they shall no more stubbornly follow the dictates of their own evil hearts.

I saw in Revelation 21 and 22 a new heaven and a new earth and a Holy city where nothing unclean or evil shall ever enter. Only those whose names are written in the Lamb's Book of Life will be allowed to enter and creatively inhabit this city for Infinity.

The Lord unveiled Holy revelation of Himself that granted me Holy Insight to know how His Rule of Righteousness is to be carried out in a new heaven and a new earth through those He is rewarding for their faithfulness in bringing Him an investment on what He entrusted to them while they lived on earth.

The Lord unveiled distinct revelation to know that there is an overseer appointed and set by God to oversee a city on the new earth. An overseer can be in charge of more than one city. The overseer assigned by God for each city can come to the Court in Heaven and make an appeal to have the Book for their city opened to them. When the overseer is granted their request, they are entrusted with the information that is written in the Book for their city; and they present it to the people in the city they oversee.

The person appointed by God to oversee their city is the one who goes back and forth from Heaven to earth to make an appeal before Heaven's Court to have the Book for their city opened for them to look into and get the assignments written in the Book for their city. This is how the people on the new earth discover their city's intended assignment. Each redeemed and resurrected person receives their assignments from the Court in Heaven from what is written in their Book that is to be creatively used on earth or in the heavens. All assignments come from the Court in Heaven. This goes on for Eternity.

The overseer for each city in the new earth also has legal access to each person's Book in Heaven's Court that reveals their unique assignment for their city that can be used in the city where they reside. Each person can come to the overseer of the city where they live asking to know what is written in their Book in Heaven's Court. Their personal inquiry releases the overseer to go ahead and access the Book that contains their assignment and relate it to them. The overseer comes into agreement with their Holy creative assignment and releases this person to freely use their God- given creative ability and creative talents in conjunction with all the others in their city who are using their unique creative abilities for the benefit of the whole community that enhances the welfare of their city.

Each person brings their assignment into existence in their city from whatever they desire and frame by their Holy words of passionate intent. This Holy design is accomplished when each person speaks creative words and does actions proceeding from the Holy intent in their hearts.

Each person operates from their own designed order as they were endowed by their Creator. These collective desires coincide and develop the creative purpose for their city for the enjoyment of the entire city and anyone who comes to see and enjoy their city.

The overseer and the people work together in harmony because there is no longer jealousy or opposition from human spirits tainted by Satan's evil. The human spirit sanctified by Jesus' Blood truly wants to put their part with another's part so all flow together and fulfill the Holy intended design for their city that brings collective enjoyment for all.

Holy and Supreme God alone has established a Holy Order that is to be followed for the welfare of Heaven and earth flowing together as One Complete Holy Operation. Actually, this is how it is meant to be on earth at this time. However, this is not being fully understood or carried out in Righteousness with an Eternal view because evil still reigns in most situations.

Ponder that at this time on earth, each city, state, region, and country has a distinct flavor or unique creativity and design as to how each person in the city or area adds their talent or creative gift to make their city a unique setting that draws people from other cities, regions, and countries to come and enjoy their city and region and country and its surroundings. Cities on earth at this time put out advertisements inviting people to come to their city and enjoy and experience their uniqueness. However, because evil reigns on earth at this time, jealousy is causing wrongly motivated competition with each city trying to outdo the other for selfish reasons.

When evil is fully removed, no one is jealous or tries to overthrow or overtake another's position of Authority. No longer are other people's possessions stolen nor is their creativity disrupted by evil intent. People are free to come and go as they please to each other's cities and stay and enjoy the people and their environment as long as they desire. Every single person enjoys each other and blesses each other's uniqueness and creativity by saying, "Come and see!" From this invitation, each person freely decides when they want to go and see another city and how long they want to stay. This invitation goes on for Eternity.

There are also those who especially desire to explore the new heavens. Those who desire to explore and creatively create in the new heavens can come before the Court in Heaven making an appeal for the Book to be opened to them that has the Blueprint that can be accomplished in the new heavens.

When they appeal to the Court of Heaven to have the exact Book opened that reveals what can be creatively created in the new heavens, the Book will be opened to them according to what is written in this Book that is in line with their unique creative design as endowed in them by their Creator.

When this Book in the Court of Heaven is legally opened to them, they recognize from what is written in this Book how to creatively design the new heavens according to their desired Holy intent. From this Holy Knowledge they formulate and build their desired Holy intent in the new heavens by speaking into existence what they construct by their Holy words.

Those who innately desire to creatively create in a new heaven speak their desired intent into visible existence from the Substance of Life which is the Faith of the God-Head: Father, Jesus, Holy Spirit abiding in them. They *creatively construct and create* what they desire to see accomplished in a new heaven that aligns with what is recorded in the Book pertaining to a new heaven. What *they creatively construct and create* in the new heaven remains and is useful for Eternity.

Whoa! What a Glorious existence this is, Lord! Hallelujah! AMEN!

Consider as well that redeemed people *can* live in Peace, Joy, and Harmony and perfect Rest right now in time on earth even in the midst of chaos and upheaval, because Almighty God's work of redemption was finished when Jesus declared on the Cross, ...*It is finished!*... and then committed His Spirit into His Father's keeping.

Jesus willingly agreed to be His Father's Living Sacrifice to pay for the sins of mankind who rebelled against their Creator when they followed Satan's deceptive evil. Jesus' Holy Sacrifice in dying on the cross to take away the sin of the world and then rising from the dead in Resurrection Power redeems humankind from all Satan's evil works and ways (1 John 3:8). Therefore, right now during God's ordained time-frame on earth, redeemed saints who accept Jesus' Salvation from evil and live as though they do, are truly and fully living in Eternity by living daily in Jesus' provision of Eternal Ways of Rest, Harmony, Love, Peace, and Joy. This way of Life exists no matter where redeemed people reside in time on earth or in their Heavenly abode. There is only One Circle of Life that exists on earth and in Heaven.

By Faith in God's Ability to complete His *Will* for Heaven and earth, people living in time on earth can live in the Eternal Ways of Eternity that never ends. When we understand Infinity, we know that we can presently live in Eternal Rest, Harmony, Love, Peace, and Joy in the Eternity of no time. As we live on earth in Eternal Ways by Holy God's provision, Satan has no advantage over us. Therefore, whether we exist on earth in time, which is actually a part of Infinity, or continue our existence in Heaven we live Eternally with Jesus. (Ephesians 2:1-7).

The Lord had me write this book, *Live Creatively - Fulfill Your Designed Destiny* for those of you who know there is so much more than what you are presently experiencing in your circumstances. For you who know this, you can freely choose to break out and break forth into Creative motion to fulfill whatever Holy God has innately implanted within you to obtain for Infinity. **Go for it!** Don't allow yourself to be dissuaded by unholy and ungodly influences.

Supreme God is for you. So who can be against you? No one, unless you allow them to persuade you differently than from what Holy God says to you as recorded in His Holy Word, The Bible.

As Romans 8:31 states:

If God is for us who can be against us? He who did not spare His own Son but gave Him up for us all, will He not also give us all things with Him?

122

God says in His Word many times: *I will never leave you nor forsake you.*

He also states in Hebrews 13:6, 8:

The Lord is my helper; I will not fear. What can man do to me? Jesus Christ the same yesterday, today, and forever!

Therefore, we can say what David said, The Lord is always with me. I will not be shaken for He is right beside me. The Lord shows me the way of Life. He fills me with the joy of His Presence. (Acts 2:25-28).

At this time on earth, The Lord God of Heaven and earth is openly revealing Himself in Holy celestial Ways that are far above self-thinking ways. Are you one who truly desires to know Him in celestial ways? When you seek Holy God's Heart to know Him in relationship, you will find Him. He knows and hears your heart's intent and comes to you in Ways that are unique to the way He Originally Designed you to relate to Him.

Holy God can be found by you. **If** you diligently and wholeheartedly seek The Lord God, your Creator, and keep on seeking Him, you will find Him. The Lord God says in Isaiah 45 that if He couldn't be found, He wouldn't say that He could be found:

For The Lord is God. He created the heavens and the earth. He put everything in place. He made world to be lived in, not to be a place of empty chaos. I am The Lord and there is no other. I publicly proclaim bold promises. I do not whisper obscurities in some dark corner. I would not have told the people of Israel to seek Me, if I could be found. I, The Lord, speak only what is true and declare only what is right. (Isaiah 45:18-19 New Living Translation).

The Lord is waiting on you to come to Him so He can show you His Love and Compassion. The Lord is a faithful God. He is Gracious to you if you ask Him for help. He surely responds to the sound of your cries. (Isaiah 30:18-19 New Living Translation).

How do you choose to devote and occupy your Life Holy God innately Created in you to fulfill before you were born on earth? Only you can answer this. Your free-will choices determine the way you can enjoy life on earth at this time, and also where you occupy Eternal Living that goes on forever and ever with no end. Choose wisely!

How you choose to creatively live from Original Design is your Infinite Destiny!

I, Betsy, want it to be known in the writing of this book that what Jesus and Paul declared as written in The Holy Bible, is most certainly true for me as well:

My teaching is not My own, but His who sent Me. If any man's will is to do His will, he shall know whether the teaching is from God or whether I am speaking on My own authority.

He who speaks on his own authority seeks his own glory, but He who seeks the Glory of Him who sent him is true, and in him there is no falsehood." (John7:16-18).

I do nothing on My own authority but speak what the Father taught Me. He sent Me. He who sent Me is with Me. I always do what is pleasing to Him." (John 8:28b-29).

I have not come of my own accord; He who sent Me is true, and I know Him, for I come from Him, and He sent Me." (John 8:42).

If I tell you the Truth, why do you not believe Me? He who is of God hears the words of God; the reason you do not hear them is that you are not of God. (John 8:46-47).

I do not come to you with excellence of speech or persuasive words of human wisdom, but in demonstration of The Spirit and of Power that your faith is not in the wisdom of men, but in the Power of God." (1 Corinthians 2:4-5).

I am not sufficient of myself to claim that anything comes from me; my sufficiency is from God, who has qualified me to be a minister of a new covenant written in me by The Spirit of god who gives life. (2 Corinthians 3:5-6).

I have this ministry by the mercy of God... I do not preach about myself, but I preach Jesus Christ as Lord, with myself as a servant for Jesus' sake. For God said, 'Let light shine out of darkness,'. who has shone in our hearts to give the light of the knowledge of the glory of God in the face of Christ.

I have this treasure in an earthen vessel to show that the transcendent power belongs to God and not me. (2 Corinthians 4:1, 5-7).

I want to give all Glory, Thanksgiving, and deference to Supreme and Living God for exhibiting His Creative Personality to me in so many manners and ways to indelibly inscribe on my heart and in my spirit how to transcribe all the ways He displays His many-sided facets of never-ending Beauty and Creativity that can be discovered for Infinity. Without His abiding Presence expressing Himself through us, we can do nothing. His sublime and Creatively Designed Preordained Plan Created us in His Image and Likeness in order to display Himself to evil principalities, powers, and rulers of darkness as The One and Only True Supreme God. In your face, devil! God is having the last laugh (Psalm 2:1-6).

Won't you join in the fun God is having in using you in His Holy Plan of restoring the world back to His Original Design for Heaven and earth to function as one complete and Holy operation?

Know God Through Relationship

Before you can truly fulfill your *Designed Destiny*, you must take a journey-adventure to discover that there is a GOD Who wants to have a Love Relationship with you and Who definitely desires to cooperate with you so that you fulfill your *Designed Destiny* He innately put in you before you were born.

I have intentionally written this book, *Live Creatively - Fulfill Your Designed Destiny* to the many *ones* who think nobody cares. I want you to know in your troubled heart with no doubting that you are indeed Loved! You just need to know Who truly Loves you.

Maybe you have personally experienced an unusual experience that you know was good and is nothing like you have ever experienced before, but you do not understand your unusual encounter. This genuine encounter was so real that you want to believe that it was God with whom you had this unusual but pleasant encounter. Yet, you are not sure that there is a God who really exists; and if He does exist, you have always believed that He cares nothing for you. But this encounter was so real to you that you cannot dismiss it or stop thinking about it, no matter how hard you try.

I want to assure you that this reality encounter was True God coming to you and engaging you to get your attention. Through this encounter He is coming to you and making Himself tangibly known to you. He is letting you know that He wants a personal relationship with you, and so He is not allowing you to forget or dismiss this most unusual reality encounter. True and Living God wants you to know that He most certainly sees you, and hears you. He wants you to know He Loves you and in Truth is right beside you engaging you in relationship through this most unusual experience. He is coming to you and offering you a brand-new life of true Freedom, Peace, and Joy that you have never known in fullness. Living God Loves you and in Truth is right beside you. He is offering you the way to turn away from old ways that are not working for you and turn to Him who Loves you and will never forsake you.

True and Living God came to you in this unusual encounter because He wants a personal relationship with you. You must decide if you truly want a personal relationship with Him. If you truly want a personal relationship Him just say, *"God, I truly want to know you in a living relationship. Come into my life and help me to know you."*

When you tell True God that you want to personally know Him through a living relationship, He hears you. He will most certainly come to you and teach you how to live in personal relationship with Him. Your life will be renewed beyond what you may be thinking or expecting so that you can live a life of Peace, Joy and adventure that allows you to accomplish your Creatively Designed Destiny that He innately put in you before you were born. Living God, your Creator, certainly will empower you with the ability to fulfill your *Designed Destiny* if you truly desire an ongoing relationship with Him and continually pursue engaging Him in a Forever Relationship.

I cannot logically tell you how you can intimately and personally discover how to relate to The God of all Creation, His Son Jesus, and Holy Spirit whom The Father in Heaven sent on earth to help you know True God in relationship. I only know unmistakably that as you persistently pursue Living God to know Him in relationship, He will personally come to you and engage you in relationship and you will know with no doubting that He Loves you with an everlasting Love. In your pursuit to personally know this God who has come to you in this unusual encounter, He wants you to learn to know the way He personally knows you and the way He uniquely speaks to you. When you honestly and deeply seek True God to know Him in personal relationship you will find Him, and you will never be the same. You will have a joy and a peace beyond your personal understanding. You will know Pure Love as you have never before known or experienced.

How Living God Almighty makes Himself personally known to people is different for each and every person. But as you keep pursuing Living God in relationship, you will learn to know His Voice above all other voices vying for your attention wanting you listen to them. You will truthfully and indelibly know that Holy and Living GOD is speaking directly to you, and you will understand with certainty that He truly knows you.

When you hear God's Voice speaking personally to you, you will know it, and nothing can ever change your mind. The God of Love will never let you go; and you will never want to let go of Him.

When you have made your choice to want to know True God, your next step is to obtain a Holy Bible so that you learn how to have an ongoing personal relationship with Him. If you have snuffed out or dismissed reading The Holy Bible for whatever reason, pick up a Holy Bible and make a concerted effort to start reading it. You will come to know True God as you read your Bible, and continue seeking to know Him in a true and lasting relationship.

I deliberately wrote this book, *Live Creatively - Fulfill Your Designed Destiny,* to be interactive so you learn how to use your Bible. When you come to the places in this book, where I direct you to read a passage or a specific book that is recorded in your Bible, stop immediately and take the time right then to go to your Bible and look up these references and read them. Don't rush to move ahead. Rather, pay attention to what God is saying to the people to help them. Then consider how you can apply this to your own life. This is how you learn the ways Living God comes and speaks to people and helps them. He will certainly do this for you too. Don't just read these accounts in the Bible one time and go on your way thinking, I *got it*. You learn to *get it* when you go through similar situations that the people in the Bible faced, and then choose to apply God's solution for them into your own life.

Don't read this book or the Bible passages just to say you read them. Use this book as a training tool to learn how to use your Bible and how to know Living God in a personal relationship. Take time to consider what you are reading so that you learn how to know God. Practice what you read in your Bible and you will discover how to know Living God in a personal relationship. Don't rush yourself. It takes time to learn to know God and His Ways. The world tells you everything is to be instant. This is not so in learning how to know and talk with Holy God in Holy relationship. As you read your Bible, start asking Living God questions that you have always wondered about but never asked anyone. Ask Him questions and expect Him to answer you according to how He knows you. When I was learning to know God in relationship, He said to me, *"Ask Me things! I can't tell you things because you are not asking Me anything. If you ask Me things, I will tell you. I want to make Myself known to you; and I will, when you ask Me things."*

Write your questions down on paper and keep them with your Bible so you can refer to them over and over while you are reading your Bible. When you recognize that True God is answering your questions, write the Bible book and reference passage beside the question you asked Him. By doing this, you will begin to learn that God did answer you.

You will see with understanding that what He revealed to you in the Bible is so very personal to your situation. You will understand that He indeed heard you and is answering the questions you asked Him. This is how you learn to know what True God says in The Holy Bible and how to apply what He is saying to your own life.

Deciding to use this book, *Live Creatively - Fulfill Your Designed Destiny,* together with the Bible, even when you have no idea what you are doing, begins an unmistakable journey that leads you how to know a Holy God you have never known or may not have even heard about. If you choose to immediately stop, look up, and read the stated Bible passages I direct you to go to and also the surrounding information before and after the Bible passage and journal your questions, you will gain invaluable training in knowing True God and the Way in which He is directing you to hear and obey Him. This is the way to have your own Bible School experience. Holy Spirit is personally teaching you how to have a Living relationship with The One True and Only God.

When you experience True and Living God speaking directly to you, and you willingly choose to surrender your own *thinking* to Him, you will come to know with certainty that The God of all Creation is speaking to you in the Way He personally knows you. The first time you recognize GOD is personally speaking directly to you and your personal circumstances, you will never be the same.

His personal involvement with you will make an indelible impression on you. When you personally experience Living God, addressing your issues and helping you know what to do in a particular situation, you will be fired-up to keep on seeking Him. When you recognize that you truly heard True God speaking to you, you will want to keep on seeking Him to know Him in a personal relationship. Know that taking this journey-adventure to know Living God through a personal relationship never ends. It goes on throughout eternity which is forever and ever with no end.

This book in your hands guides you step by step in learning how to engage True God in relationship so that you can talk to Him as you would to a friend or someone you want to be your friend. It also helps you learn how to use your Bible. The Lord's Purpose for this book, *Live Creatively - Fulfill You Designed Destiny*, is to come alongside you and engage you in an interactive relationship so you know Him in Spirit and in Truth. **Truth is a person, not an idea.** Holy Spirit is God's Breath of Life revealing Himself to you as Truth.

Now would be a good time to pick up your Bible and read in the book of John chapters 14-17 to learn how Father, Son, and Holy Spirit work together inside of you to establish you in Truth so you can have a living and forever relationship with The God of all Creation who genuinely Loves you and truly desires personal fellowship with you.

The Lord asked me if I would be willing to write this book for *the one* that He said He wanted to reach so they could learn how to know Him in personal relationship. Therefore, if you have this book your hands, then you are the one Living God wants to reach so you can learn how to know Him in an everlasting relationship. The God of all Creation wants to speak directly to you.

Your surrendered will to seek to know His Perfect Will for your life defines you as *the one* He wants to reach and have a living relationship with. Your determined choice to know True God in a personal and ongoing relationship leads you to learn Living God's Truth and Ways through engaging with Him in The Holy Bible, and in this book you are reading.

Supreme God honestly speaks and reveals Himself to you and to everyone who wants to know Him? Will you hear Him? Will you obey Him with all your heart? The decision is yours! When you know Creative God through personal relationship, you will fulfill your Designed Destiny!

I am praying for you to hear God's Voice of Truth speaking directly to you through His Words in this book that leads you to The Holy Bible. This is my earnest prayer to Living God for you:

"Lord, motivate within each person reading this book a genuine desire to want to know You in a personal and interactive relationship. Inspire them to want to read, study, and write down in a journal or diary what grabbed their attention and caused them to notice that You are personally speaking to their heart. Guide them to know what personal insights You want them to learn and know from studying their Bible. Show them what to record in their personal journal so they have a permanent record of what You said to them; and so, can easily and regularly refer to what You personally revealed and said to them. Put in them the Holy desire to obey what you reveal to them through The Holy Bible and through their personal relationship with You.

"Thank You for being right beside them as they step out and begin their own journey- adventure in knowing You in Truth and Love. Grant them Holy understanding and Wisdom to know how to truthfully search out the way to know You in a personal relationship. Reveal to them the way You Creatively Designed them and uniquely fashioned them to know You in the way You want to be known so that each one fulfills their Creatively Designed Destiny that You innately Designed in them before they were born onto the earth. Thank You. Amen!"

How God Speaks

The Holy Bible Reveals How God Speaks

You *can learn* to know and hear God's Voice speaking to you. But first, you must make a quality and definite decision to seek Him with all your heart and mind. Always keep in mind that the way God speaks to you will be different from the way others hear Him speak to theme. Each person has been uniquely Designed by their Creator, so they hear His voice in the Way He Designed them to hear Him speaking to them.

Before you begin your adventure to know Living God in Truth and in Wisdom you must freely choose to admit that you don't know True God. You must willingly surrender everything you *think* or may have been taught by the world's standards and willingly choose to commit yourself to know The Lord God of Truth and Love. When you fully surrender yourself to True God, and freely choose and desire in your heart to truly know Him in relationship, He will make Himself known to you. You can never find true and lasting peace and contentment in your life until you willingly surrender yourself to The Lord God of Truth and Love. When you choose to admit you don't know Living and honestly desire to have a mutual relationship with Him, you are ready to begin your adventure to know Holy God.

God is continually speaking through His physical Creation. Go to The Holy Bible and read in the Old Testament book of Job chapters 33-41 to see with understanding how Supreme God reveals Himself through His Creatively Designed Creation. Because Holy God is revealing who His is through His Creation no one can ever excuse themselves saying they never knew there was a Supreme God; nor should they ever question if there even is a God.

Consider these New Testament words in your Bible:

*But God shows His anger from heaven against all sinful, wicked people who push the truth away from themselves. For the truth about **God is known to them instinctively**. **God has put this knowledge** (of Himself) **in their hearts**. From the time the world was created, people have seen the earth and sky and all that God made. They can clearly see His invisible qualities – His eternal power and divine nature. **So they have no excuse whatsoever for not knowing God**.* (Romans 1:18-20)

Logical thinking can choose to dismiss that there is a God. However, True God shows every living being who He is through His physical Creation; and He, as well, has indelibly imprinted Who He is into the heart and DNA of each and every human being. There is a God-given knowledge of Living God innately or genetically designed into every living person. So, each person ever born on earth is without excuse, saying they never knew there was a God; or blatantly say there is no God. Therefore, all people are without any kind of excuse and cannot truthfully say that God does not exist.

The Lord of Life truly comes to each and every person again and again and again; and certainly, at some time in their life span on earth. However, when people are full of themselves, they do not recognize Jesus or His Father coming to them, so they say, "There is no God."

God of Life continually comes to people in their situations attempting to get them to turn to Him so that He can help them and deliver them out of evil ways that are trying to destroy them. God's heart is Good. His desire is for all people to come to a saving knowledge of His Truth and Love and Goodness to them, so that they enjoy a life of Peace, Joy, and Rest free from the entanglements of sin and evil. To learn God's plans for your life, you must believe what The Bible says:

*Without faith it is impossible to please God, for whoever draws near to God **must believe that He exists** and that **He rewards those who diligently seek Him**.* (Hebrews 11:6)

When you choose to truly believe that God exists and you fervently and diligently seek Him, He rewards you with the reality of knowing Him in relationship.

Your relationship with Holy and Living God is to be mutual and interactive based on love and respect toward one another. When you choose to want to know Living God in a mutual and interactive relationship, He speaks to you in the way He uniquely Designed you to hear Him speaking to you. Therefore, you also speak to Him in the way He Designed you to speak or talk. You have a voice pattern that is uniquely yours. No one else has your voice pattern nor do you have their voice pattern. Your journey to know True and Living God is unique to you. Don't try to copy how someone else hears Living God or speaks to Him. It may be helpful to hear their stories of how God talks to them. But these stories are to encourage you not for you to try and copy.

Each human being is Creatively Designed in Holy God's very Image and Likeness to be like Himself in fullness of truth with a mind to choose, a will to use, and emotions to express love, joy, and peace. Consequently, you can know in reality that Holy and Living God's innate holy expressions are indelibly embedded within you. Therefore, you can have interactive fellowship or relationship with Him because you are Creatively Designed to walk with Living and True God in a loving relationship. Each person is Creatively Designed by Almighty God with a free will to choose to accept their Father's unconditional Love for them and to walk with Him in a loving relationship. However, people can choose to reject His Love and redemption from sin and evil and refuse to have a living relationship with Him. Each person is free to choose how they respond to Living God.

Almighty God personally speaks to you in the very way He knows you. In your personal journey-adventure you will come to know through personal relationship with Him the way He uniquely Designed you to know Him. When you truly learn to know Him in relationship, I promise you that you will never again seek to live your own way above His Holy Ways. You may falter at times in your journey-adventure. But never stop and stay there. Draw even nearer to God's Presence to get yourself back on track. As you seek to know what to do in your situation that caused you to falter, The Lord will direct you to know what to do and how to do it. This is the way you learn how to continue your journey with The Lord. He sees you and knows what caused you to falter. As you obey His instructions to you, you learn to trust Him to direct you to know how to continue on your journey with Him. This is how you build a forever relationship with The Lord of Life.

I want to share with you a personal time in my life right after The Lord delivered me from the strong hand of the devil who was too strong for me and was seeking to devour me. I decided that I no longer wanted to listen to the lies the devil was feeding me in my thinking. I so wanted to know The Lord of Truth. The Lord heard my heart's desire to leave old ways and learn helpful ways of living. As I was crying out to The Lord to know His Voice, He led me to Psalm 40 to let me know He heard my cries to Him. These words in Psalm 40 revived me and encouraged me. I wrote the following words from Psalm 40 in my own words:

"I cried to The Lord and He came near to me; He heard my cry and He pulled me up out of a horrible pit of miry clay. He set me upon a Rock (Jesus Christ) and established my steps; and put a new song in my mouth, praise to our God. Many shall hear and fear and turn to The Lord to trust Him. Blessed is the man who does not respect the proud or turn aside to lies.

I memorized these words because *I knew that I knew that I knew* this is the way I was to live from now on. I still speak these words over myself to assure myself that The Lord is with me and so, is rescuing me from every terrible circumstance I face in my life that is outside my influence to change. These words in Psalm 40 cause me to always remember that The Lord of Life delivered me out of my distress and pain. They let me know Holy God designed my destiny, which is to stay established in The Rock, Jesus Christ; to sing the new song of praise He puts in my mouth; to place my trust in Him so I do not respect the proud or turn aside to lies; and that by doing these things others would see and respect Holy God and put their trust in Him. Finally, I knew why God Created me. I knew He Created me for good purposes. I now had a purpose for living. Read all of Psalm 40. There is so much more in this Psalm that will encourage and bless you.

Jesus Speaks His Father's Words

The Bible reveals that Jesus is His Father's Sign to all Creation:

"This child - Jesus - is destined to cause many in Israel to fall, but He will be a joy to many others. **He has been sent as a sign from God**, *but many will oppose Him. As a result, the deepest thoughts of many hearts will be revealed..."* (Luke 2:34-35)

The Father in Highest Heaven sent His Son, Jesus, to be His Sign to people in all ages of time of His Love for them. But Jesus was opposed by many people all through the ages of time and is still opposed by many people on earth at the present time because Jesus exposes people's deepest thoughts and motives toward Him and His Father in Heaven. Jesus was His Father's Sign sent to earth from Heaven to reveal to people living on earth that their Father in Heaven Loves them and has sent His Only Beloved Son to deliver them from evil's lies and deception.

Jesus, God's only Son, is His Father's Voice speaking Truth. Jesus only speaks and does what He hears His Father doing. Therefore, when Jesus lived on earth in human flesh, He showed by example how to do The Father's Will on earth as it is done in Heaven. This is why you must read The Holy Bible where you learn for yourself how to do The Father's Will on earth as it is continually being done in Heaven. To be in The Father's Will for your life, you must personally choose to copy Jesus' example when He walked on earth in human flesh doing His Father's Will.

In John 8:42 Jesus clearly explains He proceeded and came forth from His Father who sent Him to earth to reveal His Father's Will. He did not come on earth to do His own will. He came on earth to do His Father's Will. He said many times to the people to whom His Father sent Him, *For I have come down from Heaven to do the Will of God who sent Me, not to do My own will.* You can read these words in John 6:38. Therefore, Jesus, did not speak or do anything on His own or by His own will. He only did what His Father in Heaven directed Him to do on earth.

Jesus said, I have not spoken on My own authority, but My Father who sent Me has Himself given Me what to speak. ...

What I say, therefore, I say as the Father has commanded Me to say. (John 12:49-50)

Jesus comes to people over and over again in many ways and at many times during their life time on earth. Jesus comes to people and speaks what The Father is saying. The things Jesus speaks shows people that they have been duped by the devil to get them to accept his lies. By Jesus' words and actions, He is showing people that He came from His Father in Heaven to give them abundant and eternal life.

Holy Spirit Helps You Hear Jesus' Voice

Know that you are not on your own in learning to hear The Father's Voice speaking to you through Jesus. Holy Spirit is your helper. Look up in your Bible in the New Testament and read all of chapters 14-17 in the book or Gospel of John. Here are some quotes Jesus spoke:

Jesus says, I am the Way, the Truth, and the Life. No one can come to the Father except through Me. (John 14:6)

Jesus says, "If you love Me, obey My commandments, I will ask the Father, and He will give you another Counselor, who will never leave you. He is the Holy Spirit, who leads into all truth. (John 14:15-17)

All those who love Me (Jesus), will do what I say. My Father will love them, and we will come to them and live with them. (John 14:23)

When My Father sends Holy Spirit, He will teach you everything and will remind you of every everything I myself (Jesus) have told you. (John 14:26)

The Spirit of Truth will not speak on His own authority, but whatever He hears He will speak and He will declare to you the things that are to come. He will glorify Me (Jesus) *for He will take what is Mine and declare it to you. All that the Father has is Mine* (Jesus*); therefore, I* (Jesus) *said that He* (Holy Spirit) *will take what is Mine and declare it to you.* (John 16:13-15)

How Holy Spirit speaks directly to you may be entirely different than the way He speaks to me or to others. He speaks personally to each one of us in the way He Designed us to know Him. He knows us intimately. Therefore, He knows how to get us to hear Him speaking to us in the unique way He Designed each of us. There is no right or wrong way to hear True God's Voice. True and Living God speaks to you in a personal way that is uniquely the way you talk and hear because this is who He Created you to be. He wants you to know His Voice so that you know Him in the same way He knows you.

God's Proceeding Word

When Jesus was being intensely tempted by the devil, His Father said these words to Him:

You shall not live by bread alone, but by every proceeding word that comes from the mouth of God. (Matthew 4:4)

Even God's own Son, Jesus, when He lived on earth in human flesh because of His Father's Will for His Life, had to learn through suffering how to be obedient to His Father's words to Him. When Jesus was tempted by the devil's evil, He had to learn to live in His Father's Presence seeking His Father to know what to do and say in every situation He faced. He learned to live by every proceeding word His Father spoke to Him.

Jesus shouted out to the crowds who were following Him,

"If you trust Me, you are really trusting God (My Father) *who sent Me. I have come as a Light to shine in this dark world, so that all who put their trust in Me will no longer remain in the darkness.* **If anyone hears Me and doesn't obey Me,** (what I say), *I am not his judge – for I have come to save the world and not to judge it. But* **all who reject Me and My message (words) will be judged at the day of judgement by the truth I have spoken.** *I don't speak on my own authority. The Father who sent Me gave Me His own instructions as to what I should say. And I know His instructions lead to eternal life, so I say whatever the Father tells Me to say!"* (John 12:44-50 New Living Translation)

During my daily interaction with The Lord, He spoke this to me:

"Declare back to Me My Goodness and what I have done so I can hear what I have done. I don't think about Myself so I don't think about what I have done. I just do what I know to do. I am always fresh and new. I don't need to think about what I've done. I AM Life!"

I listened to these words, but thought, "You're God! You know what You've done. Why would I tell you what You have done?" As I pondered these words The Lord spoke to me, I began to understand that there are many facets or aspects to what The Lord is saying. I began to grasp with understanding that He can be pursued by personal relationship to learn the *fresh and new* that He is continually doing. The *fresh and new* that The Lord is continuously doing and speaking is His *proceeding* Word. What the God of Truth speaks is always fresh and alive and does not need to be repeated. Living God is alive and always moving in *fresh and new* ways that have never been done before. Therefore, He doesn't need to repeat what He has already done.

When you choose to pursue Living God through interactive relationship to know His *fresh and new* ways that He is doing, you are stopping the devil in his tracks. By practicing to live by God's every proceeding word to you, the devil's evil thoughts and ways that are bombarding your *thinking* are shut down.

The Burden of The Lord

The Lord personally made known to me that every person's own words they speak from what they *think* rather than seeking Him to know His proceeding word is a burden to Him and pervert the Words of Living God.

Take the time right now to read the full account in the book of Jeremiah in the Old Testament what Jeremiah, God's holy prophet, recorded from what The Lord revealed to him was a burden to The Lord. Read Jeremiah 23:33-40 in New Living Translation to get a perspective on why Jesus only said what He heard from His Father. I purposely did not write out the quote from Jeremiah 23:33-40 so you learn how to look up Scripture in the Bible for yourself. When you take the time to diligently seek to know what God is saying in the Bible, you will gain knowledge of God and His Word that you cannot learn by just reading what other people say to you. When you do your own research, it sticks with you and is imparted into your spirit. It takes diligent seeking to know what God is saying to you. There is no easy way to learn how God reveals Himself in the Bible. You must be willing to do whatever it takes to know Living God. He is with you. Are you with Him?

The Lord is revealing in this portion of Jeremiah in the Bible, that people's words spoken from a heart of unbelief are a burden to Holy and Living God. The Lord is revealing that people speaking what they *think* God is saying rather than actually living by what God says in His Word, the Bible, are a burden to Him. People's own thoughts that come from their own perspective because of being influenced by worldly thinking can distort, twist, and change God's Word of Truth. People redeemed by Jesus' Precious Blood Sacrifice are redeemed from evil thoughts. Therefore, they must learn how to bring their thoughts into alignment with every Word that proceeds out from the Mouth of God as found in His Word of Truth recorded in The Holy Bible. When you read and absorb what God says in the Bible, then what He speaks in His Word flows into you as truth. Holy Spirit reveals truth to you according to what His Father is progressively speaking.

Hear Jesus words:

A tree is identified by its fruit. If it is a good tree, it will bear good fruit. If it is a bad tree, it will bear bad fruit. How can evil people speak what is good and right? For whatever is in your heart determines what you say. A good person produces good words from a good heart, and an evil person produces evil words from an evil heart. And I (Jesus) *tell you this, that **you must give an account on judgement day of every idle and careless word you speak**. The words you say now reflect your fate then; either you will be justified by your words or you will be condemned by them.* (Matthew 12:34-37 New Living Translation)

If people remain speaking their own words from a heart that is not submitted entirely to Living God, they will be justly judged by Him for speaking their own words from what they *think* rather than living by every proceeding Word The Father gave His Son to say and do on earth that is for the good of all people who choose to obey Living God's Word of Love and Authority. Jesus was sent by His Father in Heaven to do His Father's Will and to speak His Father's Words so that

His Father was known as Almighty and Living God whose everlasting Love sustains His Creations.

Just know that if you choose to speak your own words according to what you *think*, you have chosen to exalt yourself above God's Word. Therefore, what you speak from what you *think* is a burden to The Lord.

Discover How to Hear God Speaking

Now that you have said yes to The Living God of Truth with all your heart you can begin your personal journey-adventure to discover how Almighty God speaks to make Himself known as Creative and Supreme God.

One of the ways you can know God is speaking to you is through this book, *Live Creatively - Fulfill Your Designed Destiny,* that leads you to The Holy Bible where you can learn how God personally speaks and reveals Himself so that you too know His Voice and His Ways that delivers you from dark ways and keeps you in His Light of Life forever and ever. Each person can know as much of God as they want to know. The search to know Living God never ends. The thrill of the adventure is in the pursuit. Go for it!

To begin your journey-adventure in learning to know God and how He speaks to people, you will want to get your own personal Bible. Be sure the Bible you choose includes a concordance and Bible helps. I recommend The New Living Translation (NLT) Bible, or the English Standard Version (ESV) Bible that is easy to read and understand for English readers. There are also other Bible version options you may want to choose. As you grow and mature in knowing how to use your Bible, you may want to invest in Cruden's Complete Concordance or even Strong's Exhaustive Concordance. But of course, in this modern era of electronics, you can also Google search Bible words and phrases. I call this cheating (laughter). If you will choose to discipline yourself to use hands-on material, you may surprise yourself. Diligently using hands-on material ingrains God's Wisdom deep within your spirit and your mind, because your focus is on the words at hand and you are not distracted with all the other things that come up on Google and electronic searches.

Also, you can more quickly write down on paper what you are learning. You think you will remember. However, this is not the case for most people. Somehow, what you truly believe you will remember, escapes your *I think I will remember*. It has been proven scientifically that when you write down on paper what you see or are reading, the information remains in your spirit and in your mind. Just quickly skimming over material just to get information is not the way to indelibly get the information inside you so that it remains for you to recall and use in your circumstances. If you are an electronic geek, I challenge you to try what I am saying. Another aspect to consider is this: What happens when the electronic grid goes down? Most young people think and so believe that this can never happen. But anything man designed can crash. Only what God says and performs can never be stopped. When you have your written notes in front of you, and you have access to them, you can continue without interruption. Your living and vibrant relationship with Almighty and Living God never stops, unless you cut Him off.

A concordance is very helpful in finding words you want to look up in the Bible so you learn and grow in your relationship with The Lord of your life. A concordance lists in alphabetical order the most important words or phrases in a Bible verse and gives the name of the book in the Bible and the chapter and verse where you can go and read the complete passage where that word is found. So if you are reading in the Bible and you see certain words, or names, or places you want to learn more about such as: faith, truth, love, hope, Joshua, Moses, David, Jesus, Paul, Jerusalem, Nazareth, Sea of Galilee, you can go to a concordance where you can find the words, names and places in your Bible. Diligently practicing using your Bible along with a concordance and Bible helps trains you in knowing how to use your Bible so you expand in wisdom and knowledge of Holy God and His Ways.

Almighty and Living God decisively makes Himself known as to Who He truly is in The Holy Bible. This is why you *must* have your own Bible and learn to use it. As you read and study your Bible, you will observe the ways Living God makes Himself known to people, and personally speaks to people in their situations. You are no different than the way people in the Bible thought and acted toward Holy God. Make a wholehearted effort to identify and so recognize how people acted toward True God, and how He in turn related to them.

As you read your own personal Bible, pay attention to the ways The Lord comes into the situations people are facing. If you intentionally pay attention to these situations in the Bible, you can identify when and how Supreme God comes on the scene even to people who are not seeking to know Him.

It was during a time of great distress when people were suffering greatly because of their own sin against Living God that He came to them with a message of hope. He spoke to them and related to them that He would deliver them from their distress. He made Himself known to them in power demonstrations so they would know that He is The Lord God Almighty. Even when they were sinning against Him, He came beside them and spoke hope to them. Pay attention or focus on what The Lord says in the Bible in the Old Testament book of Jeremiah 29:11-14a

I know the plans I have for you, says the Lord, plans for good and not for evil, to give you a future and a hope. ...call upon Me and come and pray to Me, I will hear you. You will seek Me and find Me; when you seek Me with all your heart, I will be found by you, says The Lord.

The Lord spoke these words of hope to His rebellious people when they were sinning against Him. Be sure to take the time to look up this account and read the entire passage in its complete context surrounding these specific verses so that you understand the circumstances when The Lord said these words in Jeremiah 29:11-14a. The people were being duped by evil. The Lord saw this and came to them and spoke these words in Jeremiah 29:11-14a to them that showed them how to resist evil by turning to Him for help. True God knew the good future He had for them. But before they could experience the Good Plans He had in store for them, they must willingly come to Him seeking to know Him in Truth through personal relationship.

A Living Encounter with Jesus

I want to share a powerful interactive encounter I personally experienced in a dream or a vision or an actual encounter. I'm not sure which it was. Nevertheless, it was as real as if it had truly happened. This holy encounter revealed to me how close Jesus is to each one of us. This powerful encounter with Jesus has profoundly affected me causing me to know how very close Jesus is to each one of us; and that He is just waiting for us to ask Him things. I will never forget this Living Encounter with Jesus.

In this reality encounter, Jesus showed me how very close He is to us. I was in a hospital room where a lady had died. There were other people in the room with her, but they were standing at a distance watching what was going on. These were people who knew what to do to obey Jesus' Words to pray and lay hands on the sick and they would recover; but they didn't do it. I was perplexed as to why these people didn't do what they knew to do; and so they just let her die. Observing this, I was crying out to Jesus saying: "Jesus, You said that if we lay our hands on the sick they would recover." Instantly, Jesus was there and said this to me, "Well, then go ahead and do it."

A prayer started formulating within me and as I reached out to touch her, I started to say "in the Name of Jesus...". I didn't even get the Name of Jesus on my lips as I touched her forehead. Immediately, she coughed and sneezed and came back to Life and threw off the body bag she was in, and we started hugging and dancing all around the room in exuberance. I kept exclaiming, loudly "Thank You Jesus! Thank You, Jesus! I knew You could do it! I knew You could do it! I love You."

As I was hugging and dancing and swinging with the young lady who was around 23 years of age, and was celebrating with her and with the many people who were rejoicing at her being alive again, I felt and saw the feet of Jesus' sandals and His flowing robes. His robes brushed up against our legs, as we danced and hugged each other. It seemed as though He was dancing with us. He was so happy and laughing with us.

Then, I heard Jesus say to me so very clearly, "I want to walk into every situation of their lives, but they aren't asking Me to. I Will, if they ask Me. If they knew how close I am to them, it wouldn't take them very long to ask Me. Go tell them how very close I am to them and if they ask Me, I'll walk into their situations with them."

As I heard Jesus speak these words to me, I sensed a weeping and a deep sadness in Jesus because He so wants people to ask Him to come into their situations to be with them and meet their needs. But very few ever come to Him to ask Him anything. He is waiting for you to come to Him and ask Him things so He can answer you. Will you?

Seek True God and Find Him

You must personally seek The Lord to know Him in personal relationship. There was a time in my life when I deeply desired to expand my personal relationship with The Lord. Therefore, I began to seek Him and draw near to Him. He personally came to me in many and various ways. He opened the spiritual ears and eyes of my understanding to hear His Voice speaking to me. This is what He personally spoke to me:

"I want people to seek Me with all their heart, and they will find Me! Most people don't think about Me until there's trouble and then they want Me to jump in and rescue them out of their trouble only to repeat the same pattern time after time. I long for My people to come into My Presence to enjoy Me and to receive My Goodness. Come into My Presence often! As a Father, I delight in My children and their questions and laughter."

Living God tells His people in the Bible in the Old Testament through Jeremiah, His holy prophet, that if they call upon Him, and pray to Him, He will listen to them; and **if they seek Him with all their heart, He would find them**. You can read God's message for yourself in the Old Testament book of Jeremiah 29:12-14.

There was a time in my life when I was struggling with knowing what to do in a situation, Holy God, boomed these words into my ears,

"Ask Me things! I can't tell you what I want to tell you because you aren't asking Me anything. I have so much I want to tell you, but you aren't asking Me to know. Ask Me big things. Nothing is too big for you to ask Me!"

Take the time to absorb Jesus words:

You can ask for anything in My name, and I will do it, because the work of the Son brings glory to the Father. Yes, ask anything in my name, and I will do it! (John 14:13-14)

Living God speaks in answer to your questions. He listens to your verbal questions, your heart (emotion or mood) questions, your questions you don't even know how to ask. It may seem to you that your questions are not heard by God. There is nothing that Supreme God does not hear or know. Nothing escapes His listening ear. He knew you before you were born and He already knows the questions you will ask Him before you ask Him. He is just waiting for you to ask Him so He can answer you. The Lord your God delights in your questioning heart. He wants you to know Him in personal relationship so you recognize when He answers your questions. You can be sure that God hears your questions, because Living God hears and knows everything.

Gods' Still Small Voice

I am going to share with you an indelible truth that I personally learned from reading my Bible. I was reading 1 Kings 18-19 in the Old Testament about Elijah, God's prophet, who was running away from trouble and was asking God to die. This is a very interesting story in the Bible. Take the time to read this Bible story to gain understanding how God prefers to speak to you so He can reveal Himself to you in a way you can understand Him. Tune in to this story and discover that The Lord prefers to speak in His *Still Small Voice* to those who choose to quiet themselves before Him to hear His *Still Small Voice* speaking to them.

In this story, Elijah was fleeing from someone who was trying to kill him. Elijah obeyed The Lord to go and do what He asked him to do. By Elijah's obedience to The Lord, mighty demonstrations of Supreme God's Power over enemy forces was experienced, which caused others to want to kill Elijah. However, rather than turning to The Lord in his distress to seek God's proceeding Word in his dire situation, Elijah ran and hid in a cave and was whining to God saying, "I did what You told me to do and they are trying to kill me, and I am the only one left." The Lord told Elijah to go and stand before Him on the mountain. The Lord passed by Elijah through a great and strong wind, then an earthquake, and then fire but The Lord was not in any of these. Then *a Still Small Voice* spoke and Elijah heard this *Still Small Voice* speaking. But basically, Elijah was so full of himself and his problems that he dismissed what God was trying to say to him in a *Still Small Voice*. Elijah just repeated his problems to God and so dismissed the *Still Small Voice* that wanted to tell him so much more.

As I took time to truly ponder this encounter with Elijah, The Lord let me know that He had so much more that He wanted to speak to Elijah that would come from His *Still Small Voice* that would encourage him and renew his strength to continue living on earth. But Elijah was so full of himself and his problems that He didn't pursue hearing what God wanted to personally speak to him in His *Still Small Voice* concerning things in their relationship. Therefore, The Lord heeded Elijah's words that he wanted to die and removed Elijah from the earth and brought him to Heaven because Elijah refused to allow Holy God to speak to him in a *Still Small Voice* directing him to the *more* He wanted to do on earth through Elijah.

As I deeply considered Elijah's response to Almighty God in this Bible account, I noticed that Elijah chose to complain to God rather than to seek Him for help and comfort in his distress. Elijah's self-absorption caused him to dismiss what The Lord wanted to say in a *Still Small Voice* to encourage him. Therefore, Elijah forced God to speak to him in power demonstrations to get his attention. Even though these power demonstrations did get Elijah's attention, he only continued his tirade of complaints. As I was thinking about this account before The Lord, He personally spoke to me and revealed to me even more about hearing His *Still Small Voice* speaking. He spoke to me in the way He speaks to me:

"I have never been truly known in My *Still Small Voice* as I sovereignly choose to be known. I openly disclose Myself through My *Still Small Voice*. I reveal Myself in My *Still Small Voice* through what is written in My Holy Word, and through My Creation, as well as in personal relationship. This is how I want to make Myself known to all people made in My Image and after My Likeness. But they must choose to quiet themselves before Me. Then, I will come to them in My *Still Small Voice* and personally speak to them.

"I am not a shouting boisterous God in the way people suppose I should make Myself known. I am Supreme God who speaks to be known in quietness and stillness of Purpose. My *Still Small Voice* reverberates into you by your stillness that is not clamoring for attention to be heard above My *Still Small Voice*. Boisterous clamoring cannot hear My *Still Small Voice*.

I wanted to make Myself known by My *Still Small Voice* to Elijah in ways he never knew Me, BUT he was too full of himself and his problems. Therefore, Elijah never knew Me by My *Still Small Voice*. He only knew Me by My power acts.

"If you quiet yourself before Me in My Presence, I release My words in you and around you so you stop your clamoring and listen to Me from whence comes your strength to persevere. This is why you keep hearing these words reverberating within you, ...*In quietness and confidence is your strength*... You have pondered why you keep hearing these words. I want you to know that hearing My *Still Small Voice* strengthens you and builds your confidence to trust and obey My *Still Small Voice* speaking to you.

"Clamoring voices make noise. Quiet voices speak volumes in their stillness. I am stillness personified so I can hear My Creation talk to Me by their unique design I Created within them for My Pleasure. I don't hear My Creation in noisy commotion. I hear them in their quiet vibrations of Life I placed in them that speaks to Me and brings Me Pleasure.

"Only in stillness can My *Still Small Voice* be heard inside you. I hear you by your *still small voice* that seeks Me because you want to know Me and hear My Voice speaking to you. Seek Me in quiet confidence to know Me for Myself not for what you can get from Me."

Because I wrote in my journal the Bible account of Elijah's encounter with God's *Still Small Voice* and what The Lord spoke to me concerning Elijah's experience with The Lord, I can refer to what The Lord spoke to me again and again to encourage myself to stop and listen to The Lord's *Still Small Voice* speaking to me when I face seemingly unsurmountable problems in my life. You too *can* truly learn to be quiet and still in His Presence. When you choose to be quiet and still in His Presence, He will speak to you in His *Still Small Voice* in the way He designed you to hear His Voice speaking directly to you in your circumstances. Jesus' Voice speaks to you so you know how to obey what He is saying to you that keeps you in His Light of Life and out of the darkness of evil.

Jesus said, I am the Light of the world. If you follow Me, you won't be stumbling through the darkness, because you will have the Light that leads to Life. (John 8:12 New Living Translation)

If you personally choose daily to come before God of Truth and Life and sit in His Presence to learn of Him, He comes to be with you. When you are still and quiet before Him, He comes as if He were sitting with you in person. He does this so you learn to know how He personally speaks to you. Each person is uniquely Designed to hear and know God's Voice in the distinct way He Designed you to hear His Voice speaking to you. No one is exactly like another person in the way they hear and personally know God. He wants you to know His Voice in the same way He knows your voice. As you continually come into His Presence and listen to His Voice in the way He speaks to you, you will discover the way that He personally speaks to you. When you know the way in which He personally speaks to you, then you can relate with Him in interactive communication.

Living God only speaks Truth. Supreme God is not a liar. He doesn't change His Mind. He never speaks and fails to act. He never Promises and fails to keep His Promises. He never Blesses and then reverses His Blessing.

Listen to God's Voice speaking through Isaiah in the Old Testament:

I have sworn by My own Name, and I will never go back on My Word... (Isaiah 45:23)

I am God, and there is no one else like Me! Only I can tell you what is going to happen even before it happens Everything I plan will come to pass, ... Isaiah 46:9-10 – Old Testament

And through David in the Old Testament:

The Word of The Lord holds true; and everything He does is worthy of our trust. (Psalm 33:4)

And through Jesus in the Gospel of John in the New Testament:

The Spirit of Truth comes, He guides you into all the truth; for He does not speak on His own authority, but whatever He hears (from The Father) *He speaks and declares to you the things that are to come. He glorifies Me,* (Jesus), *for He takes what is Mine from My Father and declares it to you. All that The Father has is Mine,* (Jesus); *therefore, I said that He* (Holy Spirit) *takes what is Mine and declare it to you.* (John 16:13-15)

God states in the Bible in Hebrews 6:17-18 that He took an oath binding Himself with an oath, so that those who receive His Promise can be perfectly sure that He will never change His Mind. God has given us His Promise and His Oath and these two things are unchangeable because it is impossible for God to lie. Holy God's Promise and Oath to us gives us courage to hold on to His Promises with confidence.

Therefore, you can fully trust God of Truth to come and speak to you in His *Still Small Voice* when you meet with Him daily and then quiet yourself before Him. As you train yourself to be quiet and listen for His *Still Small Voice*, He trains you to know when you are hearing His Voice, or other human voices who do not know Him, or the devil speaking lies, or even your own human voice. There is a difference. When you fully know the difference between the voices vying for your attention, you will only want to hear Holy God's Voice of Truth. Holy Spirit makes sure that when you ask Living God to know His Voice above the voices of the world clamoring for attention, the devil's lies, and even your own human voice, you will know with certainty without doubting which voice you are hearing. You choose to hear the voice you want to hear.

You can truthfully and certainly learn to know the difference between the voices speaking to your mind and heart. You must determine to take the time to be alone with God so you can honestly learn from Him the difference between the voices vying for your attention. When you know the difference, you can then discern and so decide which voice you will listen to. When you learn by experience to know God's Voice above the voices clamoring for your attention, you will definitely know God's Voice, and the voice of a stranger you will not listen to or follow.

Jesus is your Good Shepherd who guides you by His Voice so you know and learn to follow His Voice because you know His Voice so well that you will not follow a voice you don't know.

As you read the following account of the Good Shepherd in the New Testament, absorb into you heart how to know the Good Shepherd's Voice from the voice of a stranger:

Jesus says, I assure you, anyone who sneaks over the wall of a sheepfold, rather than going through the gate, must surely be a thief and a robber. For a shepherd enters through the gate. The gatekeeper opens the gate for him, and the sheep hear his voice and come to him. He calls his own sheep by name and leads them out. After he has gathered his own flock, he walks ahead of them, and they follow him because they recognize his voice. They won't follow a stranger; they will run from him because they don't recognize his voice.

I assure you, I am the gate for the sheep, all others who came before Me were thieves and robbers. But the true sheep did not listen to them. Yes, I am the gate. Those who come in through Me will be saved. Wherever they go, they will find green pastures. The thief's purpose is to steal and kill and destroy. My purpose is to give Life in all its fullness.

I am the good shepherd. The good shepherd lays down his life for the sheep. A hired hand will run when he sees a wolf coming. He will leave the sheep because they aren't his and he isn't their shepherd. And so the wolf attacks them and scatters the flock. The hired hand runs away because he is merely hired and has no real concern for the sheep.

I am the good shepherd; I know My own sheep, and they know Me, just as My Father knows Me and I know the Father. And I lay down My life for the sheep. I have other sheep, too, that are not in this sheepfold. I must bring them also, and they will listen to My voice; and there will be one flock with one shepherd. (John 10:1-16)

Ask Holy Spirit to help you distinguish whether it is Jesus' Voice speaking to you, or the devil's voice, or human voices, or your own voice. **Continually ask Holy Spirit to help you to personally know The Lord's Voice above all the other voices vying to be heard.** Holy Spirit gives you understanding to know the truth Jesus is speaking to you. Holy Spirit sees and knows the intent of your heart. Therefore, He knows when you are listening to Him and obeying Him. Always thank Holy Spirit when you recognize He is showing you the difference between the voices speaking to you. Thanksgiving is the way you receive more and more from The Lord.

Never, never, never give in and give up learning how Living God personally speaks to you. So many people quit right at the point when the God of Love and Peace is coming to them and answering their questions. Never allow yourself to *think* this is too hard for you to do. The Lord never gives up on you. He is always right beside you. So don't give up on Him. God is never late. He is always on time; His time, not yours.

Remember, GOD is GOD! He deeply and intimately knows you. He comes to you exactly on His Time, not when you suppose He should come to you. He knows what you may not yet know. He knows what you need before you know what you need. Sometimes you have to experience some things in your personal life before you are prepared to hear God's Voice speaking to you. He knows the exact time you are ready to hear and accept His Voice speaking to your personal situation. He is waiting for the exact right time for you to know He is speaking to you for your situation. Then, He reveals Himself to you in the way You can recognize and know He is speaking directly to you in your situation.

Also, life is not always about you and what you want. While you are waiting for The Lord to meet your need, He may be working in another person's life getting them ready to come into your life to fulfill His good purposes for all concerned. Just recall how long it took The Lord to get you to listen to Him. Be patient with yourself and with The Lord. While you are waiting for The Lord to answer what you are asking Him, pray for the others whom He is getting ready to bring into your life. Even though you may think you are ready for them to be in your life, you may not be as ready as you think you are. Just know that The Lord is still working in your life to get you ready to receive this person or persons. He is also working in the person or people He going to bring to you. When the time is just right from The Lord's perspective, He will arrange the circumstances for you both to come together. The Lord is never late. He is always on time. Only Living God knows when the time is right for everyone and everything involved in the situation, for Him to bring to you those who are to be with you.

You have to choose to trust The Lord is working in your situation to bring the best answer for all involved in the entire situation. Most likely there are other things involved that have to line up before the answer you need is answered by Living God. The Lord is never in a rush to remedy your situation. He knew the situation and how to remedy it before you ever knew you would be in this situation. The Lord uses every situation of your life to train you to know His Voice so you can forever follow and obey Him in all your ways. This is part of your journey in walking with Holy God in interactive relationship. This is the way you learn to know the way The Lord speaks to you in your personal situations.

Consider that Jesus also had to trust His Father and wait until His Father let Him know it was the exact right time for Him to be in people's circumstances. He knew The Father's exact time to go and be in people's circumstances because He spent much time in fellowship with His Father in Heaven. So He knew when to go and what to do in a situation. He also knew when not to go and be in a situation. Because Jesus walked and lived among the people, He knew their needs. He took their needs before His Father in Heaven asking Him to know what to do in the situations He faced daily in His life. Therefore, Jesus personally knew when the people, and especially *the one* He was praying for, were ready or not yet ready to receive The Father's answer through Him. Jesus lived among people doing and speaking what His Father showed Him and gave Him to speak. He did these things to leave an example for His disciples to follow.

Persevere and remain steadfast in your pursuit and spiritual journey to know True God. Remain steadfast and do not allow yourself to move away from learning how Living God personally speaks to you. If you *never, never* give up, you will learn to truly know yourself as you have never before understood yourself so that you know why you do what you do. In your unrelenting pursuit to know True and Living God as He truly exists, He reveals Himself to you and fills you with Holy Wisdom and Truth. Only you can decide if you want to know The Lord through personal relationship. When you truly and freely decide to pursue Living God in relationship, then all you have to do is ask Him to teach you how to hear and know His Voice of Truth. The Lord hears you and comes close beside you and teaches you what you want to know.

If you will personally, commit to read and study what is written in your Holy Bible considering all the Ways Almighty God reveals Himself and makes Himself known even in the midst of evil, you will be amazed at how The Lord God Almighty of Heaven and earth comes to you and personally reveals Himself to you in the way you can understand. He knows you by name; and, He calls out your name so you hear Him calling to you to come and follow Him into better ways for you to live life on earth and forever in His Presence.

As you diligently read, study, and meditate in The Holy Bible who God says He is, you learn with understanding why Jesus came on earth to save you from your selfish ideas and ways and from the lies the devil puts into your mind. You as well will learn how to live and walk with Holy God in relationship by righteousness, peace, and joy, and holy rest. You must give yourself permission to search for God with all your heart so that you come to personally know His Voice speaking to you. You must allow yourself to be led by Holy Spirit in all your ways of living.

Choose to get a personal journal so you can write down what you are learning from your Bible, and especially the way God speaks to people in the Bible. Write in your journal what you ask God, and also write down what you believe God personally spoke to you in response to your questions. Then, from time to time go back to your journal and read what you wrote. As you continually do this, you will see a pattern of growth in knowing the way True and Living God is personally speaking to you. You will actually see yourself expanding in knowing and experiencing the Love, Knowledge and Wisdom of True God. You will learn how God personally speaks to you and how you respond to His Voice. Then you will never want to stop having interactive relationship with Him. Neither will you ever want to stop giving thanks and praise to the God of your life.

Unforgiveness and God's Voice

If it seems to you that you are not receiving answers to what you are asking Living God, it may be because you are carrying unforgiveness or offenses toward others in your heart that you may not recognize. Unforgiveness causes God's Voice to diminish and even stop from speaking to you. However, God sees this and wants you to forgive others in the same way He has forgiven you.

Jesus said to His disciples, "Have faith in God. Truly, I say to you, whoever says to this mountain, 'Be taken up and cast into the sea,' and does not doubt in his heart, but believes that what he says will come to pass, it will be done for him. Therefore, I tell you, whatever you ask in prayer, believe that you receive it, and you will. **And whenever you stand praying forgive, if you have anything against anyone so that your Father also who is in heaven may forgive you your trespasses.** (Mark 11:22-26)

For if you forgive people their trespasses, your heavenly Father also will forgive you; but if you do not forgive people their trespasses, neither will our Father forgive your trespasses. (Matthew 6: 14-15)

Therefore, you **must** closely and regularly examine your heart and ask yourself questions to make sure there is no unforgiveness toward anyone, and that you are not holding onto offenses toward others, and this includes even your enemies who hate you and persecute you.

Stop right here and pick up your Bible and go to Luke 6:27-49. Read these words to gain an understanding as to how Jesus says to treat those who hate you, and who take advantage of you, and who are mean to you. This is the way you are to always live no matter how you are treated by other people. Practicing this way of holy living assures you that when you stand alone before your Father in Heaven to give Him an account of your life before His Holy Presence, you stand before Him forgiven. You want to hear Him say, *"Well done good and faithful servant. Enter into your eternal rest and rewards."* You don't want to hear these words from Him, *"Depart from Me. I never knew you."* Read Matthew 7:21-23. The same way you have forgiven or have not forgiven others will be the same way you are forgiven or not forgiven by Your Father in Heaven when you stand before Him giving an account as to how you lived your life on earth toward Him and toward others in your life.

A very important truth you must know and believe and live is this: When you choose not to forgive those who have sinned against you, you are truly hurting yourself more than you are hurting the one who offended you. A false belief people have is that if they forgive a heinous crime against them or a loved one, they are condoning (overlooking, excusing, disregarding, ignoring) the sin that was committed. To accept the devil's lies as truth comes from the pit of hell to get you to agree with this lie so that you are not forgiven nor is the person who committed the crime forgiven so that they too are free to explore knowing God in relationship. This is how the devil steals people from God's Love and forgiveness that Jesus died to extend to all people. When you willfully choose not to forgive others in the same way Jesus forgave those who hung him on a cross to die, neither will your Father in Heaven forgive you your sin against Him and other people. Go to your Bible and read in Luke 23:34-43 where Jesus forgave others when they were killing him. As Jesus was dying on a cross, He cried out, *Father, forgive them, for they know not what they do!*

Another very, very important aspect connected to unforgiveness are worthless words carelessly spoken that have no value and are at times spoken with malice or evil intent. These careless words cancel truth. The careless words people speak without even thinking are hurtful, harmful, and baseless according to God's Word of Truth. Consider these words or phrases that are carelessly spoken:

I love you to *death*.
I just *died* laughing.
That *kills* me.
I *hate* you.
You are so *stupid*.
I don't believe that!
Who says so?
You can't do anything right.

These words can bring a curse on yourself or someone else. Here is another cultural slang phrase people are speaking over and over and over in today's world: **OMG or Oh my God**! Saying **OMG** incessantly and carelessly is using God's Name in a frivolous way rather than truly calling on God's Name to save, heal, and deliver you from evil. Consider why you are always blurting out **OMG** or **Oh my God!** The reality is that when you don't truly know God or believe He can save, heal, and deliver you from evil, the devil is using you to mock Living God who does save, heal, and deliver every person ever born on earth from the devil's evil and lies.

These are only a few words and phrases that cancel God's Word of Truth. I'm sure you know of other words and phrases people carelessly speak. Speaking words that do not add good to your life or another's life, cancels God's Word of Truth written in the Bible. Saying careless words hurt and damage people including yourself, and dishonors Holy God whose Holy and Creative words bring a good outcome.

As a child I heard these words over and over and over: *"Sticks and stones will break your bones, but names will never hurt you."* As a child, I did not recognize how damaging these words were because most of the children kept on calling each other not so nice names. These death and curse words come straight out of the devil's mind into your mind and then out through your mouth. The devil is using you to curse God but most people do not recognize the devil is using them to curse True God. They just say these damaging words because they think it's cute and this makes them part of the *in-crowd*.

Seriously consider that you will have to answer to Holy God for every careless and negative word you speak and do not ask God and others to forgive you for saying them. Don't think you can just flip out these words, "I'm sorry God." and then go on saying whatever you want to say with no intent of changing your behavior or your negative words. Living God hears you and has recorded your words in His Book. The day will come when you will give an account to Supreme God for your words and your behavior.

Listen to Jesus' Words:

I tell you on the day of judgement each person will give an account for every careless word they ever spoke; for by your words you will be justified (vindicated or blameless), *and by your words you will be condemned* (sentenced to everlasting punishment). (Matthew 12:36-37)

Holy God does not overlook the intent in the way words are spoken. Words have power to create or to destroy.

Supreme God Created the world and all that is in it by the words He spoke. Living God Designed you to love yourself as He Loves you. Read: Genesis 1. You will see these words over and over: *And God said...* What God said was GOOD and brought Life to His Creations.

Deeply take hold of these words from the Bible:

The tongue can bring death or bring life; those who love to talk will reap the consequences. (Proverbs 18:21)

Watch your tongue (what you say) *and keep your mouth shut and you will stay out of trouble. Mockers are proud and haughty; they act with boundless arrogance.* (Proverbs 21:23-24)

Absorb and practice these words:

Let no evil talk come out of your mouths, but only such as is good for edifying (helpful to others including yourself) *as fits the occasion that it may impart grace to those who hear. And do not grieve Holy Spirit of God, in whom you were sealed for the day of redemption. Let all bitterness and wrath and anger and clamor and slander be put away from you, with all malice, and be kind to one another, tenderhearted, forgiving one another, as God in Christ forgave you.* (Ephesians 4:29-32)

There is no human sin ever committed that is unforgiveable by Jesus' Blood Sacrifice. Pride and self-will attempts to keep you believing a lie which is that the sin you committed is too great for Jesus' Blood Sacrifice to forgive. To accept this lie comes from pride and self-will, which is the ultimate sin the devil committed against Supreme who God Created him in beauty and for good in serving Him. The devil's sin of pride and rebellion caused Holy God to throw him out of Heaven, which separated Him from Supreme God and all the good he could have had and done. His free will rebellion caused Holy God to Create hell which is a place of eternal torment where the devil and his angels who followed him will be forever and ever living in perpetual torment and pain that will never end. Hell was not prepared for human beings. It was prepared for the devil and His angels who rebelled against God's Ultimate Love and Authority. Read Jesus' words in Matthew 25:41. However, if you freely choose to side with the devil, you too will go to this place of torment to spend eternity. This is most certainly true. So don't flip this off and say, "It doesn't matter that much right now. I have time to live as I want and then I will repent before I die." God says:

"Fool! This night or today your soul shall be required of you." (Luke 12:20)

The devil's rebellion and false perception of Supreme God is always at work attempting to get you and anyone who will side with him to believe that his lies are truth. By getting you to side with him and his lies, he wrongly believes that he can get back at God for kicking him out of Heaven. If you freely choose to side with the devil by receiving his lies, you will receive the same result or end that the devil receives. You will be separated from Holy and Living God forever with no way to escape from hell, which is a place of perpetual and never-ending torment. God prepared hell for the devil and his angels when they rebelled against His pure Love and Authority. Read God's words in the Bible:

Depart from Me, you cursed, into the eternal fire prepared for the devil and his angels. (Matthew 25:41)

Always keep in mind what The Holy Bible reveals about not taking revenge. Revenge is not yours to take. Go to your Bible and read Romans 12:17-19 and listen with all your heart and heed what Holy God says about not taking revenge and why you are not to do this. Only Holy God avenges sin, which He did when He died on the cross for you and for the person who sinned against you. When you freely choose to do God's Will which is to forgive every person who committed sin against you, and as well forgive yourself, you are releasing yourself and the person who sinned against you to Holy God who cares for each person with Holy Love and Grace. He will deliver you from your pain and the sin committed against you, if you choose to trust Him with all your heart not leaning on your own understanding. Read Proverbs 3:5-8.

When you learn to walk with The God of your life wrapped in His Love, then you can choose to love yourself and the people in your life with His unconditional Love and forgiveness. Pure and Living God Designed you to love yourself as He loves you, and to love all people in the way He Loves them and Created them. You have a free will to choose to love True God, and to forgive yourself and other people as God through Christ Jesus extends forgiveness to all who accept His Love and forgiveness. Go to 1 Corinthians 13 in your Bible and learn how God's Love is to be lived.

The only unforgiveable sin is the sin of blasphemy, which is to reject The Father's Breathe of Life emanating from Holy Spirit whom The Father sent to live inside you. Holy Spirit teaches you The Father's Will. The Father's Will is that you willingly receive The Father's free gift of Salvation through first admitting you have sinned against Holy God, and then accept His Son, Jesus Christ's Blood Sacrifice that He paid by dying on a cross to redeem you back to The Father' s Love.

Blaspheming or denying Holy Spirit's Breathe of Life is saying that you will not receive The Father's free gift of Salvation from sin for yourself or for others. You are emphatically stating that you will never forgive a person their sin against you. Once you have adamantly and willingly chosen to ultimately refuse Holy Spirit's Love and Truth, you can never be forgiven by Holy and Supreme God. You have committed the unforgiveable sin. By refusing Holy God's Salvation from sin and evil, you have freely decided where you want to live for eternity. Your decision not to ever forgive yourself or others, forever separates you from Living God and what you could have had that is good and beneficial for abundant and joyful living.

Through my personal and interactive fellowship with Holy God, I share with you a truth He revealed to me about the unforgiveable sin. He spoke this to me:

"When you lavish love upon My Holy Spirit, you are surrendering yourself to My Love that abides in My Holy Spirit. Receiving Holy Spirit's Perfect Love and Truth frees The Father's Love to be poured out upon you to protect you from the terrible Day of Judgement that is coming upon the whole world for refusing My Love through My Holy Spirit. There is no forgiveness for sin to those who refuse the Love of My sweet and gentle Holy Spirit. The unforgiveable sin is to refuse the wooing Love of My Holy Spirit. Doing this breaks My Heart, kindles My Anger, and brings My Wrath." Read: Matthew 12:31-32; Mark 3:28-29; Luke 12:10

Holy and Almighty God speaks convicting truth:

If a man sins against a man, God (Jesus) *will mediate for him; but if a man sins against the Lord* (Holy Spirit), *who can intercede for him?"* (1 Samuel 2:25)

Jesus speaks what His Father gave Him to say:

Truly, I say to you, all sin and blasphemy can be forgiven, but anyone who blasphemes (curses) *Holy Spirit will never be forgiven. This is an eternal sin.* (Mark 3:29)

It is Holy Spirit who woos (pursues, persuades, encourages) you to turn away from the devil's lie to not forgive yourself or others. When you intentionally choose to side with the devil's lies, there is no other help for you. You are on your own with no way to receive The Father's forgiveness for your sin through Jesus' Blood Sacrifice that forgives all the sins you will ever commit. If you choose not forgive the sins others commit against you, then you will not be forgiven your sins. Holy Spirit convicts of sin. If you adamantly refuse Holy Spirit's wooing Love prompting you to forgive others as you have been forgiven through Jesus' Blood Sacrifice, then you are in danger of receiving the eternal penalty for choosing not to forgive others their sins, which is to live in the unrelenting agony of hell forever. Stop right now, and search your heart.

Say before Living God,

How can I know all the sins lurking in my heart? Cleanse me from these hidden faults. Keep me from deliberate sins!

Don't' let them control me. Then I will be free of guilt and innocent of great sin. Psalm 19:12-13

Search me, O God, and know my heart; test me and know my thoughts. Point out anything in me that offends You, and lead me along the path of everlasting life. Psalm 139:23-24

How Faith Operates

Faith is Living Substance

What actually is Faith? It is supposed by many people that Faith is something you have to enough of to receive anything from God. However, according to God's Word, Faith is not something you have to have enough of before you can receive from God whatever you ask Him. Faith is actual Living Substance, which truly lives or exists; and so, is alive and actively working when applied through words that are spoken, and actions that are taken.

Paul, God's apostle states in the New Testament that without Faith it is impossible to please God. Those who come to God must believe He exists and rewards those who *diligently* seek Him. (Hebrews 11:6)

Let's look at God's Word and examine Faith from God's point of view to understand His true meaning for Faith, and how to use Faith as an action that when used brings results.

*Faith is the **substance** of things hoped for and the **evidence** of things not seen.* (Hebrews 11:1)

Living God is revealing that Faith is Living Substance which can actually be seen. In the Old Testament and in the New Testament, God reveals His Purpose for activating Faith, that is Living Substance. Check out Romans 4 and Hebrews 11 in the New Testament to explore Faith from God's perspective or point of view.

Holy God's meaning and use for Faith has never changed. It has just been misunderstood or misinterpreted. The devil is a liar and has been from the beginning and always will be.

Jesus reveals Truth about the devil:

...the devil was a liar from the beginning and has always hated the truth. There is no truth in him. When he lies, it is consistent with his character, for he is a liar and the father of lies. (John 8:44)

Therefore, the devil is the one who has twisted truth and persuaded and so convinced people that you have to have enough Faith in order to receive anything from God; and sad to say, people have chosen to believe a lie rather than truth. Because people choose to believe a lie rather than truth, they blame God of Truth for not receiving what they ask Him.

Faith is Living Substance which resides within Living God and also lives in those who receive Him. The Bible reveals visible manifestation by speaking words of Life. Faith is Living Substance which is alive and active and comes into actual existence or reality by what is spoken. Stop right now and read James 2:14-26 in your Bible to learn that God says Faith does not exist without action. So if there is no action, there is no viable Faith. True Faith brings into visible manifestation what is spoken.

God says in the Bible:

Faith is Living Substance which resides within Living God and also lives in those who receive Him. The Bible reveals that Father, Son, and Holy Spirit live in those who allow Him to live in them:

You will know that I am in My Father, and you in Me, and I in you. (John 14:20)

Therefore, if you freely choose to allow Living God to live His Life through you, you are to speak from His Faith, which is Living Substance, that lives in you. When you receive and so believe Faith is Living Substance that resides within Holy God and also lives in you, then the words you speak from God's Faith living in you visibly manifests and so becomes the evidence of what you spoke.

But when you ask Him, be sure your Faith (which is Living Substance that is alive and lives in Holy God and you) *is in God alone. Do not waver, for a person with divided loyalty is as unsettled as the sea that is tossed by the wind.* (James 1:6)

Jesus says, "I tell you, you can pray for anything, and if you believe that you have received it, it will be yours." (Mark 11:24)

Faith is Living Substance which resides within Father, Son, and Holy Spirit and also lives in those who receive Him and allow Him to live in them:

You will know that I am in My Father, and you in Me, and I in you. (John 14:20)

According to Galatians 2:20 Holy God's Faith works in you as Living Substance because you live by His Faith living in you:

I have been crucified with Christ (in other words I have died to myself and what I think)*; **it is no longer I who lives, but Christ who lives in me**, and the life I now live in the flesh, **I live by the Faith of the Son of God**, who loved me and gave Himself for me.* (Galatians 2:20)

Therefore, if you freely choose to allow Living God to live His Life through you, you are to speak from His Faith, which is Living Substance, that lives in you. When you receive and so believe that Faith is Living Substance which resides within Holy God and also lives in you; then the words you speak, from God's Faith that lives in you, visibly manifest; and so, is the evidence of what you spoke.

I have chosen to obey The Lord to speak words through God's Faith living in me knowing the words I speak will manifest tangible evidence in all my situations. I am getting bolder and bolder in saying what is needed in each situation I face. I say out loud: *I say what I have, and I have what I say.* Therefore, I believe what I say before I walk into a situation is going to happen the way I say it and it does. You too can choose to speak good words that manifest into visible evidence from God's Faith which exists in you as Living Substance. It truly works. Believe this and do it. To True God alone be all the Glory!

When I say what is to happen in my personal situations, I am putting God's Faith as Living Substance into action according to Jesus' words:

Whatever you ask in My name, I will do it, that the Father may be glorified in the Son; if you ask anything in My name, I will do it. (John 14:13-14)

If you abide in Me and My words abide in you, ask whatever you will, and it shall be done for you. By this my Father is glorified that you bear much fruit, and so prove to be My disciples. (John 15:7-8)

You did not choose Me, but I chose you and appointed you that you should go and bear fruit and that your fruit should abide; so that whatever you ask the Father in My name, He may give it to you. (John 15:16)

Have Faith in God! Truly I say to you, whoever says to this mountain, 'Be taken up and cast into the sea, 'and does not doubt in his heart, but believes that what he says will come to pass, it will be done for him. Therefore, I tell you, whatever you ask in prayer, believe that you receive it, and you will." (Mark 11:22-24)

And this is the confidence which we have in Him (Jesus), *that if we ask anything according to His will, He hears us. And if we know that He hears us in whatever we ask, we know that we have obtained the requests made of Him.* (John 5:14-15)

However, for the Living Substance of Faith to tangibly manifest by what you say, you must willingly choose to give up your former ways of *thinking* and doing. For God's Living Faith to produce holy evidence by what you say, you must be truly dead to what you *think* and alive to what God *says*. You must learn to put Holy God's *Faith* as Living Substance into action by the words you speak which produces results.

In this book, *Live Creatively - Fulfill Your Designed Destiny*, you are learning how to put Faith, which is Living Substance that actually exists as a living entity, into action which produces actual results. This book is designed to be used interactively as a hands-on book that instructs you to know what Faith is and how Faith literally functions so that actual results are experienced in your life. You are using this book interactively when you stop and take the time to ponder what you are reading and then look up the Bible passages; and as well, ask God the questions that are arising in your heart from what you are reading in this book and in The Holy Bible.

I want you to know the books The Lord asks me to write and publish for Him are not just for others, they are for me as well. As someone who read one of my books said to me, "Betsy, it is evident that The Lord wrote these books through you. There is no way you could write what you write." And WOW do I recognize this! I must as well live and put into action what I write. I am learning along with you how to put the Living Substance of Faith into action by saying what The Lord is saying to me and asking me to write for Him in these books. We must all mature together so we are the fullness of True and Living God on the earth that demonstrates who He is, not only to ourselves, but as well to the other people He brings into our lives.

At a time when I was in the Presence of The Lord fellowshipping with Him, this question rose up in me: *"Lord, show me what I need to know that I don't know that I need to know? Thank You."* I recognized that The Lord put this question in me to ask Him. I truly understand that because I asked The Lord to know what I didn't know, He revealed Truth and Wisdom to me that He wanted me to know.

The Lord revealed to me that **I am to live and act by Jesus' Faith living in Me**. He gave me understanding to know that of myself I could never have enough Faith to do anything. Therefore, I am to live my life in my human flesh by Jesus' Faith living in me. I can do this because Jesus Loved me and gave His Life for me so that I could know how to live my life on earth by His Faith that lives in me.

Never have enough Faith to carry out or bring to pass what I ask Him. Suddenly, *I got it!* True Faith was activated in me to know with no doubting that it is God's Faith living in me doing what I say or do. God's Truth canceled what I *thought.* God's revelation encouraged me to know it is not me who brings the answer to what I ask Him because of what I do or the way I say it. It is Living God's Faith as Living Substance residing in me that is doing what I say. God's revelation Truth is so right on because I can know and not doubt that God's Holy Faith is Living Substance doing what I say or do at His direction. Therefore, I am not stealing His Glory. It is God alone working His Faith as Living Substance through me to bring the answer that is needed in a situation by what I say and act on.

Jesus clearly states that before you can operate His Faith, which is Living Substance, you must give up your own selfish ways.

Listen to Jesus words:

If any of you wants to be My follower, you must put aside your selfish ambition, shoulder your cross (anything you might have to suffer for following Jesus)*, and follow Me. If you try to keep your life for yourself. You will lose it But if you give up your life for Me, you will find true life. And how do you benefit if you gain the whole world but lose your own soul in the process? Is anything worth more than your soul? For, I Jesus, who is the Son of Man, will come in the glory of My Father with His angels and will judge all people according to their deeds.* (Matthew 16:24-24)

Just remember, there can be no selfish motives for self-gain and recognition in using God's Faith as Living Substance in your circumstances by the words you speak. You must be empty of any selfish motives and full of God's Truth and Love for all people. Then what you speak becomes tangible evidence in your circumstances because you truly believe God will act on or arrange to happen what you say.

You can truly learn how to say what is needed in a situation, because you truly believe it is God's Faith as Living Substance living in you doing what you say. You are not relying on yourself and what you *think*. Rather, you are trusting God's Faith living in you to do what you say in your situation. Therefore by God's Faith residing in you as Living Substance, speak into evidence those things you hope (have confident expectation) will happen. Say with no hesitation:

"In the Name of Jesus, I say the exact right people will come into my life today who will help me in my job and who I can help do their job well. Today, by Holy Spirit Wisdom living in me I will make wise decisions that are good for all the people I work with and for the customers who I come in contact with. I choose to say only those things which are good and helpful to the people around me today which are pleasing to The Lord. So, I say with confidence that I know what to do and say in every situation I face today."

Faith as Living Substance is activated and brought into actual existence by saying what is to happen in your situations, not only for you personally, but for all the people involved in the situation. Never selfishly ask God to help only you. What you say for your situation is to be for the welfare of all people involved. The words you speak and the actions you take are the substance of God's Faith living in you that becomes what you say. What happens from what you speak is the actual evidence of what you spoke. Because I have learned God's Truth about Faith, I practice speaking into every situation I face in my daily life through God's Faith living in me. Speaking by God's Faith living in me as Living Substance brings me Peace to believe and therefore know that God is with me and is doing what I say in the situations I face. Therefore, I say what I have and I receive what I say.

Be sure to notice and then write down or journal what became apparent in your circumstances from what you stated by Jesus' Faith living in you. Then you can refer back to your journal and encourage yourself to keep on speaking what is to happen by the Substance of God's Faith living in you. Faith manifesting Living Substances into tangible evidence only works when you are truly dead to what you think and alive to what God says.

I share with you an example from my own life when I was learning to activate Faith as a Living Substance. Here is my Faith in action story:

I was interacting with my publisher on a book I was writing and editing with their help; and I needed to immediately send them from my computer what I was working on. I was ready to send it, when suddenly my computer stopped working. It completely shut down. I knew I needed help in getting this fixed right now. I knew I had to call my Internet carrier. Yet, resonating in me was my children's words to me, "Mom, it takes forever to get someone to talk to in person when you call them with a problem you are having." I emphatically said, "Well, not this time!"

Immediately, I said before calling my Internet carrier, "I will call and get the exact right person to talk with. It will be quick and easy and they will come out today and fix it, in Jesus Name! Thank You, Lord."

I made my phone call to my Internet company, and immediately, a very nice lady answered and she worked with me over the phone trying to solve the problem. Finally she said, "I think we need to send a technician out. Would tomorrow morning work for you?" I hesitated and said within myself, "But I said today, they will come out." Then I heard myself saying to her. "Well, I guess that would be okay." And we set up a time for them to come out tomorrow morning.

I went about my day. About a half an hour later, my phone rang and I answered it. And a man's voice said, "Hello, Betsy? I am the manager of my Internet company. I know they set up an appointment for you for tomorrow morning. But we could come out today. Would that be okay with you?" Without thinking I shouted out loud to him over the phone, "Praise the Lord! I asked The Lord to send someone out today to fix this problem, and I told him that I truly needed this fixed today as I am an author and I need to get in touch with my publisher today."

Then, what he said next to me astounded me, yet it shouldn't have. He said, "Well The Lord tapped me on the shoulder and told me to call you." We both rejoiced together.

Then, it gets even better. The technician came in a very short time. I needed a new router. He fixed it within a very few minutes. And I was up and running and I then sent what I needed to send to my publisher. Then I started talking with the technician and sharing with Him about The Lord. We shared so many things together. He shared with me that his family so needed The Lord in their lives. My husband was home that day and he joined in our conversation in our kitchen. The technician said that he had a short day and we were his last call. As we spoke and shared our lives together, The Lord put it on my heart to give him one of the books I had written at The Lord's direction, *Apocalypse Here and Now! Are You Ready?*

So I went and got a copy and gave it to him. He leafed through it and became exuberant. He said, "I will read this! I want to give this book to four people I know right now." I had more copies and went and got him 4 more copies. So what I spoke that day that I needed to happen for me expanded into so much more than even what I said I needed to happen in my circumstances. When I said what I needed, I watched The Lord touch other people with His Love for them. I cried out to The Lord, "Thank You, Lord for all that happened today. I give You thanksgiving and praise for being with me and helping me, and for blessing the people who helped me."

Because I am learning to truly know God is with me in what I am facing, I bravely step out trusting He is with me to do or say what is needed in my situation with His Love for me and for all those involved in this situation.

This is why we must, must, must learn to put God's Faith residing in us as actual Living Substance into action and bring into manifestation what we need in any situation we face knowing God of Love and Truth is with us performing what we say is to happen.

I greatly encourage you to absorb what I write in this book that trains you how to use God's Faith as Living Substance that manifests tangible evidence in the way God Almighty Designed for His Creation to function. As I share with you in this book, I too must draw near to GOD and listen to His Voice speaking to me. When I hear His Voice speaking to me through The Bible and through our personal relationship, I step out using His Faith Living in me to do or say what is needed in the situation I face in my life. I pray that you do the same so that together we can fulfill our Creatively Designed destinies that bring Supreme God all the thanksgiving and fame He deserves; and as well, ensures us that we will enjoy an eternal destiny of Peace, Joy, and fellowship with Holy God and one another, and with all the company of Heaven. I have determined in my heart to draw near to Him often and listen to His Voice speaking Truth to me so that I keep on hearing His Voice speaking personally to me.

I never think that I am above learning. There is always something new and fresh to learn. This is why I stay close to Living God to hear His Voice speaking personally to me. I am still learning and expanding from what I write in the books The Lord asks me to write and publish for Him so that His Voice is known the way He wants it to be known. I willingly submit to Holy God's Truth in all my ways. It is so much easier than anything I may want to do and brings lasting results.

Thanksgiving Brings Action

Always practice thanking The Lord in advance for whatever you say is to happen. This is how you let Him know that you believe that what you say is happening with His help; and you are also encouraging yourself to know with no doubting that He hears you and is working with you to achieve what you say.

When you speak what you need to happen in a situation, you are putting **The Lord's Faith as Living Substance into action**. Once you have spoken what is to happen, you do not need to keep saying what you already said. Holy God heard you the first time you spoke and He is already working from what you spoke. Therefore, just keep thanking The Lord of Life. Say, "Thank You, Lord. I know You are at work doing what is needed in this situation." No request made to Living God with thanksgiving is ever unheard or not answered by Him. He always hears the prayers of people, and answers what is best for all concerned in this situation.

When you thank The Lord before you see the answer to what you say, you are clearly stating to Him that you confidently expect Him to answer what you say and you no longer want what you *think* is to be done in a situation. You are trusting The Lord to do what brings His Blessing to you and to all the people involved in your situation. Also, consider that God is answering in His Perfect way what needs to be done in a situation that you may not even know needs to be done. The Lord of Life delights in your trusting Him. By thanking The Lord before you see the evidence of what you say, you are relating to Him that you are expecting His Faith that exists as Living Substance to become the evidence in this situation by the words you spoke.

God of Truth reveals in the Bible how to ask Him for whatever you need:

Always be full of joy in The Lord! Let everyone see that you are considerate in all you do. Don't worry about anything; instead, pray about everything. Tell God what you need, *and **thank Him** for all He has done. If you do this, you will experience God's peace, which is far more wonderful that the human mind can understand. His peace will guard your hearts and minds as you live in Christ Jesus.* (Philippians 4:4-6)

Supreme God's unveiled revelation truth that Faith is actual Living Substance that visibly manifests into tangible evidence by spoken words must be absorbed into your very being and then practiced in your daily living because this is the only way to abundantly live and thrive in this world of chaos and evil and actually forever.

Choices Establish Destiny

God is Faith and Creates what He speaks. Read Genesis 1-2. Almighty and Living God formed human beings in His very Image and Likeness and instilled in their very DNA the same ability He has to create by speaking words. Spoken words create. The devil knows this and so is trying to mimic Creative God by planting false and evil ideas in your mind. Then by skillfully lying to you appeals to your human nature so that you believe what he puts into your mind is truth. When you fall for his lies and believe as truth what he puts in your mind, he is using you to build his own evil kingdom.

If you allow the devil to use you for his own evil purposes, then you are separating yourself from Living God and are choosing to suffer eternal separation from Holy God to live in eternal torment with no way out. Nevertheless, if you choose to turn to The Lord with all your heart, He will come to you and deliver you from evil. God gave you a free-will choice to choose His Way of Living or the devil's evil way of living. Decide well. You have to live forever with the consequences of your choices, good or evil.

God says to choose life, but He gives you the free-will to choose death, which is separation from Him forever with no way out. Pick up your Bible and read and absorb Deuteronomy 28-30 in the Old Testament. God The Father in Heaven sent Jesus Christ His only Son to earth supernaturally conceived and naturally born in a virgin's womb to redeem you from the devil's lies. Therefore, you can freely choose to be delivered from the devil's lies by accepting Jesus' Salvation He died and rose from the dead to give you so you can live forever in true freedom from sin and evil. Read John 3 in the New Testament.

Exactly What Is Prayer?

Prayer is Communicating with God

Prayer is you communicating and talking with God of Love, and God of Love communicating and talking with you. When this happens, you are automatically praying and know how to pray. Prayer is interacting with the God who Created you and Loves you, and so wants to be with you telling you things that you don't know. He longs for fellowship and friendship with people He Created like Himself with whom He can communicate. You interact with Holy God when you speak and pour out your heart to Him and He speaks to you and pours out His Heart of Love to you. Therefore, you are talking *with* Him and He is talking *with* you. Each person is uniquely Designed by their Creative Creator to interact with Him in the unique way He Designed each person to hear Him and so personally know Him. Don't ever *think* that you have to hear The Lord speaking to you in the same way other people say they hear Him speaking to them.

When you want to be with Living God as your friend, you cannot help but pray or communicate with Him. The way He is known and speaks to you is according to the way He Created and Designed you to know Him and to hear Him speaking with you. When you submit yourself to Him in the way He speaks to you, then you know how to interact and communicate with a Holy God who Loves you the way He made you. You cannot help interacting with Him because you and God are connected in a personal interactive relationship. He knows you, and you know Him. Never stop or give up communicating with the God who Created you to love and enjoy Him.

You can be assured your prayers or communications with God are heard by Him in Highest Heaven. His Perfect response to you is on the way and is coming at the exact right time that is for the good of all involved in your request.

Prayers Are Heard in Heaven

There are many, many accounts or stories in The Holy Bible telling how Living God came and communicated with people on earth. This communication with True God by those who lived on earth was heard in Heaven. Communication with True God is still being heard in Heaven. All the eras of time are as one complete scenario before God of Creation. He Creatively Designed His Creation to operate this way so that all the eras of time are one distinct yet fluent and ongoing operation that He sees from Heaven.

As you read and study your Bible, you will see the accounts of people's interactions with Holy and Living God. Pay attention to these accounts. Take time to absorb the reasons people communicated with God. Your circumstances are no different than those people in the Bible experienced. We all need to know True and Living God is with us and is helping us in every situation we face.

While Jesus lived on earth in human flesh, He constantly talked with His Father in Heaven. As you read how Jesus communicated with His Father in Heaven, you will learn by His example how to pray or talk with God, your Father in Heaven.

What is spoken on earth to Supreme God of Heaven and earth from people who love Him and want to communicate with Him is received by Him in Heaven as a sweet-smelling aroma or fragrance. He responds in various or different ways depending on the situation and what is involved in communicating His response of Love.

Sighs, Groans, and Wails are Prayer

I share with you a tangible vision that I cannot explain. I saw circles as spheres of substance or tangible matter circling around and around. Instantly, The Lord caused me to know with understanding that what I was seeing were the prayers of people being expressed in sighs, groans, and wails that were going around and around as encircling spheres that are always in the atmosphere and are never lost.

I intuitively knew that these inaudible prayers being expressed as sighs, groans, and wails are circling and encompassing the atmosphere of Heaven as a continual action. I saw people continuously thanking and praising Holy God in the midst of their sighs, groans, and wails. I saw God's holy angels going to these ever-circling prayers and fulfilling these inaudible prayers. The answers to these sighs, groans, and wails were bringing more and more Glory to God, The Father. Hallelujah to the King of kings and Lord of lords Forever and ever! Amen!

I knew in truth that during times of distress, human prayers on earth may be only sighs, groans, and wails of unspoken human language that appear inaudible to us; but nevertheless, are heard as a language by Living God. These deep unspoken prayers are not silent before Almighty God. He hears every sigh, groan and wail as words that cannot be expressed in human language. These sighs, groans, and wails are audibly heard in Heaven and bring a response.

As I sat in silence absorbing Holy God's revelation knowledge to me concerning unspoken and silent prayers being expressed to Him as sighs, groans, and wails, The Lord spoke to me in the way He speaks to me:

"I heard your silent comment and question, *"Jesus was perfect in all His Ways. Was He ever unable to pray during suffering?"*

"Yes! Jesus endured suffering quietly in the face of great opposition. There were times in His human flesh when He could not audibly pray to Me in Heaven because of His unbearable suffering. I saw His suffering. Because He submitted to Me in His suffering for My sake, He could endure without audible words. I heard the sighs, groans, and wails of His heart in the midst of his pain and suffering. I kept Him true to Me in all His Ways. I saw Him silently endure suffering and pain when He was being unmercifully persecuted. I received His sighs and groans as prayer to Me. I am drawn to this kind of deep heart prayer."

When there are times in your life that you can only pray in sighs, groans, and wails because your suffering and pain seems to be unbearable, go to your Bible and read Matthew 26:36-46 and Hebrews 12:1-3. Know that God of Love and Truth sees you and hears you. Your sighs, groans, and wails are not unheard by Him.

During times when you cannot express in words what is needed in a situation you face, keep in mind that Faith, which is Living Substance, is activated by what is truly in your heart that only God Almighty sees and knows. As you are learning in this book, *Live Creatively - Fulfill Your Designed Destiny,* Faith is Living Substance and is activated by the words you speak and the actions you take at the direction of The Lord as He reveals Himself in The Holy Bible. Faith as well is activated by unspoken words that are expressed in sighs, groans, and wails. This is especially true during all the disruption on earth that God is doing and is allowing to remove evil powers of darkness to show Himself as Almighty and Supreme God of all Creation. During this time of disruption and upheaval on earth, no one knows how to pray with right words. These are the times that Living God hears people's prayers as sighs, and groans, and wails that are unspoken human language that God hears and answers. Believe this!

I want to share another story with you so you know how much God Loves you and hears even what you may consider a small thing to ask Him. This story will show you that nothing you ask God is too small for Him to answer. He knows and hears, and answers whatever concern you have in your heart and in your life no matter how insignificant you may *think* it is. Know that God cares for you and hears your heart desires.

My daily prayer partner who lives in Florida called me asking me to agree with her that her mentally challenged sister's kitty would find its way home. The kitty had escaped from their home and so was out in strange territory. Her sister was terribly upset that her kitty was missing. So we agreed in prayer saying that kitty would come home. Later, she texted me to let me know the kitty was home. I said, "Thank You, Lord, for guiding kitty home."

Put deep inside you, that no situation or circumstance you face is too small to ask The God of Life to help you. When you personally invite Jesus to come and be with you in each situation of your life, He comes to you. But you must believe that He will come to you when you ask Him to come and be with you and help you know what to do. Faith is Living Substance and is activated when you trust what you say will happen. Agreement with another person or other people in saying what you want to happen ensures The Father in Heaven will do what is agreed upon for a situation.

Hear with understanding what Jesus says:

I also tell you that if two of you agree down here on earth concerning anything you ask, My Father in Heaven will do it for you. For where two or three gather together because they are Mine, I am there among them. (Matthew 18:19-20)

Our agreed prayer that kitty would come home, brought kitty home Our Father in Heaven did what we said and agreed for together.

Prayers Prayed for Years Being Answered

I awoke recalling a dream I was in where The Lord let me experience first-hand seeing all the prayers that I had prayed for years being answered. I cannot explain this supernatural dream just as I cannot explain any of the holy and supernatural encounters The Lord allows me to experience with Him. I just know that each supernatural encounter with The Lord is real and is happening. I knew what I saw in this dream was not just for me. It pertained to all people who have been praying for years and years and it seems to them that the prayers they prayed were never heard and may never be answered by God as they asked Him.

Through this dream encounter, I was greatly encouraged to know with no doubting that The Lord is now in the process of answering people's prayers that have been prayed for years and years. The Lord is faithful in all His Ways. Even when people are unfaithful to Him, He remains faithful because He is not a liar and He certainly cannot deny who He is, which is a God who hears and answers prayer to Him.

I saw in this dream that we are going to be pleasantly surprised and greatly pleased (ecstatic, yet calm and joyful) as to how The Lord answers our persistent prayers. Most likely our prayers are not going to be answered in ways we expected or even desired. The answers are definitely going to be far greater and immensely better than we could ever have imagined. Read Ephesians 3:20.

I indelibly knew that by The Lord's doing, we will step right into each situation we have been praying for and literally see them answered. We will go from one answer to the next to the next. Somehow, we just step into each answer and see it fulfilled.

I saw with understanding that as we experienced the answers to our prayers, we had such unspeakable joy and contentment. We were in awe of how God answered so perfectly. I knew unmistakably that we don't need to beg God to answer us. I saw that all we need to do after praying and asking The Lord is to stand in faith by praising and thanking God for answering our prayers through His ability to work in Ways that are so much greater than we could ever imagine.

I also saw in this dream that The Lord was taking us from one answer into the next, and we saw its completion. Then, we picked up a trophy, so to speak - not a trophy as we think or know as a trophy, but something from The Lord that will be a reward to us for standing in faith trusting Him and believing that He will answer in the Way that is best for all involved in the circumstance that we are asking Him for help.

Through this supernatural encounter, I knew that Holy God is revealing that all the prayers that have been prayed for years are being answered. However, it may not be in the way people are expecting. These prayers will be answered in far greater ways than people even asked. These prayers prayed for years are being answered either while we live in this life on earth or when we are in Heaven where we live forever and ever. The Lord will take us and show us and let us see the answers to our prayers. He is GOD! Therefore, nothing it impossible or too difficult with Him.

God Hears and Answers Children's Prayers

I am going to share a personal life circumstance that caused me as a child to pray one of the most profound prayers, at least to me, I ever prayed. It was not until years and years later that I recognized my earnest childlike prayer to God was heard and answered by Him, and to this very day is still being answered.

My twin brother and I were given up by our birth parents as soon as we were born. Our birthparents requested that we be kept together and be placed in a Christian environment and eventually in a Christian home with parents who would care for us in the way they could not because of their circumstances. Their prayers were answered by a God who heard their prayers.

We were cared for by Salvation Army, then put in an orphanage, and then finally around 5 years of age were adopted and taken into a Christian home. Now that we were in our new home, we were taken to Sunday School where we learned what the Bible said about True God. At about the age of 8 or 9, I had a Sunday School teacher who had a profound impact on my life. I can still see her coming down the stairs to the basement of the church with her Bible and our lessons tucked under her arm carrying her cane and holding onto the rail as she carefully came down the stairs. She was an elderly lady. This immensely touched me as I knew it was a struggle for her to come down these stairs faithfully each Sunday to tell us children about a Jesus she knew so well. She made Jesus so real to me. I don't remember exactly what she taught us about this Jesus she knew from the Bible stories she told us. But I do know that she made Jesus so real to me that I wanted to know Him in the way she knew Him.

This precious lady knew Jesus in a very personal way. She shared with us children that her husband had just died and she was so afraid and felt all alone. So, she asked Jesus to come and help her. She related that Jesus came to her in a bright Light and then she had a warm feeling go all through her. She said that from then on, she was no longer afraid or felt alone. She knew Jesus was with her helping her. What she shared, deeply moved me. I too was afraid and felt all alone because of my personal situation as a child having been in in an orphanage. Hearing what she shared caused me to want to know this Jesus in the way she knew Him. I wanted Him to come to me in a bright Light and give me this warm feeling inside me so like her I would no longer be afraid or feel all alone.

So one night I stayed up all night long laying in my bed with both my arms raised straight up and my hands opened pointing upward. I have no idea why I raised my arms and hands up in the air and kept them there as I prayed to this Jesus I did not know. I didn't even know that you can and should raise your hands to God. I just instinctively did this. With my arms and hands raised up, I said, "Jesus, I want to know you like my Sunday School teacher knows you. I want the warm feeling, and I want the bright Light to come into my room." I kept my arms and hands held high in this position for what seemed to me to be all night. I just stayed in this position and didn't fall asleep. Suddenly, an unmistakable warm feeling went all through me. I didn't get the bright Light in my room. Many years later I experienced the Glory Light coming to me. But at this time when I was a child, I knew unmistakably that Jesus came to me and now He was inside me. I believed because He was truly inside me, I didn't have to be afraid or feel all alone.

Then, shortly after my very personal encounter with Jesus, I was at a Vacation Bible School when an invitation was given to come forward and give my life to Jesus. I jumped up out of my seat and went forward with no hesitation. As I went forward, this song was being sung, "Into my heart, into my heart. Come into my heart Lord Jesus. Come in today! Come in to stay! Come into my heart Lord Jesus." This song was indelibly put into my heart.

After I went forward to ask Jesus to come into my heart, I knew beyond any doubt that Jesus was in my heart and would never leave me. I rode my bicycle up and down the Pennsylvania hills where I lived singing this song to the top of my lungs. I didn't care who heard me. I knew my Jesus would always be with me and so I didn't have to be afraid any longer or feel all alone.

However, there were still some stressful issues in my life that needed attention before I would be totally free from the deep-seated harmful distresses of being in an orphanage and the other things that happened to me before I was adopted. How The Lord set me totally free is in the book *Infinite Destiny Truth and Wisdom* The Lord asked me to write for Him to make Him known as He wants to be known.

Never discount or dismiss any prayer you ever prayed and especially that you prayed as a child. You may not even remember the prayer you prayed when you were a child, but God heard your prayer, and He is still answering your simple childlike prayer. Stop right now, and ponder what you may have asked God as a child but have forgotten. God has never forgotten your prayer to Him. He will bring to your remembrance what you prayed to Him if you ask Him. Holy Spirit who is living in you will bring to your remembrance what you prayed as a child. Jesus promised you that His

Father in Heaven would send Holy Spirit to teach you all things, and bring to your remembrance all that He said while He lived on earth. You can find where Jesus says this in the New Testament book of John in chapter 14.

I am still recognizing and personally experiencing Living God bringing to my remembrance the things I asked Him when I was a child, and that I am still asking Him. Know that The Lord is always in the process of answering all the prayers you have ever prayed. You just may not recognize it yet. But you will. Pay attention to your circumstances trusting Holy Spirit to trigger you to remember the prayer or prayers you prayed. Ask Holy Spirit to help you recognize when a prayer you prayed is being answered. Your Father in Heaven wants to show you how much He Loves you. He wants you to know that He is a God who personally interacts with you. He longs to prove Himself to you as a God who hears and answers your prayers.

Getting To Know Holy Spirit

Who is Holy Spirit?

Because people are not familiar with Holy Spirit, they tend to ignore Him and eventually dismiss Him. When you truly understand Holy Spirit is a person who wants to be your friend and helper, you will never want to act as if He doesn't exist. So let's get to know Him.

Supreme God is One God. But He sovereignly chose or elected to express Himself in three distinct personalities: Father, Son, Holy Spirit. This solemn truth that God is One God expressed in three distinct personalities cannot be explained in human terms or human understanding. So, don't try. Don't attempt to dissect the elements of God. It cannot be done. However, there are many distinct characteristics that Supreme God demonstrates in human terms that we can understand. All people have fathers; and fathers have sons, and fathers and sons have friends. So God expresses Himself as father, son, and friend.

This unfathomable aspect of God Supreme being three distinct persons or personalities expressed in One God can never be explained by the finite human mind. So again, don't try. You could spend your lifetime trying, but to no avail. You can never fully know. You have to trust that God is who He says He is. You learn who He says He is in The Holy Bible. You also discover in the Bible how people chose to trust God in their situations. Yet what is written in the Bible is only a glimpse or a peek into who Supreme God truly is. He can never be fully known. He is fathomless, incomprehensible, and immeasurable. This is why He alone is GOD SUPREME.

Each person has to personally accept Supreme God in the way He chooses to reveal Himself. When you choose to accept True God as He chooses to make Himself known, you will have true peace, joy, and success in all your ways. He will be your God and you will be His friend who willingly serves Him forever.

When I was in my early twenties, I had someone try to explain God to me on a piece of paper. I did not know God in a personal relationship the way I know Him now. But as I listened and watched their drawings to explain God, I could not understand one thing they were saying or drawing. I just listened. Then I heard come out of my mouth, *"If God could be explained on a piece of paper, He wouldn't be God."* They had nothing to say and never came back to try to explain God to me. What I heard come out of my mouth astounded me. As I grew in my relationship with True and Living God, I learned that this was Holy Spirit speaking to me giving me what to say when I had no idea how to respond to their description of God. To this very day, I have never forgotten this experience.

Through years and years of getting to know Holy Spirit as my friend, counselor, and helper, I now know with no doubting that He is always ready to come and help me know what to do in any situation I find myself. Therefore, I write and speak about Him from the perspective of having chosen to believe and trust Holy Spirit is my friend and helper. He helped me when I didn't even know I needed His help when someone was trying to explain God to me on a piece of paper. You too must choose to want to know Him as your friend and helper and adviser. I hope I can help you see Him as a person who is truly alive and real and ready to be your friend, helper, and adviser. I am trusting Holy Spirit to help me make Himself real to you.

I have freely chosen to accept Holy Spirit as a true person who lives inside me with Jesus, and His Father and all together they guide my life in wholesome and everlasting ways. I know that I am never alone or on my own in making life choices and decisions. I can choose to ignore that there is a True God and go on doing my own thing as I see to do it. However, why would I want to, when I have learned by experience that The Lord my God is with me all the time in all my ways, and His Ways are so much better than what I was trying to do alone.

Maybe at this point in your life you are beginning to see that what you have been doing, isn't working for you. Well then, this is a perfect time to switch and try something that is guaranteed to work for you; and that is, to learn how to develop a personal living relationship with Holy Spirit who is your counselor, advisor, and friend who sticks with you in all your circumstances directing your path of life to know what to do in every situation you face.

There are many, many good books about Holy Spirit you can search out on your own to learn more about Him. I leave this up to you to search out books that can expand your knowledge and understanding of Holy Spirit. Just know Holy Spirit is more than theological knowledge. He is a person with the same feelings you have. Anyone can have a theological knowledge of Holy Spirit. But it is when you know Him as your own personal friend, helper, and guide that you will never want Him to leave you nor will you ever want to leave Him. He knows you want to know Him. So ask Him to direct you to the very books that are just for you, and are expressed in the way you can learn to personally know Him.

Here are some words in the Bible that David spoke over himself: during a time of great distress in his personal circumstances:

O, Lord, You are my hiding place.
You protect me from trouble.
You guide me along the best pathway for my life.
You advise me and watch over me. (Psalm 32:7-8)

I took these words and made them my own. I continually speak these words over myself knowing Holy Spirit hears my desire for Him to help me. Speaking God's Word over yourself in your situations gives Holy Spirit something to work with in your behalf because He knows what you desire in your heart. Take time right now to go to Psalm 32 and read how David related to God during times of fear from enemy attack. Teach yourself how to use Scripture to encourage yourself and say what you want and need in your circumstances. If you will determine to learn to find Scripture in the Bible that relates to your situation and then speak it out over yourself and your circumstances, you will experience a significant change in you and in your circumstances. This is how you learn to trust Holy Spirit as your friend, counselor and advisor. Don't do this just once and quit. Do this as a way of life from now on.

Teach yourself how to take Bible verses and personalize the words and make them your very own. Here are the words David repeated to himself:

I know the Lord is always with me. I will not be shaken, for He is right beside me. No wonder my heart is filled with joy, and my mouth shouts his praises! My body rests in safety and in hope. For you will not leave my soul among the dead or allow your holy one to rot in the grave. You will show me the way of life, granting me the joy of your presence, and the pleasures of living with You forever. (Psalm 16: 8-11; Acts 2:25-28)

I took these words from Psalm 16 and Acts 2 and wrote them out in my own words to make them my own personal declaration over myself in order to encourage myself in The Lord.

I wrote:

The Lord is always with me. I will not be shaken for He is right beside me. My heart is glad and my tongue shouts His praises! My body rests in hope. The Lord shows me the way of Life. He fills me with the Joy of His Presence.

Teach yourself to take Bible verses that grab your attention and make them into your own personal declarations. Taking the time to do this empowers you to know Holy Spirit is with you and helping you. Doing this also gives Living God and His holy angels something to work with in answering your words of faith declarations. God's holy angels listen for His Word of Authority and go and do His Good Will:

Praise the Lord, you angels of His, you mighty creatures who carry out His plans, listening for each of His commands. Yes, praise the Lord, you armies of angels who serve Him and do His Will! (Psalm 103:20)

So according to Psalm 103:20-21, Speaking God's Word with your mouth gives angels assignments to know what to do to help you. Speaking God's Word, rather than your own words, also aids you in replacing unnecessary words with words that are effective and bring lasting results.

Holy Spirit's Involvement

I am going to share with you some personal encounters that let me know Holy Spirit is a real person who hears you and answers you. He saw me and He knew I would need His help.

You too can have your own personal encounters with Holy Spirit that lets you know without any doubt Holy Spirit is your friend, comforter, helper and advisor. So here goes.

I call these personal encounters with Holy Spirit, God-stories. I love to hear people's God- stories and to share my God-stories with people. We need to always encourage each other to keep on keeping on when at times things are really tough and hard for us, and we may not want tos continue. But just hear a God-story from someone who like you is experiencing some really hard times, and you are greatly encouraged to get up and start running full steam ahead. Here are some personal God-stories I didn't learn were truly God-stories until I matured in knowing Holy Spirit.

I lived in an orphanage in Philadelphia, Pennsylvania during the very early years of my life. It was at this time, unknown to me, Holy Spirit came to me and was beside me comforting me. Of course, I did not know anything about God at this time in my life. When I learned later in life who Holy Spirit was and how He was sent from The Father in Heaven to be a comforter and helper, I knew it was Holy Spirit who came to me in the orphanage, and put a song in my heart and in my mouth that has never left me. I know He came to me to let me know He would always be with me.

My adoptive parents told me when they first took me to church with them, I would stand up in the pews and sing to the top of my voice the hymns that were being sung. Once I heard a song, I knew it by heart. Not just one verse, but all the verses in a song. This is true to this very day. I can recall and sing songs I hear and not forget the words. I was told this was unusual. But it wasn't for me. For me songs, and words, and music are part of me and something I cannot stop from coming up out of me. The words and the melodies in the hymns I heard and sang were not just words or music to me. They were my very life because I sang them out from my very being to God Himself. I knew God was there listening to me. I don't know how I knew; I just knew. I heard His voice and felt His music going all through me. And by the way, I still do.

When I was 6 years old, I began taking piano lessons and took them until I was 16. During my early years of piano lessons, I wanted to stop taking piano lessons. I wouldn't practice and when I came to my lesson time, I had not learned the piano pieces my teacher had assigned me because I had not been practicing them on my piano. My teacher pulled me aside and asked me what was wrong. Why wasn't I practicing my lessons. I told her because I wanted to learn to play the hymns from my hymn book. So from that time on, she told me to bring my hymn book to my lessons and she would assign me a hymn or hymns to practice along with the pieces of music she was giving me to learn.

Many, many years later I returned to Pennsylvania to attend a class reunion with classmates who were my very close friends in junior high school. One of my friends said to me, "I remember after school coming to your house and you played the piano and we sang hymns while you played the piano. I remember us all singing, *Holy Spirit Fall Afresh on Me*, as you played the piano. Don't you remember?" I had to admit I did not remember this. But her comment deeply touched me. I knew Holy Spirit was letting me know that He came to me in the orphanage and put His Song of Life in me. He was also letting me know His Song He put in me is always touching others because of my continuing personal quest in wanting to know more of Him. I thank Him and give Him all the praise and glory for causing people to want to know Him because of my life touching their lives.

Another life-changing circumstance took place in my life when I was 12 years old and in the seventh grade. This life-altering event changed the course of my life and re-directed the path in life I would take. Up to this point, kitties and dogs were a great part of my life. God used these animals in my life as a way of helping me cope in adjusting to my life of pain because of being abandoned at birth and placed with Salvation Army and then foster care and lastly an orphanage. Around 5 years of age my twin brother and I were adopted and taken from the orphanage into our forever home. When we were 6 years old, we moved from Philadelphia to northwestern Pennsylvania. It was at this time our adoptive parents presented me with my first kitten. Soon after getting this kitten, our parents brought into our home for my twin brother and me a brother and sister blond cocker spaniel puppies, whom they named Peter and Penny. And so, began my continuing love for animals especially kitties, dogs, and eventually horses. I could relate to these animals when I would not open up to people because of being so closed up on the inside by fear stemming from rejection and abandonment since birth.

My love for horses began when I was 9 years old. A boy who lived in back of our property had a pony, and he let me ride his pony. Thus, began my love for horses. I loved the feeling of freedom I felt from riding fast on the back of this pony. From this time onward, I wanted my own horse to love and to ride.

I was 11 years old when we moved to another small town in northwestern Pennsylvania. This small college town had a horse stable. I would ride my bike to this stable to be with the horses dreaming of being with these horses and riding them and taking care of them. I spent much of my free time at the horse stable petting and talking to the horses and observing all that was going on. When I was twelve years old, the stable owner saw my dedication and asked me to work for him caring for the horses and teaching people to ride and taking them on horse riding trails. He trusted me to run the stable when he had to go out of town. I ran the horse stable operations doing all the things it takes to run a riding stable. This was my first official and paying job.

While working at the horse stable, I also began taking in stray cats and dogs. Some were starving and some were severely injured. Some of them were so severely injured that they stayed in my bedroom with me all night long so if they needed anything, I would be right there to help them. I would care for them until they were fully healed and then I would find a home for them. I developed an ongoing relationship with our college town's veterinarian. I brought the severely hurt animals to him. I was getting a weekly allowance of twenty-five cents for doing home chores, and I was also getting a little money from working at the horse stable. So, I used this money to pay the vet for whatever needs these animals had and to buy their food. I also helped to pay for their vet cost by helping out at the vet clinic. When I didn't have the entire cost needed to pay for their care, the vet just smiled at me and said that's OK or he would take my few quarters and not say anything.

I had a reputation of taking in stray animals and caring for them. My parents said they were sure people were dropping off animals in our small town because they knew I would take them in and care for them and find them homes. I was seen in my small town riding my bike with a kitten on my shoulder on my way to the local meat market to get scraps to feed the dogs I was caring for. The meat market man always saved scraps for me to feed my dogs and was always waiting for me to come in and take them for my dogs. Of course, I also bought them dog food. Because of the working relationship I had with the veterinarian in this animal clinic, I decided I wanted to be a veterinarian. So I was heading toward a life career as a veterinarian. At this time, I lived in Northwest Pennsylvania so I chose Cornell University in Ithaca, New York where I would go to college to be a veterinarian. Learning came easy for me and I was making top grades in school – all A's and A+'s without much effort on my part.

But, at age 12 my life took a dramatic turn. A good school friend and I made plans to take a horseback ride after school. When we returned from our ride, my friend said she had to get home and couldn't help me unsaddle and rub down the horses. So she left and I attended to the horses. While I was rubbing down the horses and bedding them, I heard voices outside the barn. I remember leaning on the rump of Lady, the mare my friend rode, to look outside to see who was talking. I saw it was the owner of the stable talking with another man in a pickup truck. That's the last I remember. No one really knows what happened that day. But when the men heard the commotion inside the barn, they come running into to see what happened and found me bleeding and unconscious. I was rushed by the man in the pickup truck to a hospital twenty miles away. There was no ambulance service in our small town. It took an hour to get to the hospital because of the Pennsylvania hills and winding roads so that you had to drive slow and could not pass cars and trucks. This was a direct truck route and once you got behind a truck you stayed there because you could not pass them. I arrived at the hospital totally unconscious and bleeding from my nose. I remained totally unconscious for three days. The doctors diagnosed me as having a severe brain concussion and a broken nose. The only thing t I do know is the owner of the horse stable previously brought into the barn the most beautiful horse I had ever seen. He was a stallion and really rambunctious. There was only a 2x4 plank separating this stallion from the mare I was rubbing down that my friend rode. No one witnessed what happened so it was never determined what happened.

But this traumatic event changed the course of my life's direction. Because my brain concussion was so severe I was in the hospital for a very long time. When I was brought home, I had to lay flat on my back for months on end with no visitors or any kind of commotion whatever. I had to stay very still so my brain would heal. Whenever I would move, I had severe pain in my head. As I reviewed this incident in my later years of life, I recognized how prayer by others played a significant role in my recovery. The people in my church fervently prayed for me during this horrendous time in my young life. I was active in youth activities, choir, and playing the piano accompanying my father who was a soloist, and my twin brother who was accomplished in playing the trumpet. We used our God gifts for church worship services. I understand now because of people's prayers for me, during this time in my young life, why prayer is so very important to me. Prayer saved my life and sustained my life so I could fulfill my destiny God had planned for me.

Before I continue with my God-stories, I will interrupt here to interject something else that happened to me before this traumatic horse accident that changed the direction of my life. What I am going to share shows Holy Spirit was an integral part of my life even when I was not recognizing that He was right beside me helping me. This God-story is connected to my horse accident that brought a definite change into my life.

I remember staying up all night praying to God for a dog of my very own. This was during the time I was taking in dogs and cats to care for them, but I did not have my very own dog to be with me as I rode my bike and went to the horse stable to work. I so wanted this and would dream of having my own dog running beside me on my bike going everywhere with me. I explained to God down to the very detail what this dog was to look like and what his name was to be. I wanted a male Collie, and stated his exact markings, and I would name him Shep. Somehow, deep inside me I knew beyond any doubt that I would get this dog. I finally fell asleep, and got up for school the next morning. I had forgotten this and went off to school with my friends and my twin brother.

In this college town, our father bought one of the college professor's homes and so we basically lived on campus next to the boy's dormitory, and the track and field and sports fields were in conjunction with our property. So every day we walked through the college campus to go to school that was part of the college campus. As we were walking to school across the college campus on this particular morning after I had prayed all night for this specific dog, suddenly I saw a dog seemingly coming out of nowhere who perfectly fit the description of the dog I had asked God for. This dog was bounding toward me. I froze in my tracks pondering if I should call him. I said, "Here, Shep! Here Shep!" He came running up to me and jumped up on me acting as if he had known me his whole life. I saw that he was a male collie with the exact markings that I had asked for and he came to me by the name I called him, Shep. All the way to school he stayed right beside me and never left me. I knew this was my dog and God had answered my prayer. I was overjoyed trying to decide how I could stay in school all day without him leaving until I could take him home and ask my parents if I could keep him. All day long, when I could, I looked out a window to see if I could see him. And sure enough, he never left the school yard all day long. He was just lying there as if he was waiting on me. When I went out to recess, he was still there and came to me, and when I had to go into school again, he stayed and never left. After school left out for the day, Shep followed me all the way home never leaving my side. I asked my mother if I could keep him, and she said you will have to ask your father. My father said yes.

So began my journey with Shep. He was my constant companion and the whole town knew me and my dog Shep. He accompanied me into the meat market to get his waiting treat from the meat man. He was beside me when riding my horse or when I was riding my bike with my friends. Then during a really bitter cold and snowy Pennsylvania winter around Lake Erie, I put Shep outside for his potty duties. When I returned to bring him in, he was not there. I called and called and called him. But no Shep. This went on for days. I was heartbroken. My dad would take me in the car riding all around letting me get out of the car to call him. But no Shep. Every night I would work on my homework, but I would stop now and then and go and call Shep. Then as suddenly as he had left, he mysteriously returned to me. He was full of snow and ice balls in his fur and in his paws. I nursed him back to health. There was yet another time Shep left me; and again he mysteriously returned to me because I would not give up looking for him and calling his name.

Shep came into my life right before my severe brain concussion from the horse accident. All during this time when I could not have visitors or be out of bed, Shep laid right beside me on my bed. He never left my side except to go potty or to eat or drink. He stayed right beside me where I could lay my hand on him and feel his love and warmth. This brought me so much comfort and aided my healing.

When I could finally be out of bed and return to school, I discovered I could not learn to retain my school work no matter how hard I studied. I was devasted because I love to learn and learning always came easy to me without a lot of extra studying. I was planning on going to college to become a veterinarian. Now even though I studied and applied myself to learning, I could not retain or remember how to do my school studies. By doctor's orders I also could not play any sports, which I was very active in and loved, or do any gym classes. This was extremely hard on me. I kept on trying and never gave up. I truly believe Holy Spirit was with me helping me during this very difficult time when I could have become bitter and angry. I don't remember becoming bitter and angry, but certainly painfully disappointed. I cried a lot. As I look back over my life and especially ponder this painful time in my life, I recognize Holy Spirit was right beside me the entire time.

Now I will continue with more God-stories I experienced. While I was still recovering from this traumatic brain injury, our family moved from Pennsylvania to Indiana. My learning disability stayed with me all during high school. It was so very evident to me I could not go to college because I could no longer to the academic work it required. So I changed my high school major from college prep to taking business courses. I excelled in shorthand and taking dictation, and typing was easy for me because I could play the piano. I continued my piano lessons. I also began seeing that playing the piano and typing was causing my brain to develop in new ways of learning. I didn't fully understand this at the time. But I recognized that I was able to learn more quickly, and I associated my increased ability to retain what I was learning in school to playing the piano and typing. Later in life, I learned music enhances and stimulates the brain to learn and retain facts. Holy Spirit knew this before I knew this. So again, I knew The Lord was with me guiding me down the path He had for me to fulfill. Learning to efficiently type also played a part in fulfilling my God-ordained destiny, which is to be an author of published books to make God known as He wants to be known. I type and edit my own writing being led by Holy Spirit.

Yet, all during this time of not being able to learn which used to be easy for me, God drew near to me and became even more real to me as I relied on Him to help me do what I used to be able to do but no longer could do. As the years went by, I grew in my relationship with God and I recognized He had allowed this horse accident to change the direction of my life. I was headed in my direction, but The Lord had another plan for my life that was greater that my plan.

It was during this difficult time in my life, that God became even more real to me. I had to rely on Him to help me with my school lessons. By this time, I was training myself to learn in the way I could learn and have some recall of what I studied. I learned that if I wrote down what I wanted to learn I could remember better. Doing this seemed to help me retain things better because I first saw it on paper and this seemed to transfer to my mind. This became a way of life for me to learn, and still is to this day. I discovered that as I read my Bible and trained myself to memorize Bible verses which spoke into my heart, I could learn and remember what I read. I recognized I was retaining more and more from my school studies. The Bible stories I studied in depth and memorized stayed with me and gave me direction for my life.

I was married and raising four children when The Lord directed me to go to Bible College. He fulfilled my dream of going to college. However, it was not to be a veterinarian as was my plan. I now know that The Lord directed me to go to Bible College to let me know I could do academic studies at a higher level. I made the dean's list for high academic studies. The Lord wanted me to know I could learn, but I was to learn what He wanted me to learn; and this was to know Him and His Ways of living that had eternal value.

Shortly after I had begun to recuperate from this horse accident, and I began to regain somewhat normal living, Shep once again disappeared. This time never to return no matter how long I looked for him or called to him. I cried and cried and cried for my Shep to return to me. But he never did. As the years went by and I learned more and more about the Bible and how angels helped people, I came to believe and still do that an angel took on the form of dog who I named Shep for the purpose of being beside me during a time in my life when God was changing my life's direction. Of course, I did not know this at the time. I just knew God answered my prayer for a dog named Shep.

My God-stories continue to this very day. There are way too many God-stories for me to include in this book. Some of them are in my other books I wrote at The Lord's direction. I have learned by experience to never take any happening in my life for granted or think it was just a coincidence. Nothing that ever happens in our lives is a coincidence. God, our Father in Heaven, has a distinct and Creatively Designed plan for each and every one of us to fulfill, if we willingly choose to trust Him and so follow His Ways above our own.

Choose to Know Holy Spirit

You must choose to want to know Holy Spirit. You can freely choose to know Holy Spirit and believe He is with you and is arranging your circumstances to bring you into your Creatively Designed destiny. He will never force you to do what you do not want to do. He is the gentle and loving side of The Father's personality. He is always coming beside you and wooing you to have relationship with Him. Because you may presently be in a painful situation, you may not believe this right now. However, if you choose to give Holy Spirit an opportunity to be your friend, He will be a friend who never leaves you.

Holy Spirit is tender-hearted and can be easily hurt, offended, or grieved by your ongoing rejection of Him when He is trying to get you to respond to His Love and Truth. If you continue in this pattern with no turning to Him, He eventually just quietly leaves you and you won't even know it. He will never, never force you to do anything you do not want to do. But remember He is always ready to come to you to help you, if you sincerely call on Him to come and stay with you forever. You can count on this.

Just know True and Living God always comes to people to make Himself known to them. He especially comes to them in their times of distress. He comes to you wanting to be your friend, and helper, and adviser. Choose to step out, even in your fear, and especially when you are so very afraid. Honestly ask Him to come to you and be your friend and helper. He is always listening. Also choose to stop focusing on yourself and your pain and problems. Tell Holy Spirit you are sorry for not coming to Him for help. Tell Him you need a friend and you want Him to be your friend forever. He is a person as you are. You are made in God's Image and Likeness. So you have the same feelings Holy Spirit has: love, hate for evil, grief, joy, pain, rejection, peace, justice. These feelings are not wrong or bad. They are part of who you are because Supreme God made you in His Image and Likeness and so you have the same feelings of Holy Spirit, Jesus, and your Father in Heaven.

If you ask Holy Spirit to know things about yourself and your circumstances, He may show you things where you were wrong in what you did that also hurt other people, and as well hurt yourself more than you realize. When He shows you, ask Him to forgive you and help you not to do this again. If you are truly sincere in admitting you sinned against Him and others, and yourself and truly want to be forgiven, He instantly forgives you and cleanses you from all sin against Him and other people, and yourself. Read 1 John 1:5-10 in the New Testament for assurance that you are forgiven when you admit you are wrong in what you thought, or said, or did that hurt other people, yourself, and Living God who Loves you beyond your comprehension.

We must all truly humble ourselves before Almighty God admitting that we need Him to help us. We must be honest with ourselves and admit when we are wrong in what we are doing. More than anything else, Living God draws close to you the moment you admit you are wrong and so ask Him to help you. Your honest confession of being wrong and asking to be forgiven, immediately draws Him close to you to be with you and help you. Believe Holy Spirit is right there with you; and then talk to Him in your very own words. He hears what you say in the very way He knows you. You don't need to copy someone else's words or prayers to God. Holy Spirit wants to hear your voice and your heart talking with Him just as He hears the way others talk to Him in the way He knows them. Every person is uniquely Designed by Creative God to know Him and hear Him. God purposely chose to Create people uniquely different in how they respond to Him and how they live their lives being directed by Him. No one else is exactly like you, nor are you exactly like them. So you don't have to try to be like someone else. Just be who Living God made you to be. He likes you and enjoys who He Designed you to be. You should too. Allow yourself or give yourself permission to be who He Created you to be.

When you choose to surrender yourself entirely to True and Living God asking Him to be your friend and helper, He will come to be with you. He will be your forever friend, helper and lover. If your family is broken and is not with you, know Holy God is the mother, father, brothers, sisters, friends you may have never had in the way you needed them to be. He will bring people into your life to be to you the parents, siblings, friends you may have never had, but truly want.

Don't ever dismiss that Holy God is a God of restoration and reconciliation. He can easily bring families who have been broken apart and so separated for whatever reason together in harmony to love and help each other. This is truly God's way for families to live with each other. Do not ever give up asking God to restore your family. He Loves them more than you could ever love them. Because Holy Spirit is helping you to truly know Him, you can know in truth He will help your family to know Him because you are asking Him to make Himself known to them. Trust Holy Spirit. Believe He hears your prayers and is answering them in the way that is best for all concerned. This may take longer than you would like. But always remember God is never late. He is always right on time. I share with you something an old lady who knew God well and walked with Him for years said to me when I was young and impatient in wanting to see God answer my prayers. She said to me, "The greatest thing I know about God is that He is the slowest man I know. But He is always on time." This should bring a smile to your face. It did to mine.

Only you can decide what you truly want. When you decide how you will act and respond in your circumstances, then your life will follow that path, good or evil. Living God says choose Life, which is relationship with Him. If you choose good, which is a living relationship with Him, then you will be joyful and successful in all your ways both now and forever.

I have chosen throughout my life to surrender to Living God, even when I didn't want to. But I learned when I surrendered to Him and asked Him to help me, He came to me and helped me. He has never left me and I never want to leave Him. He is my best friend. I can count on Holy Spirit to be with me and help me in every situation I face.

I share my personal God-stories with you to encourage you that no matter what your circumstances, God is there to help you as He did for me when I had no one to help me. He continues coming to me to help me, because when He comes to me, I respond to Him by listening to Him and obeying what He is revealing to me. As I matured in learning to know Holy Spirit, I recognized the times He came to me during my life and was with me and helping me when I did not know it was Him who was with me and was helping me.

I will venture to say there was a time or times when you knew something good happened in your circumstances that was beyond your ability to understand, but deep down inside you, you wondered if it was God. You felt a flicker of hope and sensed someone was with you or helping you. Something told you there was no way this could have happened unless it was God or His angels. You have always wondered about this, but you have never told anyone. This could have been Holy Spirit coming to you. Ask Holy Spirit about this circumstance and if this was truly Him who came to help you. The devil can come to you disguised as God to get you to follow his lies This is another reason why you must read and know what God says in The Holy Bible. This is how you learn what is truth and what is the devil trying to get you to *think* that he is helping you. You can also ask a trusted person you know who faithfully and truthfully knows Holy Spirit to help you know if this was truly God who came to you.

Ask Holy Spirit to show you a time or the times He was there with you and came to you in your distress. He will help you remember and will tell you the exact time or times He was there with you. He will bring to your remembrance details you have forgotten, but He has not forgotten. When you remember, with His help, a time or times He was there for you, stop and thank Him with your whole heart.

The Lord of Life was with you all during the times you felt and thought you were all alone and no one cared about you or what you were suffering. He heard your cries, saw your tears, and heard the silent groans and sighs that erupted out from you as a silent language that had no human words. Yet, God Almighty heard your silent groans as an audible language.

The Lord of Creation knew you so well He knew the time would come when you knew you could not go on the way you are any longer. He has been waiting for you to turn to Him. Living God is standing before you with open arms and an open heart of Love wanting you to turn to Him so He can teach You His Ways of Living so that you never again want to go back to old and evil ways that were seeking to devour you. There is no where you can go or anything you can do that separates you from your Creator. Only you can choose to separate yourself from Him.

As you read my God-stories in this book, please stop and take the time to consider before Holy Spirit your own life from childhood to right now. You too have your own God-stories even though you may not yet recognize them. Stop and think about your life so far. Take time right now to review your life, no matter how difficult or painful it is or has been. You may not yet recognize that all that has happened in your life are your God-stories. Even the pain you experienced that you didn't understand and did not want to happen is shaping you to become who God Created you to be to fulfill the Creative destiny He Designed in you before you were born. Your circumstances, no matter how painful, only arrange the way, the place, and the time for you to fulfill your destiny. Your circumstances prepare you to fulfill your destiny even though at this time in your life you can't see how. This is why you need to learn to trust and follow Holy Spirit. I am 81 years young. So I can truthfully prove that my life-long painful circumstances prepared me to write what I am writing for you, so you can also fulfill your destiny your Creator planned for you to fulfill.

I am not sharing my God-stories with you to make you think I am someone special to God. You too are someone special to God and He wants you to know this. Please search deep within yourself and think back over your circumstances. Look with new eyes of understanding and consider that Holy Spirit has always been with you directing your circumstances even though you were not aware He was right there with you. He was always right beside you even during those times you thought God didn't care and neither did anyone else. Just know that He was right there with you. If you do not yet see this, the time will come when you truly understand this, and you will forever thank Him for being with you even when you didn't recognize He was there with you.

The Lord is letting me know at this time in my life that what I am writing in this book, *Live Creatively - Fulfill Your Designed Destiny,* is to leave a legacy for upcoming generations. Supreme God is Faithful to all generations. Each generation believes they can outdo the preceding generation. However, each generation needs the preceding generation in working together to fulfill what Holy God initially designed for His Creations. The former generations as well need the present generation to proceed forward in carrying out what Holy Spirit taught them during their lifetime on earth so all generations work together in cooperation with Supreme God to fulfill His predetermined and unending plan for human beings to cooperate with Him in ruling His Creations.

True Authority

What is True Authority?

Holy and Supreme God rules over His Creation using a Righteous Government set-up. Government on earth conforms to how the Government in Heaven functions. According to Genesis 1:26-28; Psalm 8; Hebrews 2:5-8 in the Holy Bible, Supreme God of all Creation Created human beings in His Likeness and Image and gave them dominion to rule over the earth and the heavens. Therefore, human beings have Supreme God's legal and rightful Authority to rule and govern God's Creation in cooperation with Him. God's Righteous Government includes angels, heavenly beings, and human beings whom He Created and Designed to rule with Him in Governing His Creation.

However, the Bible reveals one-third of God's angels who were Created with free wills chose to betray their Creator's holy purpose for Creating them, which is to help Him rule His Righteous Government. They purposefully chose to attempt to dethrone Holy God from His position of Righteous Authority over them to set up their own government or kingdom to rule over. These rebellious angels truly believe they can overthrow God's Kingdom to govern or rule over a kingdom of their own making. God calls them fools. These evil angels do not understand that even if they could overthrow Supreme God's Rule of Power and Authority, they would not have the ability to stay in rule because they were Created by Him with limited knowledge and power; therefore, they can never sustain permanent rule. This is why there is chaos and upheaval on the earth today. These rebellious angels are fiercely opposing Holy God and His Righteous Kingdom of Authority or Government.

The Created angels who chose to rebel against their Creator are attempting to usurp or take away your God-given right to rule the earth and the heavens. You must truly learn through studying your Bible that these evil angels who rebelled against their Creator are lying and deceiving you to get you to join their coup to overthrow God's Holy Kingdom Rule of Authority over His Creation. They want to overthrow and take over God's Kingdom so that they can have a kingdom to rule over using their perverted thinking and evil ways. Just know, God laughs at them.

Why God Allows Evil

You are probably asking the age-old question, *Why does God allow evil to have a place to harass His Creations?* The only plausible answer is that Supreme God sovereignly chose to Create angels and human beings with free wills to choose as they desire to live or exist because Perfect Love does not demand its own way. Perfect Love allows free will choices. If you are not permitted to choose how and when you want to do something, you are forced to do whatever the one dictating to you requires you to do. Supreme God is not a dictator. He freely chose to Create angels and human beings with a free will to choose how they desire to live and act. Creative God desires that His angels and human beings use their free will to choose to be faithful and obedient to His Perfect Love and Holy Will. However, Perfect Love demands Justice.

One of Holy God's Created angels decided to use his free will to rebel against his Creator and to influence other angels and human beings to follow his rebellion. Sadly, human beings fell for his plausible lies and they too rebelled against their Creator. This angel's free will decision to rebel against Supreme God's Perfect Love, Rule and Authority, forced Holy God to Create a time system to bring this rebellious angel and all those who choose to follow him to a final end because Perfect Love and Authority demands Justice. Therefore, Sovereign God Created a time system within His Eternal Design. Supreme God's ingenious Plan was to set a boundary around the devil and limit the operation of his evil activity. Time designates limits. Time sets a perimeter around this evil angel so that he cannot operate his evil forever, but only for a specific or allotted time designated by Supreme God, who is Sovereign and therefore limitless in ultimate rule and dominion. The devil can never overthrow God's Holy and Righteous Kingdom, but he never stops trying. He continues to lie and deceive people into following his evil plots to overthrow Supreme God.

Created angels and human beings are Designed by their Creator to exist forever. Therefore, this angel's free will rebellion against Holy God required Sovereign and Creative God to prepare a final abode for him and the angels who followed his rebellion. According to Matthew 25:41 and Revelation 20:10 the *lake of fire* known as *hell* was prepared for the devil and the evil angels who followed him; as well as, for anyone who chooses to join this rebellion against Holy God. *Hell* is their final dwelling place. You have a free will to choose how you live your creatively ordained life on earth. If you choose to use your free will to follow the devil's lies, you too will receive the same end and living place as he does. How you choose to use your free will confirms your eternal dwelling place either the *lake of fire* known as *hell* where you will live with the devil and his lies forever or Heaven where Holy God and those who follow Him live in peace and safety and good that can never be eradicated or eliminated. How will you choose?

Yet, there are angels who chose to remain faithful to their Creator. They faithfully and obediently serve their Creator to minister to human beings who inherit Jesus' Salvation from sin. Go to your Bible and look up Psalm 103:19-22, Psalm 104:1-

4 and Hebrews 1:14 to learn how these holy angels respond to Living God's directions to go and help people on earth in response to their prayers or communication with Him. As you read the stories in the Bible pay attention to how God's holy angels are involved in people's circumstances. Human beings are Created to have reciprocal or mutual relationship with their Creator. Angels are not relational in the same way human beings are. Angels are made to be obedient servants of Living God. Yet they can choose to rebel against their Creator.

Angels are not Created to have legal authority or power to sovereignly rule God's Creation. Therefore, these rogue or rebellious angels must persuade human beings to agree with them and get them to join in their sinister plots to usurp God's Righteous Authority and Power. Evil angels get away with their sinister tactics because people continue to allow them to influence their lives. These evil angels fool you by their believable lies that convince you to join them and follow their dastardly deeds. Because the devil does not have legal authority to rule the earth and God's Creations, he has to get human beings, who do have legal authority to rule and govern God's Creations, to agree with his evil plot to overthrow God's Authority. The devil uses the pride of rebellious human beings who side with him to get what he wants. You must know in truth that these rebellious angels are unrelentingly attempting to get you to follow their sinister plots so you side with them in overthrowing God's Holy Way of Governing His Creations so they can take over ruling the earth and the heavens. The devil is a master at deceiving you to agree with his evil plots to overthrow God's Righteous Government and Kingdom. Getting you to agree with his evil plan to overthrow Supreme God is his perverted way of taking revenge against Holy God for dismissing him and throwing him out of Heaven.

You will learn in all the books The Lord of Creation asked me to write and publish for Him that the only way these evil entities will be completely stopped from their sinister plot to rule or govern God's Creation is when redeemed people go forth with His Authority and take the dominion to rule the earth and the heavens in cooperation with Him and His holy angels who do not rebel against their Creator.

This how-to, hands-on book you are reading instructs you how to cooperate with Living God so that you rule with Him thus taking dominion of the earth and the heavens as He Created you to do. Pay attention to what The Lord reveals in His Holy Word, The Bible, as to how you are to take your Rightful Authority to rule and have dominion of the earth and the heavens as God Almighty has legally appointed you to do.

Holy God will never override your free will He Designed in you. He has Sovereignly chosen to cooperate with human beings He Created in His own Image and Likeness to whom He gave Holy dominion of the earth and the heavens. Therefore, you have legal Authority to join with Him in bringing these evil entities, who oppose their Creator, to their final end **if** you willingly choose to cooperate with Living God and His Holy angels in bringing these rebellious angels to their final end. Supreme God is counting on you to cooperate with Him in eradicating these rebellious angels. Supreme and Holy God will never do this alone or without your cooperation. This is why these rebellious angels have not been wiped out by Him before now.

In fact and in truth, Holy God is waiting on you to take dominion in your personal circumstances by using the Authority Jesus gave you from His Father in Heaven at the time He ascended from earth and went back into Heaven to sit at His Father's Right Hand. Read Matthew 28:18-20 and Mark 16:15-19;

Ephesians 1:20-23 in your Bible. When each person rules or takes dominion within their own sphere of influence by using their God- appointed authority as described in Matthew 28:18-20 and Mark 16:15-18, then legal and authentic dominion takes place on earth.

Take time right now to pick up your Bible and read Matthew 28, Mark 16, and Luke 24 to recognize that Holy God authorized you to take dominion of the earth and the heavens. Some Bibles only have the short ending in Mark 16, so be sure and read the longer ending in Mark. Then search your Bible to find examples where people used Holy God's Authority in their circumstances and how He delivered them from the strong hand of their enemies.

Through your obedience to follow Living God's instructions, you too can learn how to use God's Authority He has given you to use in your own personal circumstances. Each circumstance you face is different. Therefore, you must learn how to cooperate with Holy Spirit to know what to do in each circumstance you face. He is your Counselor and Advisor who leads and guides you to know what to do in every situation you face, **if** you consult Him. He is waiting for you to come to Him and ask Him what to do in each situation you face and how to do it.

Supreme God allows evil to turn people to Him because Holy and Supreme God gave legal authority to human beings to rule His Creation in cooperation with Him. He will never overthrow these rebellious angels on His own and without the cooperation of human beings. This is the reason you see all the wars going on in the Bible and to this very day. Holy God Supreme is still waiting for people He Created like Himself to carry out and do what He Created them to do, which is to have rule and dominion of the earth and the heavens in cooperation with Him. Know in truth that you can choose to cooperate with Living and Almighty God and His holy angels in eradicating these evil angels. Will you?

If you are waiting for Living God to do it all for you, forget it! He Designed you with a *free will* to choose as you will. *Free will* includes taking full responsibility in directing the course of your life with Holy God' help, and with the help of other people in your life. Your *free will* choices determine your present and eternal outcome. Know that choosing God's Holy Will over your own human will cause you to suffer at this time on earth. However, the eternal rewards you will receive for suffering for Jesus' sake will never end. Choose wisely with God's help.

You must look at the BIG picture or overall outcome for the decisions you make at this time of your existence on earth. You could look at your journey on earth as a school in learning how to live with Eternal and Living God forever. See yourself during your existence on earth as being in Supreme God's school of learning. As in all schools of learning, you are given tests to see how well you learned your lessons. God is no different. He presents you with tests all through your life on earth so you can see with understanding how far you have come in listening to Him and obeying Him. When you see that you are not quite where you should be in listening to and obeying Living God, you can adjust *your thinking* to line up with His perfect Will for you. Then, through your obedience to Him in all your ways, He rewards you both now on earth, and even more when you graduate to be with Him forever.

Each person has their own personal journey in knowing Living God of Truth. Never stop your quest in knowing God of all Creation as outlined in your Bible. Be willing to choose to go forward in God's School of Learning. He gives you His Power, Strength, and Wisdom you need to do this. Go for it!

You will never regret your *free will* decision. I am not saying that it will be easy, but it is well worth the choice you freely make. The Lord Himself will hand you His holy diploma when you graduate to eternity that promotes you to live in everlasting peace, joy, and rest. He will take you to the head of the class in eternity where you can continue learning how He functions in cooperation with you and the entire company in Heaven. Learning about this fathomless God of Creation is never ending.

How enjoyable it will be to continue our eternal journey learning together how to cooperate with Holy God and His holy beings so we expand in knowing the way Supreme God's Creatively Designed Kingdom is ever expanding. Praise be to God forever and ever!

Another secret Supreme God shared with me that you will be interested in knowing is how music restrains His unlimited power that could destroy everything He Created. This secret is written in Chapter 10 in the book *Shekinah Glory Reveals Wisdom, The Voice of The Lord Speaks,* by Betsy Fritcha. This holy revelation gives you insight into why God is counting on you to take dominion of the earth, and why He doesn't just take over and do it for you. There is so much more to learn and absorb in all of the books The Lord asked me to write and publish for Him. These books are written to enlighten and expand your understanding to know how Supreme God ultimately overthrows those trying to oppose Him and His Righteous Government. These books also mature you in knowing and doing The Lord's Will to fulfill your God-Designed destiny that expands forever.

At this time of global upheaval and unrest because of evil's clandestine or hidden and secret agendas and operations, The Lord is clearly drawing a line of demarcation and a dividing line between those who truly belong to Him in personal relationship, from those who outrightly oppose Him, which includes those people who *think* they know Him. However, those who *think* they know Holy God, but do not have a living relationship with Him, are only siding with The Lord for personal advantage to gain power, control, and earthly wealth. Those who choose to join with these evil entities to gain power control will also meet the same end as these evil entities, which is not good.

Therefore, is it strategically important to stay in constant communication with Living God. From your mutual relationship with The Lord, He protects you and keeps you from all evil plots set against you to get you to turn away from Supreme God. Your personal and ongoing relationship with True and Living God keeps you from joining these evil entities and their false authority to gain power, influence, and wealth. By your personal and living relationship with Holy God of Truth and Wisdom, you remain free from these evil influences. When you daily meet with Him, He Blesses you with Holy Truth that brings you Peace and contentment in the midst of all the upheaval on the earth. You, as well, gain His compelling assurance to know what to do in your every circumstance.

All through The Holy Bible Almighty and Supreme God executes Powerful Actions that display Him as Almighty and Supreme. There are times when The Lord intervenes on earth to disrupt the evil plots against people because these evil powers of darkness are too strong for human beings to overcome on their own. At these times, Almighty God of Power sovereignly comes to the aid of human beings and overcomes their enemies who are too strong for them. However, most of the time, The Lord works in cooperation with human beings to overcome and destroy their enemies. He does this through those who are calling on Him to help them. This is why staying in constant communication with Living and Almighty God in personal relationship is so necessary. He relates to you what to do in your situations so you know how to overcome evil plots that are set against you.

As you diligently read your Bible, you discover the ways Supreme God comes to the aid of His people who cry out to Him in their distress. These Bible events help you to recognize the ways in which The Lord always answers the people who cry out to Him for help. These Bible accounts train you to recognize how you too can overcome your enemy's plots against you. God has a part and you have a part. When you do your part, God sees this and comes to do the part you cannot do because of evil entities who are too strong for you to fight on your own. The stories in the Bible are so much better than any fiction movie you could ever see or any book you could ever read. Almighty God is always working with you for your good; that is, **if** you listen and follow the ways God Almighty works with you to gain the lasting victory over your enemies.

God reveals in Genesis in chapter 1, which the first book in the Bible, that He Created Adam and Eve in His very Likeness and Image so they could rule and have dominion of the earth and over every Created thing He made to exist upon the earth and in earth's atmosphere.

The Old Testament scenarios reveal that Supreme God placed His True Authority upon His selected prophets who carried His Holy Word of Authority into the situations people were facing for His Holy Purpose of defeating the enemies plaguing the people. God of all Might, Power, and Dominion displayed Who He *is*, through what He gave His prophets, who obeyed Him, to do and speak to the people who were being unmercifully attacked by evil entities. Supreme God's holy angels who chose to remain true to their Creator were as well involved with His holy prophets so that Supreme God's Sovereign Plan to rule the earth and the heavens with Righteous Authority was displayed.

The New Testament writings reveal our Father in Heaven sent His only Son, Jesus to earth to suffer and die by shedding His innocent Blood on a humanly designed cross. Jesus' obedient sacrifice redeemed sinful people back into the good graces of their Father in Heaven. When Jesus rose from the dead, as His Father said He would, He departed from earth to sit at His Father's Right Hand of Authority ruling with Him in heavenly places. As it is written in the New Testament, Holy God empowers those who have accepted His Son's free gift of Salvation from sin and evil by giving them His Righteous Authority to rule on earth with His help. When you willingly acknowledge and freely accept Jesus' Holy Salvation from sin, evil, and death you are seated with Jesus at His Father's Right Hand (place of power and rulership) ruling the universe in cooperation with The Father's Authority. When you choose to obey True God's Holy Sovereign Plan to rule with His Authority and Power, you have righteous authority over evil powers of darkness and evil.

There are many, many stories in the Bible which reveal how Holy God works in cooperation with human beings and holy heavenly beings to stop the sinister plots of evil powers. Evil entities are always trying to overthrow Almighty God by getting people to take part with them in their evil ways. No fiction book or movie could ever relay the way Almighty God reveals Himself in the Bible. You will read of adventures with God that defy all imagination.

In your Bible are true to life accounts of the clash between good and evil. You can use your concordance to find the names and the actual accounts of conflict between Holy God and evil beings. Look up Nephilim, Anak and the giants, the exploits of Moses and David to see how these evil entities were always opposing God and His people. These accounts will surely enlighten your adventurous soul to know how God proves Himself over and over and over that He is Supreme and Almighty in Power and Dominion.

Here is an assignment for you: look up these names in your concordance: Abraham, Moses, Elijah, David, Jesus, Paul and whoever else you want to know about in the Bible. Then look up all the places in your Bible where these people are mentioned and read the full accounts of their adventures with Almighty God. Their adventures with Living and Almighty God are recorded for you to learn how to overcome your enemies. You may also want to invest in getting a topical Bible or Bible Dictionary to find where things and people are mentioned in your Bible so you can pursue your journey to know Living God and how He lives and moves among people on earth, and also how He operates in Heaven. This is the way you can learn on your own, with Holy Spirit's help, anything you want to know about Living and Almighty God and how He cooperates with people on earth.

Authority Operates Through Love

God's Authority operates through His Perfect Love. As you pour out Holy God's Love in your divinely arranged circumstances, His Authority falls and is seen and known for the good of all. Expressing His Perfect Love in your personal situations allows Holy Authority to operate through you which changes things for the good of all concerned.

Ask The Lord for His Love to be seen through you. When His Love is demonstrated through your holy words and actions, you are using His Authority He gave you to act in

His Name. When His Holy Compassion comes on you, His Love flows through you with Authority that changes things. **You have no Authority if you have no Love.** Authority issues from Love.

I painfully learned through a God-arranged circumstance that I was not properly using God's Authority that is attached to His Love. Because I didn't properly use *both* His Love and Authority in this situation, I was greatly come against by opposing forces stemming from evil and unholy spirits who were disrupting what The Lord wanted me to do in cooperation with others in this place. I *was* acting in Love. However, I *was not* using God's Holy Authority in this situation. Love and Authority must operate together so God is seen as a Good God who has the best interest toward all involved.

When I came running to The Lord in my pain from being come against, He lovingly, yet sternly spoke these words to me:

"Exercise your Authority! Exercise your Authority! In all you do and speak for Me, exercise your Authority! My Authority is upon you when I send you into a situation or you are in any situation you face. Act like it! No matter how you are treated, you must respond with My Love and Authority so people cannot say I didn't Love them or have their best interest at My Mind and Heart."

During this time of great upheaval on earth, The Lord is arranging people's circumstances that bring His Love and Authority into a variety of situations. He puts people in dire situations trusting them to demonstrate His Love and Authority so people know His intent toward them is Love and Life not destruction and death. The Lord wants you to choose to use His Love and Authority in your personal situations. His Purpose for you to use His Love and Authority in your every situation is for people to observe Almighty God and the way He always does what is best for all concerned in each particular situation. Exercising Holy Authority with Love shuts down evil operations set against The Lord and against you and the people you are among.

Living God's Word of Truth expressed with His Love and Authority may cause you to be greatly come against by evil sources. However, remember Jesus said that before they hated you, they hated Him because He exposed their sin and revealed to them what is truly in their hearts. Listen and heed Jesus' words:

When the world hates you, remember it hated Me before it hated you. The world would love you if you belonged to it, but you don't. I chose you to come out of the world, and so it hates you. Since they persecuted Me, naturally they will persecute you. The people of the world will hate you because you belong to Me, for they don't know God who sent Me. (John 16:18-26)

Because God of Truth lives in you, when you develop a personal relationship with Him, He can then speak His Word of Truth to you and show you what to do in your personal circumstances to demonstrate His Love and Authority. As you continually draw near to The Lord of Truth to learn what to do in each situation you face, He teaches you His Ways for that particular situation so that His Love and Truth is demonstrated for the good of all.

Know in truth that when you obey God your Father in Heaven and agree with Him to show His Love and also demonstrate His Righteous Authority in your situation in the same way Jesus obeyed and demonstrated His Father's Love and Authority in the situations He faced, you are demonstrating God's Love which is attached to His Authority. Because Jesus demonstrated His Father's Holy Love and Righteous

Authority in His circumstances, He was greatly come against. You too will be greatly come against for showing God's Love and Authority in your situations. At these times, you are not to retaliate and respond in anger at any time. Knowing how Jesus responded in these kinds of situations, immensely helped me to learn how to act when I faced these kinds of situations. Yet, I know that I could never suffer to the extent that Jesus suffered. No person could ever suffer to the extent our Savior did. I say to Him with all my heart, "Thank You Jesus! You demonstrated Your Love for me in that while I was still sinning, You Loved me and gave up Your Life unto death on a horrible cross for me to give me a way out of my dilemma. I love You so much for demonstrating Your Love to me in Ways that are beyond my comprehension."

Holy Spirit's abiding Presence living in you teaches you truth. Right now, pick up your Bible and read the book of 1 John in the New Testament. It is a short book. You will learn in this book that Holy Spirit is your teacher who teaches you truth. He does not lie because He cannot lie. Let the truth in this New Testament book, 1 John, sink deep into your heart and mind so you know with no doubting that you can trust Holy Spirit to teach you truth.

I am going to share with you my personal experience when I was learning to know Living God in personal relationship more than I already knew Him. I was so hungry to know Him in deeper ways. I was searching everywhere to know how to know Him in deeper ways. My friends were going to all kinds of conferences where The Lord was being revealed in profound ways. I so wanted to go to these conferences with them. My circumstances never seemed to align when these conferences were offered. I still had young children at home so I needed to be home to care for them. I was getting pretty upset because I could not go to these conferences to learn more about The Lord. But I never stopped having my personal time alone with God.

During one of my times alone with The Lord, He showed me in the book of 1 John that I didn't need to go to these conferences to know Him in deeper ways. He said to me through 1 John 2:20, 27 that Holy Spirit lived in me and was my teacher who He would teach me all things; and what He taught me would be truth and not be a lie. Instantly, I had a settled peace and began to delve into my Bible to learn more about the God I was so wanting to know. I used every free time I had to get into my Bible and diligently study who Living God was and how He lived and moved among people. I came to know with understanding that studying my Bible to know truth about Him was the best way I could ever truly know God in the way He wanted me to know Him. The Lord taught me to know that by not being in all these conferences, I was not being taught by human personalities how they know God. He showed me that by being in His Holy Presence, He Himself was teaching me to know Him in the way He wanted me to know Him because of the way He Designed me to know Him.

However, there were times He allowed me to go to conferences of His choosing for His Holy Purposes. But He had first taught me to know Him personally in relationship and through His Word in the Bible. He also brought people of His choosing into my life through books and other ways to enhance what He was teaching me. Then, He allowed me to go to selected conferences to confirm to me what was being taught in these conferences He had already taught me.

When The Lord teaches you truth through personal relationship with Him, you will never forget the way in which He explained and taught you truth. No one can ever take away from you what The Lord personally taught you. It is indelibly ingrained within you. Granted you can learn from other people who know God. However, the best way to personally know True God in the way He uniquely Designed you to know Him is by spending time alone with Him in relationship and through studying your own Bible. This is how you learn to discern truth from lies, and The Lord's Voice from the voices of human wills, or the devil's voice, and even your own voice. My obedience to The Lord to spend time with Him to learn His Ways has been the bedrock or foundation I have built my life upon. I continually thank Him for teaching me and showing me how to really know Him and His Ways for my life.

When you know with no doubting that you have been redeemed by Jesus' Precious Blood Sacrifice, you can know in truth that you are the righteousness of God in Christ Jesus, your Lord, who has given you authority to use against wickedness and evil. Therefore, by an act of your will you must freely choose to use God's holy Authority and Love He has authorized you to use against all the works of evil. You must know that using God's Holy Authority and Love brings His Righteous Kingdom on earth to be done as it is being done in Heaven and also stops evil beings from stealing what Holy God has endowed within you for your good. When you truly believe and accept this truth, then you can go forth in peace and joy using His Authority and Love to stop evil powers of darkness from operating in every circumstance you face. When you use Holy Authority and Love in your circumstances, you are making known to evil powers that Supreme God is Almighty and the Supreme God of all Creation.

God's Will and Your Circumstances

There are many circumstances recorded in the New Testament in the Bible where Jesus went to His Father to learn what He was to do in each and every circumstance He faced in His life on earth. Pay attention to how Jesus acted in the situations He found Himself. Always remember Jesus was sent to earth in human flesh by His Father in Heaven to be an example to those on earth who would be willing to be His disciples. You are Jesus' disciple if you freely choose to be His disciple in doing what Holy Spirit reveals to you to do in in your situation in the same way Jesus acted in His circumstances while He lived on earth in human flesh. These examples are written in your Bible. To be a disciple is to be an imitator of the one whom you choose to follow.

You must learn, as Jesus had to learn from His Father, that you are not to go anywhere or do anything until you know it is The Father's timing for you to go into a situation and do what He is asking you to do in this situation. You must learn from Holy Spirit when and where to go and be in a situation by listening to Him. Then you can go in obedience to His Voice and do what He gives you to say and do for that particular situation. If you choose to act by your own will, you are on your own. God is not backing you. To be on your own, is a precarious or dangerous place to be. You are an open target for the devil or disobedient human wills to attack you to stop what The Lord wants to do through you in your circumstance for the good of all involved in this situation. Because Jesus spent much time with His Father in Heaven, He learned how to know when He was to go and be in a situation. You too can learn this by taking the time to be with Holy God in relationship asking Him questions about your situation and also reading your Bible to learn how others faced their situations with God's help.

There will be times in your life and circumstances that others may prod you to go places and do things that they believe are for you to do. But, be careful not to rush to go anywhere or do anything until you seek Living God to know His Will and timing for you to go and be in any situation. Because you totally belong to The Lord, you are not to operate by the world's standards or ways. You must know The Lord's Voice of Truth in the way He speaks to you through your personal relationship together. Then, you will know when and where to go and what to do in every situation you find yourself.

When you are reading in your Bible about the circumstances Jesus faced, take the time to pay attention to the times when people were trying to kill Him and how He acted. Concentrate on the times Jesus knew from His Father, that it was not yet His time to do what people were asking Him to do.

Jesus had to rely on His Father's timing to know when to go into a situation. He knew when to go into a situation because He spent much time in His Father's Presence listening to His Father's Voice speaking to Him and directing Him when to go and be in a situation. Then Jesus went and did what His Father related to Him to do. Stop right now and look up in your Bible these two accounts that reveal Jesus knew from His Father in Heaven the timing for Him to go and do His Father's Will in these situations. In the first account in John 2:1-12 there was a wedding at Cana that Jesus was asked to attend. In the second account in John 11:1-44 Lazarus Jesus close friend died and He was asked to come and raise Lazarus from death. Jesus did not go and act in either of these situations until He knew from His Father in Heaven it was His Fathers' time for Him to go and act in these situations. Jesus also knew from His Father, the exact place and time for Him to die and be resurrected from death, and then to ascend back into Heaven. Read in your Bible: Matthew 26-27; Mark 14-15; Luke 22-23; John 18-19.

As you continue to read and study your Bible, closely examine the circumstances and the exact timing Jesus went to do what His Father gave Him to accomplish in the situation. Pay close attention to how Jesus acted when He found Himself in situations where He was hated and people were literally trying to kill Him. Through Jesus' examples, you too can learn how to know God's exact time for you to be in a situation. It is very important for you to learn from Jesus how He knew when to go into a situation. When you obey True God to go in His timing using His Holy Authority wrapped in His Love, no one can touch you outside of God's Will for you in that situation. God, your Father in Heaven, protects you because He sent you to a certain place in His perfect timing for this situation.

There may be times, however, when God of Truth allows you to go and do your own will in a situation to teach you how important it is to obey Him in all your circumstances. Nevertheless, He is watching over you to protect you. When you experience the absence of God going with you because you are doing what you want to do, then hopefully you learn not to ever again go anywhere without asking God if you are to go. Or at least you should learn this. You do have a free will to use as you choose. The Lord never overrides the free will He endowed within you and all people. Always ask The Lord to go with you when you know from Him that you are to go and bring His Presence and His Words into a situation. Then you can be sure He is with you and helping you.

Also, keep in your mind and in your heart that The Lord may take you into circumstances of His choosing to teach you what you could not have learned in any other way. I share with you a personal circumstance where The Lord truly arranged for me to be. I knew from The Lord that I was to be in this place. I went in obedience to The Lord. While I was in this place, I discovered that I had walked into a den of evil unknown to me. After I came out of this circumstance, I yelled very loudly at The Lord saying, "Lord, I asked you to never let me be deceived into doing something I am not to do. I asked You to keep me from going where I am not to be and from doing what is not from You for me to do. Why did you not stop me from going into this situation?" I was completely unnerved and totally upset that I found myself in this situation that I was invited to go by people I trusted. I was totally baffled as to why I allowed myself to be in this place. The Lord gently and lovingly said to me, *"How else would you learn how evil operates?"* His Words to me brought me comfort and peace. I knew He had arranged this circumstance so I could learn what I could not have learned in any other way. This circumstance surely made an indelible impression in me that I will never forget. I praise and thank God to this day for His protection of me in this learning experience. I learned from going through this experience something that I could not have learned in any other way. I also recognized that He protects me in these learning situations. To God alone be all Glory and Honor!

The Lord is in the process of training you for this very hour in your life on earth, so you can stand with His Love and Authority saying and doing what He is asking You to do in your personal situations you face. It is your personal relationship with The Lord that prepares you to know where to go, when to go, and what to do in your circumstances. Because you have developed your personal relationship with The Lord, you can trust Him to be with you and help you.

The Lord taught me to pay attention in my circumstances. He related to me that in my circumstances His Will is being done even when I may be in circumstances where I would not ordinarily be or where I would choose to be. He instructed me to yield to Him in every circumstance I find myself to get His instructions for me to do or say in this situation. I learned from Him that My willing obedience to seek Him in an ongoing personal relationship gives Him permission to act in any situation I find myself so His Good Ways are made known in the situation. He let me know that if I obey Him and allow Him to lead me and guide me, He arranges my circumstances to always be in the right place, at the right time, with the right word, among the right people.

God also instructed me that I was not to rely on logic or on my own understanding in any situation I find myself. But rather, I was to depend totally on Holy Spirit by yielding to Him in my circumstances He either arranged for me or I was part of for whatever reason. He related to me that I am not to prepare beforehand what to say or speak before I go into any situation. What I am to do and say in a situation will be given to me at the very time and place I need to know what to do and what to say. At that precise moment, He will give me a boldness to know with certainty what to do and what to say in this situation. What The Lord instructed me to do is based on Jesus' words in Matthew 10:16-20; Luke 12:11- 12.

I have made these words my life's confession:
Trust in The Lord with all your heart, and do not rely on your own insight or understanding. In all your ways acknowledge Him and He will make known the path you are to be on. (Proverbs 3:5-6)

I say to myself continually, "Lord, I trust You with all my heart. I will not rely on my own understanding. I choose to allow You to direct me to be in the right place, at the right time, with the right word, among the right people. Thank You."

The Lord further instructed me to keep watch over my mouth so I don't say what I may want to say. When I order my conversation rightly, He is always with me. I am to guard my conversations and keep silent until I know from Him what to say. I am not to go into a situation to do anything unless He lets me know it is His timing for me to go into a situation. I am to keep silent until I know from Him what I am to say in this situation. If I obey Him, He protects me and brings success in what He gives me to say and do in my situation. If I do not obey Him, I am on my own and He is not with me in my situation. Here is a declaration I make over myself continually, "Lord don't let me hold back when I should speak; and don't let me to speak when I should hold back. And let me know the difference in every situation I am in. Thank You."

Another nugget of truth I learned is that when you choose to wholeheartedly obey The Lord to go and be in a situation where He sends you, you will appear to be wrong to the people He sends you to be among. This does not mean that you heard wrong and you shouldn't be in this situation. When The Lord sends you into a situation in answer to people's prayers, the people in this situation have a choice to make. This was true of Jesus too. Look up Luke 4:16-30 where Jesus made Himself known as coming from His Father in Heaven to help people. Jesus was not treated well for speaking what His Father gave Him to say. Yet, there were those who did believe Jesus was sent to them by His Father in Heaven to live among them to help them by showing them the way out of their evil and dire situations. Obedience to your Father in Heaven is always in your best interest and in the best interest of those in your personal situations.

Draw Near to God to Resist the Devil

When you draw near to God to know what to do in your circumstances, you are resisting the devil. This is how Jesus resisted the devil. He lived and acted from every proceeding word His Father spoke to Him. Jesus too, was severely tempted by the devil when Holy Spirit tested Him by sending Him into the desert for 40 days and 40 nights where Jesus had no food, or human contact, and was by Himself. The Father in Heaven was testing Jesus' obedience to do His Father's Will even in the midst of great suffering. When Jesus was at His weakest point, the devil came and tempted Jesus in His human flesh in the same way he tempts all people. Take time to read the full account of Jesus' temptation in Matthew 4:1-11. Jesus personally shows us how to stand against the devil's temptations. At this time of severe testing, Jesus resisted the devil's temptations by speaking His Father's words of Authority.

Jesus knows what it is to be severely tempted by the devil. Jesus learned through His temptation in the desert that He must live by every word that His Father spoke to Him. Through fellowship with His Father in Heaven, Jesus knew that His Father was revealing to Him that this was to be a way of life for him while He lived on earth in human flesh. Therefore, Jesus always drew near to His Father while He lived on earth. He knew that He must continue listening to His Father's words to Him in every situation He faced. Before He made any decision in his circumstances, He always fellowshipped with His Father in Heaven to know His Father's Will for His current situation. By His living relationship with His Father in Heaven, Jesus knew where to go, when to go, and what to say in any situation He faced. Keep in mind *testing* is always to learn obedience to The Father in Heaven in all the situations you face in life.

Jesus learned obedience to His Father through suffering. Take into your heart these words in the Bible:

*In the days of His flesh, **Jesus** offered up prayers and supplications with loud cries and tears, to Him [His Father in Heaven] who was able to save Him from death, and He was heard for His Godly fear. Although He was a Son, He **learned obedience through what He suffered**, and* *being made perfect* [through suffering] *He became the source of eternal Salvation to all who obey Him.*

Consider Him who endured from sinners such hostility against Himself, so that you may not grow weary or fainthearted. In your struggle against sin you have not yet resisted to the point of shedding your blood. (Hebrews 5:7-9; 12:3-4)

You too will have temptations that test you. Just know that you have a choice during your temptations to draw near to your Father in Heaven so you truly know what to do in your situation. Know with true understanding that when you draw near to God and continue to stay in personal relationship with Him, you are resisting the devil. This is the most important life truth you can know and must do in order to have peace, joy, and success in fulfilling your God-ordained destiny.

The most important way to live a holy and successful life is to draw near to God and resist the devil and his lies. The devil knows this. So this is why he is always opposing you. He is unrelentingly attempting to get you to stop using Living God's Holy Authority against him and his evil ways. The Lord God gave you His Authority and Power to use against evil forces coming against you. The devil's purpose and strategy he sets against you is to get you to stop spending time with God so you don't know what to do in your situations in life. When you neglect time alone with The Lord, the devil sees this and comes to you mixing truth with lies; and he puts half-truths into your mind attempting to get you to truly believe that everything he puts into your mind is truth and is from God. Deception is truth mixed with lies. Always remember there is truth in the devil's lies. This is how he gets you to side with him to oppose Holy God. The devil is a master deceiver. His lies are believably realistic. This is why you must know The God of Truth and His Ways. If you do not know what God

Almighty says in the Bible about Himself that is authentic truth, you accept the devil's lies as truth. Not knowing what God says in the Bible causes you to mix the devil's lies with what you *think*. Then you accept what you *think* as truth. Even if you know the Bible well, the devil can put confusion into your mind to get you to believe his lies. Keep in mind that his favorite time to deceive you by tempting you to believe his lies is when you are at the weakest point in your life for whatever reason. This is when He came and tempted Jesus. Read Matthew 4:1-11 again.

The devil is a genius strategist. He takes your questions and contemplations and twists your thinking to get you to accept his deception as truth. But his twisted strategies lead to everlasting death and torment. Death means to be separated from Holy and Supreme God forever with no way to ever again be in a loving and holy relationship with Him.

Holy God promises to never leave you or forsake you. So He is with you no matter your circumstances. However, when you decide for yourself what you will do in a situation, you are choosing to leave His Love and Truth. At this point of freely deciding to go your own way, you are choosing to separate yourself from Almighty and Living God to follow your own path. Just know that at this point you are on your own and you are on dangerous ground. When you repeatedly follow your own choices, you are choosing to separate yourself from God's Love and Truth. If you continue following your own choices, eventually this becomes your final choice decision. When you choose to follow your own will in all your ways above God's Good Ways for you, there is no way you can ever have a peaceful and successful life on earth or an eternal life in Heaven with Holy God and His holy company in Heaven.

The only way you can assure yourself and know you will have a good and prosperous life on earth that extends into eternal living in Heaven is to tell Holy God you are wrong in wanting your own way above His Good and Holy Ways. If you choose to admit to God that you are wrong for wanting your own way above His good ways for your life; then, all you have to do is ask God to forgive you. To truly receive God's forgiveness, you must admit that the Blood of Jesus He shed on the cross redeems you from the devil's lies and forgives your sins, and has the Power to keep you from wanting your own way above God's Holy Ways. When you willingly choose to receive Jesus' Blood Sacrifice that forgives you, immediately The Father in Heaven forgives you and you are back in right standing with Him. But you must freely choose to stay in this holy position of relationship with Living God, and never again willingly despise His Love and Truth. Forgiveness includes repentance. Repentance means to stop what you are doing and do what you should be doing that is good and right in the way Living God reveals true and lasting life in The Holy Bible. If there is no true repentance there is no true forgiveness. Only you can decide while you have breath on earth which way you choose: your own way or Holy God's Way of Truth. Choices establish destiny!

You and every person ever born has to answer to Holy God as to how you fulfilled your ordained destiny that He Creatively Designed in you to fulfill. He endows you with the ability to fulfill your destiny as you willingly choose to follow His instructions that He gives you in The Holy Bible and through your daily personal fellowship with Him. When you carelessly choose to fill your life with other things and dismiss your daily time of fellowship in The Lord's Presence, you form a habit that unknowingly leads you away from God to do your own thing. Therefore, you follow your own will and ultimately do not even know you are doing this. Yet, all the while you are doing your own thing, you choose to truly believe God is with you. If you continue to stay away from studying the Bible and fellowshipping with The Lord, eventually you will lose your salvation. This is a very dangerous position to find yourself when you face The Father in Heaven on the day you stand before Him to give Him an account as to the way you chose to live your life on earth.

Listen to heed the Word of The Lord:

The heart is deceitful above all things, and desperately corrupt; who can understand it? I the Lord search the mind and try the heart, to give to every person according to their ways, according to the fruit of their doings. Jeremiah 17:10

For we shall all stand before the judgement seat of God; for it is written, 'As I live, says the Lord, every knee shall bow to Me, and every tongue shall give praise to God', so each of us shall give account of their ways to God. Romans 14:10-12

Holy Spirit is your helper who teaches you how to resist the devil and his lies. Holy Spirit is your teacher and helper who trains you to know Holy God and His Good Ways for you to live both now in time and for eternity where there is no time, only endless opportunities for continuing success.

When you truly choose to believe that Supreme God's main purpose for mankind is to Glorify Him and enjoy Him forever, you will want to do all it takes to pursue having a living relationship with Him that is forever. Through your personal relationship with Holy God you will know that He Created you so He could enjoy seeing to it that you fulfill the destiny He uniquely Designed in you to fulfill that is forever. Fulfilling your forever destiny is what brings Him enjoyment and Glory.

Take Your Own Personal Journey

There is so much to learn concerning Holy Spirit and His Ways. He is ever moving and His Ways of moving never end. They go on forever. I trust you to take the time to learn how to know True and Living God in an ongoing relationship. Your search and desire to know Him is to be a continuing one; and you should never want to stop. As you will discover during your personal journey-adventure to truly know Him in relationship, your life gets more and more exciting to see what He has in store for you just around the next corner. Choosing to obey what Holy Spirit leads and guides you to do, stirs you up to keep pursuing how to know Him in relationship. When you are experiencing a living relationship with Holy God of Truth, you will never want to go back to your old habits and ways that you have experienced through your personal and painful circumstances, isn't working for you.

My goal in this book, is to inspire you enough to want to have your own personal and active relationship with The Only True and Living God who Loves you with a Love that can never be fully understood. The Lord's goal in my writing this book in obedience to Him is to inspire you to desire seeking after Living God to have your own Love relationship with Him.

What I share with you from my own personal pursuit to know Living God is to help you recognize that God has been with you your entire life. He has been watching over you when you were not recognizing He was there with you all the time taking care of you in your painful circumstances. I want my God-stories to prod you to want to have your very own personal adventures with The Lord of your life. When you have your very own personal journey with Living God, no one can ever dupe you or deceive you or into following false lies and ways. Know that when you venture out to know The God of Love and Truth who knows you inside and out, He is right there beside you training you to know Him in truth. Therefore, you can know that what He teaches you is truth, and no one can ever dissuade (discourage or prevent) you from what The Lord is personally teaching you, unless you allow them to. When you choose daily to spend time alone with Living God, you will develop yourself to know how to have your very own personal and active relationship with the God of Love who Created you to know Him.

I am trusting The Lord to use this book to ignite a Holy Fire in you to pursue having your very own personal and active relationship with Holy God who Created you to have fellowship with Him. I had to truly desire to know Living God in relationship. Because I wanted to know True God in true relationship, I had to do something about having an active relationship with Him. I had to willingly choose to do whatever it took to get to know Him in personal relationship. I did this and I know in truth with no doubting that knowing God in relationship is the only way to live a peaceful and joyful life on earth. Therefore, if you too want to truly know True God in a personal and active relationship, then you must pursue developing your own personal relationship with Him. I know with all knowing that no one can ever take away from me how I personally learned to know Holy God in personal relationship, unless a I let them. But I have made a personal decision this will never happen. So can you.

I share with you the greatest commandment that Holy God gave people so they can enjoy a joyful and successful life. Jesus gave this commandment to His disciples from His Father in Heaven:

The Lord our God, the Lord is one; and you shall love the Lord your God with all your heart, and with all your soul (thinking, will, emotions), *and with all your mind, and with all your strength. The second is this, 'You shall love your neighbor as yourself.' There is no other commandment greater than these.* (Mark 12:28-31)

Make a quality decision to freely choose to trust The Lord of Life to lead you in your search to know Him in personal fellowship. He wants you to know Him through personal relationship. Even though you may not trust people for whatever reason, you can truly trust God of Love and Truth to guide you to honestly know how to have a living relationship with Him. As you choose to surrender yourself to His Love, He will teach you how to love Him with all your heart, mind, soul, and strength. When you learn how to love The Lord your God with all your heart, mind, and soul and strength, you will want to choose to love yourself without shame and anger because people hurt you. You as well will want to reach out to love others in the same way God Loves you and them.

Holy Spirit is Truth and He will never lie to you. He leads you to know Him in Holy Truth and Love. But you have to decide to trust Living God with all your heart, not leaning own your own understanding or thinking. When you choose to the best of your ability that you want to trust The Lord, He will direct your pursuit in learning to know Him. Trusting The Lord God of all Creation to help you love Him and all people with all your heart, mind, and emotions, ensures you will receive from The Lord what you need to sustain your Life forever.

Hear The Word of The Lord:

"Seek Me while I may be found. Call upon Me while I am near!

*"**When You seek Me** and call upon Me with all your heart. **I will come to you** and show you great and mighty things you don't know, that you need to know.*

"Then obey My Voice and you will bear good and abundant fruit that remains."

When you seek Holy God with *all* your heart and call upon Him to *know* Him in truth, He answers you and shows you great and mighty things which you do not know that you need to know. Read in your Bible in the Old Testament, Jeremiah 33:3; Jeremiah 29:11-14a; and in the New Testament, Matthew 7:7-8; Mark 11:22-26; 1 John 5:14-15.

No one can ever know all there is to know about Creator God. He is fathomless in His ability to continue Creating and maintaining what He Creates. He has no beginning and no end. Therefore, He is forever and ever and ever. So there is no end, or culmination, or conclusion as to how you can know Him. Who is like unto The Lord our God? No one is the answer. However, you can most certainly know True and Living God in a holy relationship of Love, Peace, and Joy and Trust.

If you willingly choose to surrender your preconceived ideas and the opinions you are holding onto and are wrongly trusting, Holy Spirit will take you on a Spiritual journey-adventure that will rock your boat and cause you to consider Truth, Who is a Person, not an idea or a philosophy. Through what is written in this book, Holy GOD of all Creation is bringing you a personal challenge and offering you the honest and only Way you can correctly and truthfully know The One and Only True God as He has been revealed to you in this book and in The Holy Bible so that you can confidently know Him the Way He wants you to know Him. **Believe** that you can truly know The One True God and that He is taking you on an incredible personal journey-adventure to know Him the way He wants you to know Him. This thrilling journey-adventure goes on forever and ever and ever with no end. How this can be, only Creator God knows completely. When you obey God of Truth and Love, you can truthfully know with no doubting that you can fully rest in His Everlasting Arms of Love forever.

Also, you must truly choose to believe that there is no such thing as making a mistake in your personal pursuit to know True God. What you may think is a mistake is only an opportunity to learn what you don't know that you need to know. Sometimes God allows you to make what you *think* is a mistake so you can learn what you didn't know until you made what you call a mistake.

Be Sure You Choose True God

If after reading this book, you are not sure you ever honestly asked Jesus Christ, God's only Son, to save you from your sins and transgressions against Him by asking Him to come and live inside you forever, take time to do this right now. There is no better time to do this.

Know in truth that only by your free will choice to receive Jesus Christ as your personal Savior and Lord can you be eternally saved from sin. Sin is choosing your human will above God's Holy Will. Receiving Jesus free gift of Salvation frees you from the devil's evil lies, and from permanent death, which is being separated from Holy God forever to never again have the opportunity to choose to receive Jesus' free gift of Salvation. There will come the time in your life when you stand before Holy God to give Him an account for your life He gave you to live for Him. You will remember all the times you could have received Jesus free gift of salvation, and you refused for whatever reason. You will painfully recognize you missed your opportunity to say yes to Jesus' Salvation. However, at this time no matter how loudly you cry out to Jesus to save you, it will be too late for you because The Lord gave you many, many opportunities to choose Him and you refused.

Recognizing you can miss your opportunity to accept Jesus' free Salvation from sin and evil should cause you to want to turn to True God right now and cry out to Him to be delivered from evil and saved from sin. The choice is yours. You can immediately choose to stop the way you are going and turn from your selfish way of living and choose to accept Jesus' free Salvation. When you choose Jesus' Salvation from evil and sin, you receive and are guaranteed Everlasting Life. His Everlasting Arms of Love are waiting to hold you forever. Will you turn from evil and choose Everlasting Life? The choice is yours.

Choosing to receive everlasting life begins in this life on earth. You must choose to believe and wholly accept that Jesus Christ is God's only Son who came on earth in human flesh to live an innocent and sinless life; and that He allowed Himself to be crucified on a cross He didn't deserve to die on that caused His Precious and Holy Blood to be unmercifully spilled out. You must honestly believe and accept that Jesus' Holy Blood Sacrifice redeemed you from sin and evil and brought you back into Your Father's Good and Holy Will for your life. You must acknowledge and publicly confess that Jesus' Father raised His Only Son from death and brought Him back to Heaven to rule beside Him now and forever. When you willingly receive God's Way to truly know you have abundant Life now and forever, you are assured that you are now saved from sin, evil, and eternal separation from The God who made you and Loves you.

These words in your Bible reveal the way you can honestly know you are saved from sin and evil:

The Word is near you, on your lips and in your heart, because if you confess with your lips that Jesus is Lord and believe in your heart that God raised Him from the dead, you will be saved. For people believe with their heart and so are justified, and confess with their lips and so are saved. The scripture says, "No one who believes in Him will be put to shame. (Romans 10:8-11)

There is no specific prayer you must pray or repeat to ask Jesus to forgive you and to come into your life and help you know Him. True God hears your heart intention to Him to want to be saved from your own evil desires and the devil's lies. So just honestly speak or talk to The Lord and tell Him what is truly in your heart. Speak to Him the way you normally speak and talk. Don't copy how others speak or talk to God. The Lord God is listening to you and He will assure you He heard you. I am not going to tell you how you will *know* that He heard you. I can't do that because how you *know* and *hear* Living God is personal to you and is different from how others know and hear True God. Holy and Living God is a personal God who fashions each person to know Him in the way He uniquely designed them to know Him. But believe me, you will know, that you know, that you know. When you *know* deep inside you that Holy God truly forgives you and you are forever delivered from the devils' lies, you are free to pursue and go after your very own unique journey- adventure with Living God who is leading and guiding your path so you fulfill your Creatively Designed destiny Your Creator fashioned for you to fulfill.

Freely choosing to accept Holy God's Way of Salvation as unchangeable truth, assures you that you are saved from sin, the devil's lies, and eternal death, which is being separated from True and Living God forever. Then, as you continually surrender to the Holy God of Life in all your ways, He makes Himself personally known to you so you learn to know Him in good ways. As you persistently pursue your personal journey-adventure with Holy God, the entanglements that kept you in bondage to lies and fear will drop away and be removed from your life, as long as you maintain your personal and active relationship with the God of Love and Truth.

Because you have decided to receive Jesus' Holy Blood Sacrifice for yourself, you will want to be baptized in water to publicly confess that you are freely choosing to believe Jesus Christ died for you personally to forgive your sin of wanting to have your own way above His good Way for you. You are confessing that you want to be set free from the devil's lies so that you receive eternal and everlasting Life. You are also announcing publicly that you freely choose to forgive yourself and all those who have sinned against you. When you choose to publicly acknowledge you are a sinner in need of salvation from sin and evil, you will never again be the same person you have been in feeling afraid and ashamed because your sins separated you from True God and from people. You will be united with True God and with people in a holy way you may have never known up to this point in your life.

Here is a truth written in your Bible that will bring you good success throughout your life's journey, if you choose to live by these words:

Do not fret or worry yourself because of the wicked, don't be envious or jealous of those who do wrong! For they will soon fade like the grass and wither like Spring flowers. Take delight in The Lord, and He will give you the desires of your heart.

Commit your way to the Lord; trust in Him, and He will act. He shall bring forth your righteousness as the light, and your justice as the noonday. (Psalms 37:1-6)

Holy Spirit's Baptism with Fire and Power

I want you to know that there is still another step for you to choose to receive from The Lord; and this is to be baptized with the Holy Spirit Truth and Fire, which is His Holy Power working through you to use His Love and Authority that brings authentic results in your personal situations and in the circumstances where The Lord directs you. You have a free will to choose to search out this truth of Holy Spirit Baptism on your own. There are plenty of books and teachings on how to receive Holy Spirit's Baptism of Fire that brings Living God's Holy Passion and Power wrapped in His Love on the scene of your circumstances that first touches your life, and then touches other people's lives for good.

Seek The Lord to know His valid Truth about receiving Holy Spirit Fire Power. He will lead you and guide you to the exact right places in the Bible to read and to apply to your life. He will also direct you to the exact right books and videos that have been written and electronically recorded that will aid you in knowing how to surrender to Living God to a deeper extent so you receive Holy Spirit Fire Power to use in your personal journey with Him for the good of all people including yourself. Do not ever dismiss or discount that Living God can individually come to you and baptize you with Holy Spirit Fire and Power as He so sovereignly chooses so that He can fulfill His Holy Purposes for your life. God is God! He knows the way He Designed you to fulfill your Creatively Designed destiny. He knows what you do not know. Therefore, He chooses as He Wills to do whatever He knows is good for you and for what He is bringing you into for His Glory and your good and for the good of all concerned. Know you can trust God to do His Good Will in your life.

To be baptized with Holy Spirit Fire and Power means to be filled with Holy Passion and Power to obey Jesus' words of Holy Love and Authority that affects people's lives for good and changes their situations from distress and despair into hope, truth, and a good outcome. Using Holy Spirit Truth and Fire Power stops the devil in his tracks.

I am going to share my own personal journey and God-story as to how The Lord led me to know that I needed to personally receive His Holy Spirit's Baptism of Fire. I was hungering for more of The Lord and His Life and Ways. I personally knew Jesus, but I didn't truthfully know Holy Spirit whom I read about in the Bible? I had no idea that He was a person in His own right. I came to realize truth about Holy Spirit by personally searching my Bible to know truth for myself.

As I searched for truth about Holy Spirit, I discovered and recognized that my personal question, *Is this all there is?* began my journey of searching out for myself all I could learn about Holy Spirit. I searched and searched Holy Scripture and read book after book and listened to cassette tape after cassette tape about what people were writing and saying from their experiences of Holy Spirit encounters that were happening all around the world and in their own personal lives. I attended meetings where people from all over the world were coming and sharing what was happening to them personally and in their churches that was spilling out into their personal circumstances and affecting their spheres of influence in good ways. People were being healed, delivered from demonic influences, and were receiving Jesus' free gift of Salvation, and were being baptized in water for the forgiveness of their sins, and then they were being baptized into Holy Spirit's Baptism. These living and actual accounts triggered me to want to know more.

I was reading these words in the Gospel of Matthew in my Bible:

I baptize you with water for repentance, but He who is coming after me is mightier that I, whose sandals I am not worthy to carry; **He will baptize you with the Holy Spirit and with fire**. (Matthew 3:11)

I could read no further. These words captured my attention and mesmerized me. The Lord ignited me and lit a Fire in me to want to know more about these words John the Baptist spoke in Matthew 3:11. I instinctively knew The Lord was beginning to answer my question to Him, "Is this all there is?" I knew there was so much more I did not know, but truly wanted to know. Deep inside me I wanted to understand John the Baptist's words **He will baptize you with the Holy Spirit and with fire**.

At this time of my personal search to know what these words *He will baptize you with the Holy Spirit and with fire* truly meant, Holy Spirit began sweeping through denominational churches in America, and really across the world, at a phenomenal pace. Holy Spirit encounters were sweeping across all denominational lines of demarcation that each church denomination had set for itself. Holy Spirit was moving so powerfully and swiftly that one either got on board or stayed dead to the things of God. I was captivated by what was happening around me in my personal circumstances and by what I was hearing being taught from the Bible and written in books and recorded on cassette tapes. I had never heard such teaching and preaching. But what I was hearing greatly stirred in my spirit, so much so, that I wanted to know all I could about how Holy Spirit was moving on earth.

As I continued reading and hearing the testimonies from what others were saying about this Holy Spirit Baptism and their extraordinary personal accounts because of receiving this Holy Spirit Baptism, I became convinced that this phenomenon was truly Living God's doing. I wanted the zeal and the enthusiasm that these people had for The Lord. But I wanted to make sure that it was truly Holy God and that it would last and was not just a passing fancy of people's own making. The main emphasis being taught from the Bible that was spreading around the world was you had truly received this Holy Spirit Baptism when you spoke in tongues or an unknown language as The Spirit gave utterance as the early disciples did in the book of Acts chapter 2. Speaking in tongues or in an unknown language was the evidence that you had received the Holy Spirit's Baptism.

It was believed that by *speaking in tongues as The Spirit gave utterance* was what caused the Power of God to manifest and heal and deliver people from demonic strongholds. As I heard and personally experienced people's lives being changed for good right before my eyes, I started to believe that this Holy Spirit Baptism was truly from God. There was some hoopla and I saw counterfeit things happening, but for the most part what I was seeing was genuine and lasting. I didn't want to get caught up in the counterfeit or my flesh nature. So I was crying out to The Lord to let me know clearly if what I was hearing and seeing was truly from Him. Almighty God protected me from error and excess and from counterfeit manifestations all the way through my heart-search to know Truth who I learned is a person, not a theological idea.

During a meeting I was attending, someone gave me a Bible teaching cassette tape *How to Receive the Baptism of The Holy Spirit.* Before I listened to this cassette tape, I asked The Lord to help me know if I was to pursue receiving the Baptism of The Holy Spirit as this cassette tape was teaching. Then, I carefully listened to this cassette tape and concluded that this phenomenon people were experiencing truly was from

God, and that I should seek Him in asking to receive Holy Spirit's Baptism.

After listening to this cassette tape several times, I went into my bedroom and closed the door and shut myself in with God. Then, I again intently listened to this cassette tape.

However, I wanted The Lord to give me Scripture that would totally convince me that I was to receive this Baptism of Holy Spirit. So I asked The Lord to show me specifically in Scripture that this Holy Spirit's Baptism was truly from Him and if it was truly from Him for me to do. I opened my Bible and began reading in the Gospel of John chapters 14, 15, 16, 17. Then Holy Spirit led me to go to 1 Corinthians chapter 2. I read these words:

*Yet among the mature we do impart wisdom, although it is not a wisdom of this age or the rulers of this age, who are doomed to pass away. But we impart a secret and hidden wisdom of God, which God decreed before the ages for our glorification. None of the rulers of this age understood this; for if they had, they would not have crucified the Lord of glory. But, as it is written "What no eye has seen, nor ear heard, nor the heart of man conceived, what God has prepared for those who love him," God has revealed to us through the Spirit. For the Spirit searches everything, even the depths of God. For what person knows a man's thoughts except the spirit of the man which is in him? So also no one comprehends the thoughts of God except the Spirit of God. Now we have received not the spirit of the world, **but the Spirit which is from God, that we might understand the gifts bestowed on us by God.** And we impart this in words **not taught by human wisdom but taught by the Spirit, interpreting spiritual truths to those who possess the Spirit**. The unspiritual man does not receive* *the gifts of the Spirit of God, for they are folly to him, and he is not able to understand them, because they are spiritually discerned. The spiritual man judges all things, but is himself to be judged by no one. "For who has known the mind of the Lord so as to instruct him?" But we have the mind of Christ.* (1 Corinthians 2:6-16)

and suddenly these words captured my attention and convinced me I was to receive Holy Spirit's Baptism because what I was hearing and seeing was truly of God to receive from Him. The words in bold print in this Scripture passage grabbed my attention. I knew I had gifts from God and I was using them some. Yet, I knew deep within me there was more that I needed but I didn't know what it was. Through this Scripture I was thoroughly convinced I was to receive Holy Spirit's Baptism. I knew with no doubting this was truly of God to receive from Him.

Immediately after reading this Scripture passage in 1 Corinthians 2:6-16, great peace and joy and contentment flooded my entire being. I knew, that I knew, that I knew God was showing me specifically, as I had asked Him to do, that I needed His Holy Spirit's Baptism in order to receive His Wisdom to know how to use the Spirit Gifts I knew He endowed within me, but didn't exactly know all about them or how to effectively use them. I distinctly knew in my heart that if I would surrender to The Lord and receive Holy Spirit's Baptism, He would enable me to know how to use the Spirit Gifts that He put within me. So, I knew beyond any doubt that I was to continue to pursue my personal search to know The Lord and His Holy Truth in deeper ways. Now I was ready to receive the Baptism of Holy Spirit.

I once again listened to this cassette tape on Holy Spirit Baptism that was teaching me how to totally surrender every part of my life to God, and not hold back from wholeheartedly yielding to Him. The teaching was about dying to myself and surrendering my tongue and mouth to The Lord so He could fill me with a Heavenly language. Then I could converse with Living God in His language. By speaking to God in His language, I could shut off my own thinking and close out Satan's words of lies to my mind. It made total sense to me.

So, I totally surrendered myself and my tongue and my mouth to God the best I knew how and followed the instructions on this cassette tape to just begin talking to God in the syllables that came out of my mouth. So I began; and lo and behold a language I did not know came flowing out of my innermost being and verbally out of my mouth. I tangibly received the gift of speaking in a Heavenly language to Holy God. I instinctively knew it was Living God doing this through me and that I was not making it up. Eventually I learned that I could speak in the tongues of angels and they would heed or do what I was saying to them in their language according to 1 Corinthians 13:1.

The Joy I knew at that moment continues to this day, and knows no bounds. I could now literally talk to God in His language. I knew speaking in a Heavenly language helped me to control my unruly tongue and unnecessary conversation. I knew this was the way I could shut off the mind of flesh, which is my own thinking, and also shut out the devil's voice speaking lies to my mind. I learned from choosing to use Holy Spirit language, that whenever I would speak in Holy Spirit language, immediately, I would get the mind of Christ to know what to do in any situation I was facing. I found that speaking in Holy Spirit language granted me a direct line to Heaven so I could hear and know with understanding what Living God had to say in every situation I faced. I also knew I must also seek His heart and mind through His decreed and written Word that stands sure Forever. From that day to this very day after I read God's Word in the Bible, I pray in Holy Spirit language and I receive understanding from God's Word that is His answer for my situation.

But there are times when I don't want anything from God, I just talk with Him in His language for His enjoyment in my telling Him of my love and honor for Him. The Lord enjoys wanting to be wanted just for Himself:

After totally surrendering myself to The Lord and receiving His Holy Spirit's Baptism, these words were indelibly written in my heart:

Abraham believed God, and it was reckoned to him as righteousness. Now to one who works, his wages are not reckoned as a gift but as his due. And to one who does not work but trusts Him who justifies the ungodly, his faith is reckoned as righteousness. No distrust made him (Abraham) *waver concerning the promise of God, but he grew strong in his faith as he gave Glory to God, fully convinced that God was able to do what he had promised.* (Romans 4:3-5, 20-21)

I truly believe The Lord imprinted these specific words in the book of Romans in the Bible on my heart and in my spirit so I would never forget I fully surrendered and trusted myself to Him in receiving Holy Spirit's Baptism. I knew He was encouraging me to know that because I am not wavering concerning His promise to me, I would grow strong in trusting His ability that lives in me to know how to use the Spirit gifts He gave me to use in ministering to people that delivers them from evil and brings Glory and Honor to His Holy Name. Now I knew with assurance that The Lord would continue teaching me to know how to live my life on earth by Holy Spirit's Power.

Nothing written in this book and in The Holy Bible will impact your life, unless you have an open and teachable heart. Listen to what Jesus spoke in parables or in life-related stories to those who came to Him seeking truth:

*For everyone who listens with an open heart will receive progressively more revelation until he has more than enough. But those who don't listen with an open, teachable heart, even the understanding **they think they have** will be taken from them. That is why I teach the people using parables* (or life-related stories), *because **they think they're looking for truth**, yet because their hearts are unteachable, they never discover it. Although they will listen to Me, they never fully perceive the message I speak.* (Matthew 13:12-13 The Passion Translation)

To receive all Holy Spirit has for you, you must completely surrender what you *think* and then choose to yield to Holy God with a willing and teachable heart. When you willingly choose to fully surrender yourself to Him, He will certainly come to you and teach you to know Him and His Ways that are far beyond your human comprehension. Having a teachable heart and surrendering yourself entirely to Holy God is the only way to have a successful life on earth at this time, and for eternity.

I was not going to share this God-story, but Holy Spirit asked me to share it because there is *one* He wants to reach through my personal God-story.

Through Holy Spirit's arrangement I became a Sunday School teacher when my oldest and first-born son, who was 4 years old, began asking me questions about God that I could not answer. This impelled me to get more serious about reading my Bible so I could answer His questions. The questions young children ask about God should never be dismissed.

God puts in their hearts to search for Him. How I was thrust into teaching a 4- year-old Sunday School class is a comedy in itself. God does have a sense of humor. When you surrender to Him and allow Him to get you where He wants you to be so you can use your Creatively Designed destiny that He put in you, you too will understand that He truly has a holy sense of humor. Chill out and let go of old *thinking* so you can enjoy your earth journey in creative ways you never thought possible.

Anyhow, here I was teaching 4-year-olds about Jesus and God from the Bible. This began an over 30-year journey of teaching children, youth, and adults about the God I knew and loved. My stories of teaching these children about the Love of God are too numerous. But they are certainly funny. I most certainly had to personally learn how to live and demonstrate Jesus' Love for them again and again and again. Children are unending delight to The Lord and they certainly are a delight to me to this very day. My God-stories with children, youth and adults are funny and also heart-rending. God sees us all as His children. He delights in the welfare of His children no matter their age. Jesus says that unless you become as a little child, you cannot enter the Kingdom of God. Read Matthew 18:1-6 in your Bible.

Well, here is the God-story I am going to share with you about Holy Spirit leading me to teach on the Baptism of Holy Spirit to second and third grade boys in the Sunday School class I was teaching at the time. I had always taught boys and girls together. I knew that boys and girls being together in a class brought a better perspective to the class and certainly brought unending adventures. But at this time and in this particular church the new wave was to separate boys and girls. There were enough teachers who came forward to teach the girls and the older boys. But no one would take the second and third grade boys who were together because of there being so few children in this age group. So I said I would take these boys. I said, "I love boys. I have three boys of my own; and five grandsons. So I know boys." In previous Sunday School classes I taught, there were some teachers who did not want the non-compliant boys who caused a ruckus at times. I always said I would take these boys because I saw potential in them that needed to be directed for good. My God-stories through the years with these boys are very interesting and fun, at least they are for me. I love action and fun.

Anyhow, back to my God-story about teaching these second and third grades boys about Holy Spirit baptism. I had been teaching what Holy Spirit was leading me teach them each Sunday from the Bible. I prayed and asked The Lord to let me know what to teach them each Sunday. Then I would teach them what He led me to teach. One particular Sunday I was teaching about Jesus' Life and how they too could do what Jesus did. I was teaching them about Jesus and how He healed the sick. Then, suddenly, the boys said together, "Mrs. Fritcha! Mrs. Fritcha! Can we pray for, and they named a boy in the class? He is deaf and we want to pray for him." So they gathered around this boy and they all laid hands on him. I don't remember telling them to lay hands on him. I just stood and watched my Sunday School class turn into a Holy Spirit led class. There was nothing spectacular that happened so that we all knew he was healed that Sunday in class. I do believe the boys knew he was healed. But they didn't say anything.

Well, this story goes on. At a family gathering, my niece who was a neo-natal nurse at a local hospital said a nurse she worked with asked her, "Do you know Betsy Fritcha?" My niece said, "Yes, she's my Aunt." Then this nurse, who was the mother of the little deaf boy that the Sunday School boys prayed for to be healed from deafness, told my niece that her son was healed from deafness in his Sunday School class when the boys in his class prayed for him. This is how I knew God healed this little boy of deafness through the boys in his class who had prayed for his healing.

Now, on to the Holy Spirit led occasion that happened among these same little boys. This particular Sunday, Holy Spirit led me to teach on the Baptism of Holy Spirit. I said, "Are you kidding? I could be kicked out of this church. They don't teach this." However, when you know it is Holy Spirit leading you, you should never say, no. And I didn't say no. I knew better.

Holy Spirit led me to know how to teach these little boys how they could talk to God in His language. So I taught from the Bible how they could talk to God in His language. Then, I asked them, "Would you like to do this?" They were so excited and wanted to do this. So I led them in speaking out loud to God in His language. I didn't push them to do this. We just did it and then went on with our Bible lesson.

After the class was over, one of the little boys came running up to me exuberantly saying, "Mrs. Fritcha! Mrs. Fritcha! I have been doing this all along and I didn't know what it was." I still have his little hand written note he gave me thanking me for teaching him about Jesus and Holy Spirit from the Bible. This is why you never, never want to say no to Holy Spirit. He always has a reason for what He leads you to do. You may find out the reason, and then again, you may never find out this side of Heaven.

This God-story gets even better. The next Sunday I was teaching what Holy Spirit led me to teach. A new little boy came to our class. Each Sunday new boys were coming to our Sunday School class and even parents were coming because they knew I was teaching the Bible and they wanted to learn. I had some parents sneaking children from the first-grade class into our Sunday School class. They wanted their children taught about Jesus from the Bible. I didn't mind. If they wanted to be there that earnestly, they could come.

Anyway, the next Sunday after teaching on Holy Spirit Baptism, a new little boy came to our Sunday School class. Before the class started, the little boy who exuberantly said, "Mrs. Fritcha! Mrs. Fritcha! I have been doing this all along and I didn't know what it was." came up to me and said, "Mrs. Fritcha can I take him back in the corner and do what we did last Sunday?" I was so busy getting the class organized to begin teaching, I said, "Sure." He came running up to me as I was beginning to start our class, again exuberantly saying, "Mrs. Fritcha, Mrs. Fritcha, he got it too.!"

Oh, the never-ending moving of Holy Spirit if we will just get out of our own thinking, and obey His leading in each situation we face allowing Him to work His Will through us in the way He wants to that brings others into a face-to-face encounter with Holy God.

You Do Have a God-Appointed Destiny

Do you know that The Lord knew your before you were born? Supreme God uniquely created you and put a Creative Design in you before you were born that no one else will ever have. He expects you to fulfill the Creative destiny He planned for you. Psalm 139 defines how Supreme Creator God knew you and uniquely Designed you before you were born:

O, Lord, you have examined my heart and know everything about me. You know when I sit down or stand up. You know my thoughts even when I'm far away. You see me when I travel and when I rest at home. You know everything I do.

You know what I am going to say even before I say it, Lord. You go before me and follow me. You place your hand of blessing on my head. Such knowledge is too wonderful for me; too great for me to understand!

I can never escape from your Spirit! I can never get away from Your Presence! If I go up to Heaven, You are there; if I go down to the place of the dead, You are there. If I ride the wings of the morning, if I dwell by the farthest oceans, even there Your Hand will guide me, and Your Strength will support me.

I could ask the darkness to hide me and the light around me to become night – but even in darkness I cannot hide from you. To you the night sines as bright as day. Darkness and light are the same to You.

You made all the delicate, inner parts of my body and knit me together in my mother's womb. Thank You for making me so wonderfully complex! Your workmanship is marvelous – how well I know it. You watched me as I was being formed in utter seclusion, as I was woven together in the dark of the womb. You saw me before I was born.

Every day of my life was recoded in Your Book. Every moment was laid out before a single day has passed. How precious are Your thoughts about me, O God! They cannot be numbered! I can't even count them; they outnumber the grains of sand! And when I wake up in the morning, You are still with me! (Psalm 139)

At a time in my life when personal situations were overwhelming me, The Lord greatly encouraged me through these words in Psalm 139 to know that He intimately knew me and placed a unique destiny in me before I was born. He personally spoke these words to me:

"All your days are written in My Book. That is why I know what you will ask Me before you ask Me. Before you ask, I have already answered. I allow you to seek Me to know Me and to know what I have written in My Book concerning you. This is Pure Wisdom. I greatly delight in making Myself known to you. I know you and when you know Me, My Joy is full. I have you hidden in Me in My Secret Place where I make Myself known to you so that My Pleasure is full. I put My Holy desires in your heart to know Me. When you receive Me and My Holy desires, and make them your own, together we accomplish My Will My Way. I see all that is in your heart, because I put it there. Not one thing nor can one person ever take away what I have put in you, unless you let them."

These words The Lord personally spoke to me are for you too. Living God, your Creator, knows the unique plan He Creatively Designed in you that He expects you to fulfill. He Creatively Designed in you that He expects you to fulfill. He Creatively Designed you so that there is nobody else exactly like you. You are you. The Lord truly wants you to enjoy who He Creatively Designed you to be. Living and True God uniquely Designed you so He could enjoy you in the exact way He Creatively Designed you. When you choose to enjoy how God Creatively Designed you, then you can choose to enjoy the way He uniquely Designed other people for His Holy Purpose of blending together each person's unique destiny for the good of all Creation and for His Pure enjoyment.

You most certainly have a Creative destiny to fulfill. However, you must want the good destiny your Creator Designed you to fulfill. Each person enjoying who Living God Creatively Designed them to be is eternal living and the way Heaven functions forever. There will be no more sorrow, no more pain, no more tears, no more jealousy, or envy, or hate. Only true peace and enjoyment because the devil and his evil plots will never again harass you. Therefore, you can enjoy being who Living God Created you to be in fulfilling your Creative Destiny.

Only you can decide if you want to know True God in a personal and active relationship so you can fulfill your Creatively Designed destiny. Do you want to?

Begin to speak these words over yourself every day and watch yourself gain confidence in who God Creatively Designed you to be:

I am Designed by my Creator to live at this time on earth. My life does matter.
I am not an accident.
God Created me to be who I am;
not who someday else thinks I should be.

Laugh with me at this saying I heard someone say:

"Be who you is. Cause if you ain't who you is, you is who you ain't."

GOD ALMIGHTY SPEAKS
Will you Listen?

"God is not a man, that He should lie,
nor a son of man, that He should repent
(change His mind).

Does He speak and then not act? (NO!)

Does He promise and not fulfill? (NO!)
Numbers 23:19

I have sworn by My own Name,
and I will never go back on My Word...
Isaiah 45:23

I am God, and there is no one else like Me!

Only I can tell you what is going to happen even
before it happens

Everything I plan will come to pass, ...
Isaiah 46:9-10

"The Word of The Lord holds true; and everything He does
is worthy of our trust." Psalm 33:4